The Complete Guide to
Coaching Soccer Systems and Tactics

by Jacob Daniel

**Library of Congress
Cataloging - in - Publication Data**

The Complete Guide to
Coaching Soccer Systems and Tactics
Jacob Daniel

ISBN No. 1-59164-068-7
Lib. of Congress Catalog No. 2003112185
© 2003

*Art Direction, Layout and
Editing*
Bryan R. Beaver

Cover Photo by
EMPICS Ltd.

Printed by
DATA REPRODUCTIONS
Auburn, Michigan

Reedswain Publishing
612 Pughtown Road
Spring City, PA 19475
800.331.5191
www.reedswain.com
info@reedswain.com

*In memory of Piotr Slomski,
Whose passion for coaching was an inspiration,
And with whom countless hours were spent talking tactics*

TABLE OF CONTENTS

Introduction

The Purpose of This Book   1
The Evolution of Soccer Tactics   3
The Evolution of the Soccer Coach   7
Characteristics of Successful Teams   11

Section 1 - Principles of Play

Principles of Attack   17
Principles of Defense   35
Team Shape and Principles of Play   43
Coaching the Principles to Youth   53

Section 2 - Systems of Play

Defending Systems   57
   Man-to-Man Marking   57
   Zonal Defending   59
   How to Decide on Marking System   63
   Pressing Systems   67
   Channeling the Ball   72
Team Formations   75
   The 4-4-2 Formation   75
   The 3-5-2 Formation   82
   The 4-3-3 Formation   87
   The 3-4-3 Formation   93
Variations of Traditional Formations   95
Positions and Their Role   107
Selecting a System of Play   111

Section 3 - Methods of Coaching

Planning a Practice Session   121
Tactical Coaching Feedback   127
The 'Situational' Approach to Coaching Tactics   131
Functional Training vs Generic Training   139
   Generic Tactical Activities   140
   Functional Tactical Activities   148

Patterns of Play   174
      Patterns in Defending Third   175
      Patterns in the Middle Third   180
Shadow Plays   186

Section 4 - Finishing Touches

Developing Forwards   195
Developing a Possession Rhythm   207
Throw-ins   212
The Offside Trap   217
Substitutions   220
Conclusion   222

INTRODUCTION

The Purpose of This Book

Coaches are responsible for elevating their team's performance. This is done through training and instruction. One of the key principles of sport science is that learning is accelerated when practice activities succeed in replicating the demands of the game. In soccer, the demands placed on the players are grouped into four areas, often described as the four components of the game. These components are technique, tactics, fitness, and psychology. Although this book is concerned with the tactical aspects of the game, it must be stated at the outset that coaches cannot neglect any of the components. They are all interdependent and all must be enhanced for a team to reach a high performance potential. Just as it is true that a team is only as strong as its weakest player, the team's performance will likely be weighted down by its most deficient component. Although performance perfection is never reached in sport, teams are capable of reaching a high 'peak performance' level when all the players are simultaneously playing at their own personal best within each component.

This book deals with the methods for training the tactical component of the game. With that in mind, the book aims to help coaches attain a better awareness in the following three areas: 1) principles of play; 2) systems of play; and 3) methods for coaching tactics. A solid understanding in these three areas is a definite pre-requisite for teaching successful tactics.

Section 1 of the book explains the attacking and defending principles of play and relates them to the game by using practical illustrations. The principles of play are the bedrock of tactics and remain the same, no matter which playing formation is used. They are like the 'Ten Commandments' of soccer, the guidelines that help players make the correct movements and decisions for each situation, regardless of the playing system or formation. Coaches should understand these principles, as well as how to teach them to their players. This section also discusses the elements of team shape. When players move according to the principles of play, the end result is a good team shape. References to team shape and how to identify and teach shape are made throughout the book since it is such an integral concept of team tactics.
Effective soccer is attained when players react to the game and not blindly follow a system like robots. Having said that, systems of play have a very important purpose. The system of play is in essence the language of soccer tactics.

Coaches use systems of play, also known as formations, to define each player's role and provide a framework for team strategy. The system of play is responsible for distributing the workload among the players in the most efficient way. It gives the team cohesion, and gets all the players on the same wavelength. Section 2 explains the most common modern systems used worldwide by professional and youth coaches. The section starts with a discussion of the most popular defensive systems, namely the man-to-man and the zonal marking systems and includes the pros and cons of each system. This is followed by an explanation of high pressure and low pressure strategies, as well as channeling the ball. The focus then moves to playing formations. The strengths and weaknesses of each formation are discussed, along with the best way to utilize each one. An in-depth analysis of modern variations to the traditional formations follows, showing how coaches manipulate formations to gain an edge over opponents. The section also provides advice on how to select the most suitable system and includes practical guidelines for teaching a system of play.

The methods for coaching tactics are addressed in the third section, in what is probably the most important area of the book. For many coaches, finding activities is the easy part. There are a myriad of books and periodicals available, full with drills and activities. However, the challenge for most coaches is how to pick the right activity, how often to use it, when to use it, and how to get the coaching points across to the players. This section attempts to help coaches bring practice activities to life. Only when one is able to take the X's and O's from a coaching manual and make it work on the field can he claim to be a real coach. Only when he can put players through a session that impacts them and improves them can he truly consider himself a teacher. This section deals with the pivotal elements of modern coaching methods: How to provide effective tactical feedback; how to teach team shape using a simple 'situational' approach; how and when to use functional training and shadow training; and how to instill successful patterns of play. This section will hopefully help the reader make the transition from a coach who is merely a 'driller' to one that is a bona fide 'teacher of tactics'.

The fourth section addresses a variety of tactical issues with which many coaches grapple. It starts with valuable tips on how to train the forwards to become more effective. The game is all about goals. Hence, coaches must spend considerable time helping their forwards create goal- scoring chances and finish those chances. Possession is another hot topic among coaches and this section presents methods for developing a possession rhythm. The section also deals with throw-ins. Getting the most out of throw-ins is a topic neglected by many coaches but one that should receive substantial attention, considering how many throw-ins occur in a game. Next, the pros and cons of the offside trap are discussed. Finally, the topic of substitution is given a consideration, both from a strategic perspective and the players' tactical development angle.

Coaches must develop the skill of using the two most important teaching tools at their disposal: observation and communication. The best coaches are able to detect through observation the important facts, such as the reasons for a successful maneuver, the cause of an attack's breakdown. Good coaches pick up on all the little details that make up the game and take care of them during preparation. And yet they have the knack for sifting through the details observed, discarding the trivial ones, and zeroing in on the key ones. These coaches can then communicate to the players quickly and expertly exactly what is needed to achieve success. Although the public side of coaching folklore often glorifies the inspirational qualities of our coaching icons, those who can coax a miraculous comeback with a stirring half-time talk, the most consistently successful coaches are those who can combine inspiration with attention to tactical detail.

To summarize, this book attempts to improve the coach's ability to analyze the important tactical details of team preparation. The methods discussed apply to coaches of both males and females. The principles of tactical coaching are the same for both genders. It's in the area of communication and player-coach relations where the main differences between the genders are manifested. For the sake of brevity and consistency, this book refers to coaches and players in masculine terms.

The Evolution of Soccer Tactics

The game of soccer was formally codified in England in the 1860's, when the Football Association was formed. In those bygone days, the contest was all about dribbling. Passing didn't exist. Players took turns dribbling solo through the opposing team, who all ganged up in a scrum to defend. If the ball was tackled away, and tackling in those days was brutal, whichever player gathered the loose ball would proceed to dribble through the opposition until he lost it. Goals were few and far between. Not surprising, considering the odds of successfully navigating the ball through a mob. Tactics and team formations were given hardly any thought and the team with the superior dribblers would usually win. Then came passing, and the game was changed forever. It was teams from Scotland who were credited with introducing passing to soccer in the 1870's. Soon, player combinations became an integral part of attacking play and soccer has become a team game, in the true sense of the word.

Over the past one hundred and forty years, playing systems have evolved from a cavalier style with the accent on attack to a more methodical, cautious approach. In the beginning, most players on the field had attacking roles, with only one or two left behind as defensive cover. In the 1870's, teams played with two defenders and eight attackers. By the 1890's, most teams were playing with two defenders, three midfielders and five forwards, in a 2-3-5 formation. The 'great migration' from front to back began in earnest. Over time, the balance between attack and defense was gradually redressed to favor defense. Teams are now conditioned to maintain a numerical advantage in their own half at all times. Nowadays, when the ball is in midfield, there are likely to be more players behind the ball than ahead of the ball, and only when it is safe to do so will players make runs ahead of the ball.

Players' roles have changed considerably as well. In the early formations, and even up to the 1950's, every player stayed in his designated area of the field, charged with fulfilling a very specific and narrowly defined task. Defenders only defended and forwards only attacked. There was hardly any overlapping of responsibilities and players rarely interchanged positions. For example, in those early days, it was unheard of for the winger to cut inside and go to goal. The winger's job was to dribble down the flank and deliver crosses. The fullback's job was to stop the winger from crossing. It was all so very simplistic and straightforward. Now, players routinely switch places and some have the license to pop up anywhere and everywhere. Tactics have become much more flexible and sophisticated.

To understand how tactical systems have evolved, it's important to recognize that, although soccer is a contest between two teams, it is essentially made up of a succession of individual duels. It's the individual duel that is the pivotal determinant of the contest, and the team whose players win the majority of these individual battles will dominate the game. When a midfielder is in the process of receiving and controlling the ball, he is engaged in a duel against his immediate opponent who is trying to steal the ball away. If the midfielder is able to control the ball and pass it accurately to a teammate, he has won his duel. His teammate is now in possession, involved in the next one-versus-one duel. This fundamental principle was true one hundred years ago and is still true today.

Coaches were pressed to find ways to neutralize the impact of the individual duel. This became the driving force behind the evolution of soccer tactics. If the old style winger kept winning his duels against the fullback and delivering a succession of dangerous crosses, something needed to be done to stop the crosses. The obvious solution was to replace the overmatched fullback with a better player. But what if there was no one better on the bench or on the field. What if the winger was superior to any individual defender the coach could muster. This forced the coach to tinker with the formation to provide cover for the fullback. Playing systems were changed to create 2v1 situations wherever the 1v1 duels were being lost. The same logic applied everywhere on the field. Coaches had to find a way to cope against teams that had better individuals. They started shifting more players to the back. The Italians took it a step further and, in the late 1950's, made sure by adding a sweeper. The Italian man-marking system, bolstered by the extra cover of a sweeper, became the pre-eminent defensive system in the 1960's and brought the Italian club teams Inter Milan and AC Milan international success.

The shift towards a more defensive strategy in turn forced coaches to find better, more effective ways to attack. Forwards had to become more mobile and crafty. With more defenders between them and the goal, attackers had to find ways to create space and learn to operate in tight spaces. Midfielders started to make attacking runs to support the forwards and to exploit the spaces created by the forwards. Gradually, midfielders and forwards started to interchange positions in order to penetrate the massed defenses.

Back on the defensive front, coaches were forever looking for ways of dealing with the dilemma of those individual duels. In the first half of the 1900's, soccer was an open game with lots of space and time to control the ball. Teams used only two or three midfielders, as evidenced by England's 2-3-5 formation or Brazil's 4-2-4 system. With players so spread out, the midfielders had plenty of time on the ball to measure passes or dribble through. Superior players had a field day, able to control the game and assert their style and tempo. There were less upsets in the game since the weaker teams could not cope with the individual skill of their midfield opponents. Coaches had to find playing systems that could minimize the damage of a beaten player. The answer came in many forms. Fitness training improved the players' speed, strength and endurance, and formations were revised by moving more players to the midfield. By the 1960's most teams were employing four midfielders, with England winning the World Cup with its famous wingless 4-4-2 formation. By the 1980's many teams were using five and six in midfield. Argentina won the 1986 World Cup with a 3-6-1 set up. In addition, players became more adept at closing down spaces quickly and squeezing together to form a more solid, compact defensive unit. Now, when one player was beaten, another one was close by, ready to apply immediate pressure. Players started to attack the ball in groups. The result was a more congested midfield with players denied any time to elaborate on the ball.

With the game becoming more defensive and players getting fitter and better organized, coaches had to invent new attacking strategies to counter the congested midfield and team compactness. Attacking play had to adopt a quicker tempo, with more one-touch and two-touch passing combinations, and a quicker transition on the counterattack. Players' technique had to adapt as well. Players improved their ability to send long accurate passes over the midfield, either into spaces behind the defense, or from side to side to unbalance the defense.

Another offensive answer to the congested midfield came in the form of the overlapping defender. With less room in the middle and the central areas well protected, wide defenders, who now found themselves with no one to mark, were increasingly mobilized to attack down the flanks, where there was more space. The modern defender has arrived. Roberto Carlos from Brazil and Real Madrid is the quintessential overlapping defender. He divides his time between attacking wing play and defensive grunt and still finds time to score a few goals as well. The modern defender, in turn, caused the emergence of the modern attacker, one that not only scores goals, but also hurries and chases defenders to try to win the ball.

In the 1970's, Holland raised the whole concept of player interchange and overlapping defenders to new heights with their famous 'Total Football'. The Dutch team had superbly fit and intelligent players whose movement off the ball bewildered opponents. In 'Total Football', wide attackers slid inside, pulling opponents with them. Defenders attacked the spaces created on the flanks. Midfielders popped up everywhere, and forwards switched places at will. The fluid mobility of the modern game is a legacy of the Dutch 'Total Football'.

Which brings us to today. In just over a century of tactical innovations, we have come a long way. Modern tactics bear very little resemblance to the primitive, embryonic, naïve systems of the past. The old school of strict positions is as extinct as dinosaurs. The modern systems are very flexible, featuring a constant interchanging of positions, with intelligent and fluid player movement designed to create numerical superiority around the ball. Today's player movement makes it difficult to even tell the team formation. Players playing off a basic 4-4-2 formation could give the team, from a bird's eye view, a 5-4-1 look one moment and a 3-3-4 look seconds later. The game is much faster now. The high technical and tactical speed of play emphasizes the economical use of the ball. In the defensive and middle thirds of the field, one touch passing is preferred and over-elaboration on the ball is frowned upon.

Today's player is a superbly conditioned athlete, with speed, stamina and power. The modern player is adaptable, tactically aware, quick thinking and capable of sliding into multiple roles. Whereas in the past, players had limited, one-dimensional roles, the modern player must be an all rounder. Today's player is best described as a versatile specialist. He specializes in his main role and is expected to excel in it but, at the same time, he must be competent in all aspects of play. Regardless of position, he must be comfortable in defending and attacking, winning tackles and dribbling like a winger, intercepting passes and distributing balls like a midfielder, creating scoring chances and scoring goals himself.

Possession has become highly valued, the common reasoning being that if you can keep the ball the opponents cannot score. At the same time, with every square or back pass allowing opponents to recover and get organized defensively, the transition to attack must be swift. Since teams are now very good at defending in blocks and pressing the ball in numbers, the moment of transition from defense to attack has become crucial in the modern game. When teams win the ball, they look to play it forward quickly, before the other team gets a chance to regroup. The weighing between possession and penetration now has little margin for error. Players have had to become better at reading situations and recognizing instantly when to go forward at speed and when to slow it down and keep the ball.

The Evolution of The Soccer Coach

Coaches have evolved as well. When tactics were simpler and players had limited roles, most coaches were not great thinkers of the game. They were less tacticians and more man-manager types, mainly concerned with motivating their players by urging and lambasting them in equal measure. But every generation of coaches had their share of progressive pioneers who took the game to new tactical levels. Those who adapted survived, and those who couldn't were found out.

The term 'tactics' has many connotations and means different things to different people. Many coaching books define tactics as players' decisions. So, if we accept this definition as a valid starting point, then coaches are responsible for improving their players' ability to think and solve problems in the game. To do that, coaches must themselves become problem solvers. It's not enough to rely on well worn clichés, such as "Put them under pressure!", or "You have to want it more than them!" to get results. Today's players are more knowledgeable, sophisticated and inquisitive. Even young players are quick to ask questions to satisfy their natural curiosity rather than just follow instructions blindly. Today's coach cannot take his authority for granted but must earn it. The modern coach must have an analytical mind and be able to dissect play and zero in on the key problem areas. Only then can he win his players' respect and help them develop the ability to make decisions on the field. The modern coach is tactically astute, innovative, and always looking to find that extra edge in training and games. The modern coach is well organized, making sure that practices are well planned, with attention to detail and all players involved with little idleness. He can converse intelligently with specialists in all the sports sciences, possessing enough general knowledge in a broad range of disciplines, from psychology to physiology to nutrition and coaching methodology.

With a few exceptions, the early generations of coaches kept in the background, in an era when soccer was clearly considered a player's game. In fact, team manager was a more appropriate description of the person in charge of running the team in those days. The managers were more administrators than tacticians. They took care of the equipment, the travel details, and the paperwork. The players were left to solve the tactical problems on their own and it was up to the senior players to pass on their knowledge and experience to the rookies. Herbert Chapman, the legendary Huddersfield and Arsenal manager in the 1920's and 30's, is reputed to be the first team manager to cross the divide from an administrator to a coach. He was one of the first tacticians in the English game who successfully imposed a cohesive and, at that time, revolutionary playing system on his players, making Arsenal the best club team in England by a mile. Chapman was the first to use a magnetic board to explain his ideas to the players and the first to recognize the importance of pre-game tactical and technical preparation.

Tactical pioneers like Chapman left such a legacy that today's coach has become a central figure in the overall scheme of things. As coaching methods improved and matured, the coach's influence and impact on the final destination of the trophy was more recognized. Today, with so much money and prestige at stake, coaches must come to grips with a double-edged sword. Given a greater role and ample rewards, they must also carry the burden of greater expectations from fans and team owners. Coaches are now as famous as the players and the successful ones have become a hot commodity.

The importance of the coach has now filtered down to all the levels, including youth and school soccer. Top coaches are sought at every grade. Youth clubs hire the best 'player development' experts and schools and professional clubs search far and wide for the most qualified coaches. Youth academies are springing up in all corners of the globe, financed by professional clubs and national federations. These academies are run by full-time specialist youth coaches who are required to be certified. Coaching Education programs are now an integral component of every national and state soccer association. The increased authority and influence of the coach does bring with it the potential for over-coaching. Coaching schools heap theories upon enthusiastic students of the game. The result: a gradual transformation of coaching from an 'art form' to a 'science based' endeavor. There is no doubt that progressive coaching methods have brought about an overall improvement in the technical, physical and tactical abilities of players. But, as methods and systems dominate the thoughts of the modern coach, the 'system' can become more important than the individual. Creating players to fit a system is not healthy for the game if it ultimately fails to nurture genius. In the wrong hands, or heads, coaching theory and methodology can sterilize the spectacle out of the game. Worse still, over-coaching can stifle player development.

A clash of coaching philosophies has emerged, with the 'organization' versus 'improvisation' argument at the core of the debate. Some coaches extol the virtues of one over the other when in fact both are essential for success. Modern teams must ally organization with improvisation since both are critical for optimum performance. Players must have the freedom to express themselves, but freedom without cohesion can become a defect rather than a merit. A basic tactical framework with well-defined roles prevents players from running into the same space, duplicating effort, or taking unnecessary risks. The best teams are those able to combine a collective team strategy with a license for individual improvisation. The best coaches are those who understand that balance.

Good coaches never stop learning. An insatiable thirst for knowledge and a natural curiosity are traits associated with the very best. The urge to travel and learn new coaching methods first hand should not be suppressed. Staying in one's neighborhood and playing against the same teams over and over leads to stagnation. Soccer is truly a global game. By traveling both domestically and abroad, coaches can discover fresh new ideas and acquire new perspectives. Just as players need to challenge themselves and break out of their comfort zone to improve, so do coaches.

Coaches must develop their own vision of how the game should be played. Every coach worth his salt should be able to close his eyes and clearly visualize his ideal of team play, his preferred style, his version of the optimum team performance. It is impossible to impose tactical concepts and strategies on a team without a concrete end product in mind. It's not important whether the team ever attains the ideal performance. Players' limitation and constraints of time and resources will likely prevent the ideal from ever being reached. But without a clear target, it is impossible to move forward. And to get to the point where a clear vision of the ideal performance is developed, a coach needs to immerse himself, travel, and become a student of the game by constantly watching top level soccer, both live and on television.

It is also highly recommended to watch taped games multiple times. Coaches are soccer fans, just like everyone else. When a coach watches a game for the first time, it's hard to maintain a detached and analytical perspective and not allow the emotions to cloud judgment or recollection of details. But when watching a game for the second or third time, the result is already known and the moments of brilliance have already been savored. Attention can now be more easily directed towards specific details. We can therefore glean much more technical and tactical information from the game after watching it a few times.

To summarize, the skills required by the modern coach, as far as tactical coaching is concerned, are:

1) An understanding of the Principles of Play. A coach fluent in the principles of play can watch a game or a practice and correctly identify the missing ones. He understands the relationship between the principles of play and team shape.
2) An understanding of Coaching Methodology. By this we mean understanding the principles of teaching, how people learn, how to structure a practice and make the sequence of activities flow in a logical and progressive manner, and the dynamics of short and long range planning.
3) An ability to visualize the Ideal Performance. This provides the coach with a clear vision of the ideal end product and becomes the standard against which both the individual players' and the team's progress is gauged.
4) The ability to Coach in The Game. The intuitive skill of reading the game. The ability to observe and zero in on the most crucial points that need addressing in order to win the game. It means having a 'feel' for the game and being able to influence the flow of the game through tactical adjustments. It means knowing how to alter the team's strategy by maximizing its strengths and minimizing its weaknesses to create the most favorable impact on the result. This ability is part science and part art.
5) Player management skills. The ability to deal with people, gain the respect of the players, convince them to follow the collective game plan, and inspire them to achieve their potential.

The first two qualities can generally be taught. Coaches can learn them by attending coaching courses and reading books such as the one you are holding right now. The third quality comes from immersing oneself in the game and becoming a keen student of the game. The last two qualities are not as easily taught, being more intuitive in nature, and in many cases take years of experience to fully develop. Some coaches are born, possessing a natural affinity to coaching. Many others never quite master the art of reading the game, or grasping the dynamics needed to get a winning result. There are coaches who are weak in the theoretical areas of coaching methodology, but possess a strong playing background, which enables them to read the game well and deal with players effectively. Other coaches understand the principles of play and can plan a good practice session but may lack the ability to convert theory to results on the field. Sometimes, winning a game depends on the art of 'thinking outside the box' or following a gut feeling, a hunch. The mere knowledge of the principles of play will not always guarantee success. It is, however, a safe bet that coaches who are successful at the highest level over a long time, with every team they manage, likely possess all five qualities mentioned above.

Characteristics of Successful Teams

In team sports, the most successful teams set the bar and become the model for everyone else. Here, success is defined as winning competitions that last over a number of games, as opposed to winning a single game. Every aspiring coach should study successful teams in order to form in his mind a standard against which he can measure his own team's performance. Analyzing successful teams also provides coaches with clues regarding the training emphasis that should be adopted for their own teams.

When analyzing successful teams at the youth level, one must be careful to discard success borne merely out of physical superiority or age advantage. The perceptive coach should be able to tell whether any useful information can be gathered from a particular competition. But all coaches, regardless of the level of players they work with, could benefit from analyzing the traits of successful teams at the top level. World Cup games, European and South American Cup games and top professional leagues provide plenty of scope for identifying the most common predicators of success.

Technique and tactics are inextricably connected in soccer. Championship teams are built on a solid foundation of excellent individual technique. Without technique, tactics are a moot point. Technical proficiency, or the ability to 'make the ball talk' is a pre-requisite to any successful team. A good first touch is vital. If players cannot control and pass the ball under pressure, they will lose the majority of the 1v1 duels and their team formation becomes irrelevant. Once players develop a sound technical base, they have the tools to carry out the tactical plan and the confidence to express themselves with the ball.
In addition to a sound technical base, successful teams are well organized both defensively and offensively. They are able to maintain a good team shape even as their players interchange positions and make all sorts of runs. There is an economy of movement, where every run has a purpose. Runs are made either to create space or to exploit space. There is no reckless, excessive running just for the sake of it. There is always a good balance between moving support and standing support, providing ample passing options both to space and to feet.

Successful teams exhibit a balance between organization and improvisation, able to transition smoothly from choreographed combinations to deceptive, unpredictable play. Successful teams have players who can solve problems on their own, with little or no guidance from the sidelines, players who instinctively know when to stick to the rehearsed moves and when to play 'off the cuff'.

Successful teams have more possession of the ball. Even if possession doesn't always translate into penetration and goal chances, it helps conserve energy. The odds are that teams who are forced to exert a lot of energy chasing the ball over long periods do not have any left to mount many dangerous attacks of their own. Teams that keep the ball can impose their style on their opponents and, more importantly, can dictate where the ball can go. Teams who can possess the ball for long periods in their opponents' half are clearly superior in every department. They are able to play the ball into the areas of the field where they hold the advantage in the 1v1 battles, and then penetrate. Also, teams who have the bulk of possession are more likely to create openings towards the end of the game, when opponents begin to tire.

Successful teams are able to penetrate both through the middle and on the flanks. Teams who vary their attack are obviously more unpredictable and harder to contain. The ability to penetrate through the middle is crucial for success. At best, it can be a devastating pierce right through the heart of the defense. At the very least, it forces opponents to concentrate numbers in the central areas and concede space on the flanks, which in turn facilitates flank penetration.

Successful teams display versatility. They have versatile players who can fill multiple roles and are comfortable in any area of the field. This allows the team to effortlessly switch from one formation to another, even in the middle of a game, and adapt to any tactical changes imposed by opponents. It also allows frequent interchanging of positions, making the team hard to contain.

Successful teams can counterattack swiftly and directly. When teams have the skill and speed to transition from defense to attack immediately and effectively, opponents are exposed because they have no time to regroup.

Successful teams regain possession often in the attacking half. This characteristic is an indication of a team's high work rate and ability to close down the ball instantly upon loss of possession. It speaks of an ability to anticipate and intercept passes and pounce on loose balls. When the ball is frequently regained in the attacking half, goal chances are more likely to occur because of the proximity to the opponent's goal.

Successful teams win the majority of the individual battles. As much as the game has changed tactically, one thing has remained constant. The game is still about the individual. And the contest is still dependent on the individual duel. Brazil won the 2002 World Cup because it had the better individuals. It was not the 3-5-2 formation or the system that brought Brazil glory. It was the brilliance of the Brazilian artists that tipped the balance. Obviously, coaching played a part, by using a system that maximized the impact of the individual superiority. But the bottom line is, if Ronaldo, Rivaldo and Ronaldinho had played for Germany, the World Cup trophy would have been lifted by a

German captain instead. Brazil has won more World Cups than any other nation because, over the past fifty years, the Brazilian conveyor belt has consistently produced players of high technique and imagination. The lesson is clear. Coaches at all the levels need to maintain the right balance between the game plan and individual freedom. Creativity must not be sacrificed in the name of functionalism.

SECTION ONE

PRINCIPLES OF PLAY

PRINCIPLES OF ATTACK

The object of the game is to score goals. Possession of the ball for the sake of possession is meaningless since the winning team is the one that scores the most goals. In order to score goals, chances must be created. Hence, the attacking side of the game is about seeking ways to create goal-scoring opportunities. Game analysis tells us that the majority of goal-scoring opportunities are created when attacking teams are able to either *1) reach the end line* (goal line) before crossing the ball into the penalty area, or *2) get the ball to an attacker who is in the 'hole'* and facing the goal. The 'hole' is the space just in front of the opposing central defenders. Let us examine why these two situations bring so many goals

Diagram 101
Crosses from the goal line

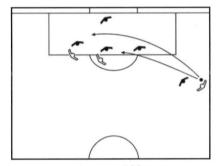

Diagram 102
Crosses from in front of the defense

Crossing from the goal line

Crosses from the goal line (Diagram 101) are more dangerous than crosses made from in front of the defense (cross A in Diagram 102). When an attacker reaches the goal line and crosses the ball, the defenders are 'turned' and forced to challenge and clear the ball while running towards their own goal. This often leads to poor clearances or conceding corner kicks. The defenders are also unable to keep their eyes on both the ball and the attackers, making it easier for attackers to sneak in front of them and head the ball home. Crosses coming from in front of the defense are relatively easy to clear away from goal since the defenders are facing up field and can keep their eyes on the attackers as the cross is coming.

That's not to say that crosses from in front of the defense cannot result in a goal. David Beckham from Manchester United is considered one of the best crossers of the ball, and his crosses from deep are devastating. That is because

Beckham has mastered the art of whipping a hard and accurate cross into the space between the defense and the keeper that bends away from the keeper, yet forces defenders to turn towards their goal, making it very awkward to clear (cross B in Diagram 102). The trajectory and pace of Beckham's crosses create a similar effect to the cross from the end line without the need to penetrate to the end line. But generally speaking, defenders prefer to deal with crosses originating from in front of them because they do not like to 'get turned' towards their own goal.

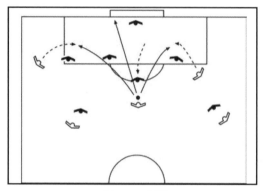

Diagram 103
Getting into the 'hole'

Getting the ball into the 'hole'

An attacker in the hole with the ball at his feet, facing goal, can be very dangerous (see Diagram 103). From this close proximity to the heart of the defense, he can dribble at the defense, or he can deliver a 'killer' pass behind the defense for a teammate before anyone has time to react. Dribbling at the defense will destroy any cover since one of the defenders will have to step up and challenge him to prevent a shot on goal. If the defense is slow in closing him down, he can shoot on goal himself. Either way, defenders do not like to deal with attackers who dribble at them from midfield. It often leads to badly timed tackles, conceding free kicks in dangerous areas or even penalty kicks.

In studying diagrams 101, 102 and 103, it should become obvious that creating scoring chances essentially depends on the attackers' ability to exploit the space **behind** and **in front** of the other team's defense. All coaches will agree with that. But there are many opinions as to the most effective ways to accomplish this. Some coaches prefer the more direct approach while others espouse the slower, possession oriented build up. Some believe in the short passing game while others like to see more long passes. The modern approach is a more pragmatic and flexible one, using a combination of all of these methods. The most successful modern teams have players who know when to speed up the play and counter quickly, when to be more direct and use longer passes, and when to slow it down and keep the ball. But regardless of approach or coaching style, for a team to consistently penetrate into the key spaces behind and in front of the defense, its players must play by the general principles of attack. Regardless of the formation used, it is the principles of attack that really dictate the positioning and movement of the players. It is therefore absolutely essential for every coach to understand these principles and to be able to teach them to his players. The next few pages provide a brief explanation of the following principles of attack:

Support
Depth
Width
Mobility
Penetration
Creativity and Deception

ATTACKING PRINCIPLE: SUPPORT

In order for a team to maintain possession, the player with the ball must have teammates in supporting positions near him. Whenever possible, there should be support on either side of the ball, behind the ball, and in front of the ball. Also, the team in possession should always strive to have 'numbers up' near the ball, meaning that it should have more players around the ball than the opposing team. The supporting players should adopt good support angles that minimize the chances of passes getting intercepted. Diagram 104 shows poor support angles while Diagram 105 shows good support angles.

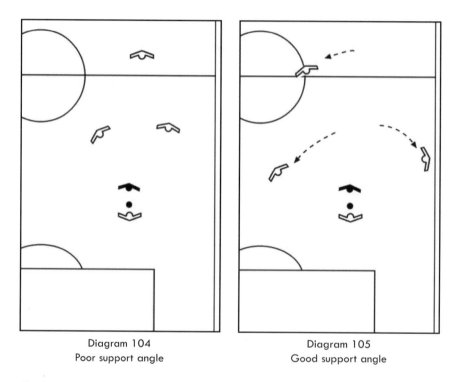

Diagram 104
Poor support angle

Diagram 105
Good support angle

The support angle also depends on factors other than the pressure on the ball. Supporting players should position themselves so that they can see both the ball and as much of the field as possible. For example, if the inside player in Diagram 106 gets a pass, he will not be able to watch both the ball and opponent X closing in on him at the same time. But by adjusting his support angle as shown in Diagram 107, he will now be able to see both the ball and the approaching opponent and will be in a better position to decide how to play his first touch.

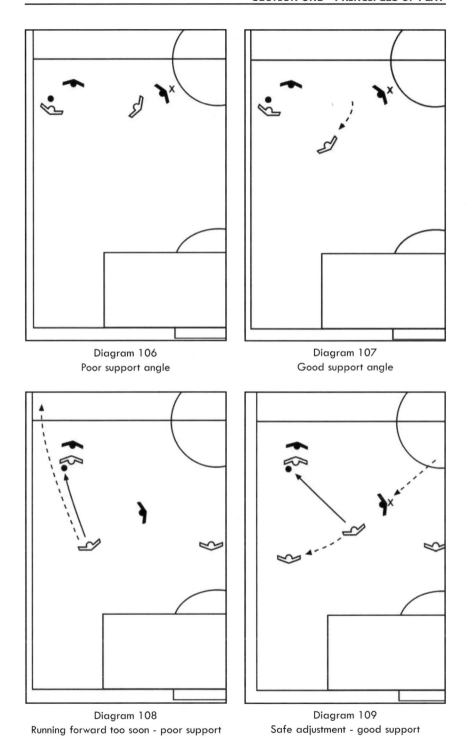

Diagram 106
Poor support angle

Diagram 107
Good support angle

Diagram 108
Running forward too soon - poor support

Diagram 109
Safe adjustment - good support

Many times, the old cliché of 'pass and move' leads inexperienced players to abandon good supporting positions by moving too early. For example, when the ball is passed into midfield from the back, the back players must suppress their urge to join the attack until the midfielder with the ball is able to turn and face upfield. Diagram 108 shows such a moment, when a defender passes the ball to a midfielder and moves up on the overlap to join the attack. The hapless midfielder is in trouble because he is under pressure and without support from behind. The defender should have stayed behind after passing. Diagram 109 depicts what should happen in a similar situation. The defender, under pressure from opposing forward X, passes the ball to his midfielder and backpedals into a new support position, away from X. This is a good decision by the defender since he is making himself available for a pass back from his midfielder who is under pressure, while adopting a safer distance between himself and forward X.

Support positions that offer many options for diagonal passes are preferred over those that lead to vertical and horizontal passes. For example, the support positions in Diagram 110 help maintain possession. But the passing options are limited to square and back passes with no penetration, since players 3 and 5 are too flat and player 1 cannot pass a ground ball to player 4. On the other hand, Diagram 111 shows good support angles that encourage diagonal passes. These diagonals create new passing lanes and better penetration.

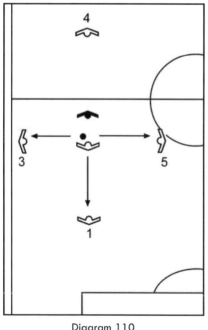

Diagram 110
Poor support angles

Diagram 111
Good support angles

ATTACKING PRINCIPLE: DEPTH

In order for the attacking team to penetrate, it must have at least one player, and preferably more, positioned as far up the field as possible. In other words, the team's strikers should always look to push up against the opponent's last defender and thus stretch the field vertically. This vertical stretch will allow the ball to be played forward and will also open up more space in the midfield, making it easier to penetrate through the midfield.

A common defensive system among youth teams features a sweeper behind man marking defenders. Most sweepers often drop back as much as 10-15 yards behind their own defenders. Many forwards do not look to see where the sweeper is and fail to take advantage of his deep position. A good forward should always be aware of the sweeper's position and push up as far as he can, in line with the sweeper, to increase his team's depth.

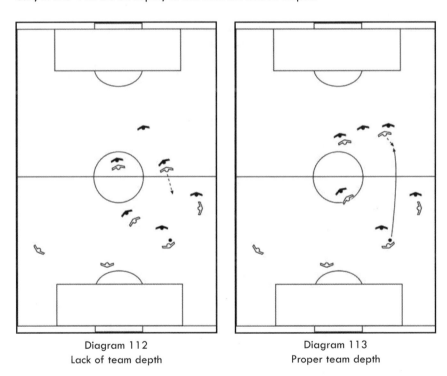

Diagram 112
Lack of team depth

Diagram 113
Proper team depth

Diagram 112 shows a failure to create sufficient depth by the forwards even though the opposition's sweeper is very deep. To make matters worse, the forward checks towards the ball, destroying what little depth there was and making it futile to pass to him since his checking run has brought him into midfield. Diagram 113 shows much better depth, with one of the forwards taking advantage of the sweeper's deep position to maximize team depth. From his advanced position, the forward shows for the ball to receive a pass to feet and penetration is achieved.

ATTACKING PRINCIPLE: WIDTH

Width in attack is vitally important for a number of reasons: Width allows a team to play the ball away from a congested area to maintain possession and buy time to regain a good team shape. Width also enables a team to switch the point of attack from one flank to the other. But, most importantly, width improves the team's ability to penetrate by opening gaps between opponents and creating 'vertical passing lanes'. When players spread wide from touch line to touch line, it forces opponents to stretch as well, opening up the passing lanes through which the ball can be played forward to advanced targets. Diagram 114 illustrates how a vertical passing lane is created when the right midfielder pushes out wide to the touch line, making it possible for the defender to pass directly to the forward.

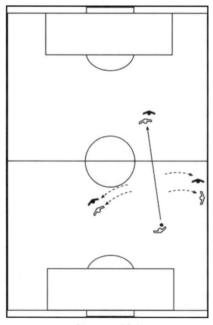

Diagram 114
Width opens up passing lanes

Diagrams 115 and 116 show one example of how width can be used to create gaps for penetration. In diagram 115, defender D4 has the ball and midfielder M4 is providing width, but opponents 1, 2 and 3 are staying very compact and are blocking any possible ground passes to the forwards. Diagram 116 shows how the width provided by M4 can help open up gaps. D4 passes the ball to M4, which forces opponent 2 to go wide and pressure M4. Midfielder M4 passes the ball back to D4 who is now able to thread a pass through the gap to the forward.

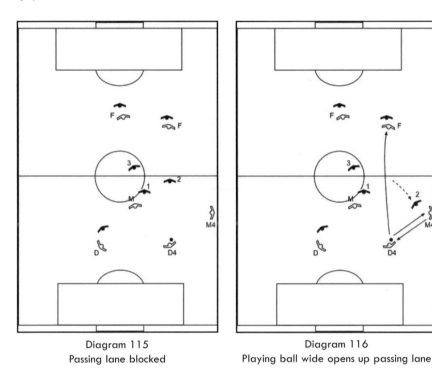

Diagram 115
Passing lane blocked

Diagram 116
Playing ball wide opens up passing lane

ATTACKING PRINCIPLE: MOBILITY

Mobility refers to the movement of the players without the ball. Soccer is a physically demanding game, where players are expected to cover a few miles in the course of the ninety minutes. But hard running without thought can backfire. It can cause a loss of team shape or lead to fatigue towards the end of the game. Successful attack requires intelligent, efficient movement and proper timing of runs. Hard running must be coupled with smart running.

Players' runs are part instinct, part choreography. Players' movement in attack is dictated by the positions of teammates, opponents, and the ball. The most critical movement involves runs geared towards achieving penetration. Intelligent running simply means that, as players are moving, they understand where they should be in relation to teammates in order to maintain the balance between safety and risk. The end product of good movement is penetration without sacrificing team shape or possession.

Generally speaking, a static attacker presents an easy task for a defender because defenders are happiest when they can position themselves such that they can see both the attacker and the ball. A moving attacker, therefore, tends to cause problems for a defender who now has to adjust his position in order to keep both the ball and the attacker within sight. Also, when an attacker makes a run, his marker has to decide whether to follow him or stay to cover his zone. No matter which option the defender chooses, the attacking team can gain an advantage. If the defender chooses to follow his mark, space is created and can be exploited by another attacker. If the defender chooses to stay in his zone, the attacker is now free to receive the ball with time and space to turn and go forward.

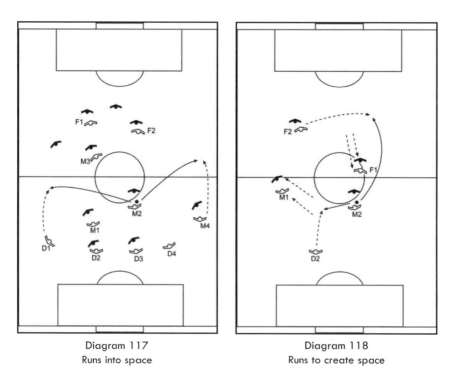

Diagram 117
Runs into space

Diagram 118
Runs to create space

As implied above, there are basically two types of runs players make: *1) runs into open space*, and *2) runs to create space*. Diagram 117 has examples of runs into open space, showing runs by defender D1 and midfielder M4, either of whom can receive the ball from M2. Diagram 118 shows examples of runs to create space. In Diagram 118, forward F1 runs towards the ball, dragging his marker with him and creating space for the second forward, F2, to exploit. At the same time, midfielder M1 runs away from the ball, taking his marker with him, and creating space for defender D2 to step into. As illustrated in diagram 118, players run to make space for teammates. Players also make many runs to create space for themselves. The movement to create space for oneself is usually in the form of short 'dummy' runs in one direction aimed at sending the defender the wrong way, followed by a quick sprint in another direction.

Coaches have coined runs with all sorts of colorful names in their attempt to teach movement off the ball to their players. Regardless of the name picked to describe a movement, all of these runs essentially fall into one of the two basic types, namely, either runs into space or runs to create space. Diagrams 119 through 131 demonstrate some of the most common types of runs.

Diagram 119
Overlapping run

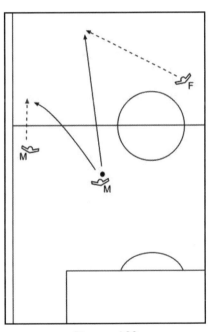

Diagram 120
Diagonal and straight runs

Overlapping runs: An overlap is a run made by a player from a point behind the ball into space in advance of the ball. Although the overlap is mostly executed by wide defenders, midfielders are also known to join the attack with an overlapping run. See Diagram 119 for an example of an overlapping run by a defender.

- 27 -

Diagonal runs: When a ball is passed into a player's run, the preferred relationship between the pass and the run fits together as follows: A straight forward pass to a diagonal run, or a diagonal pass to a straight forward run. In other words, the runner should not give his back to the ball. The logic here is that it is a lot easier for the passer to judge the weight of the pass when the run is made across his line of vision. It is also a lot easier to receive a ball if the receiver can see both the ball and the space into which he is running. Another advantage of receiving a straight pass onto a diagonal run is that it is easier for the receiver to put his body between the ball and the defender. Generally speaking, it makes more sense for wide attackers to make straight runs and for central attackers to make diagonal runs. Young players often turn their backs to the ball and make straight runs towards goal from a central position, expecting the ball to be played through. Although straight runs down the middle can slice the defense, they do not succeed very often against good teams since the sweeper, the goalkeeper, or the chasing defender can easily intercept the pass. Diagram 120 shows examples of diagonal runs and straight runs.

Blind side runs: A blind side run is usually a diagonal run behind defenders' backs. As the name implies, the defender is busy watching the ball in front of him and therefore is unlikely to pick up the runner. Diagram 121 shows midfielder M2 making a blind side run behind opponents who are caught ball watching.

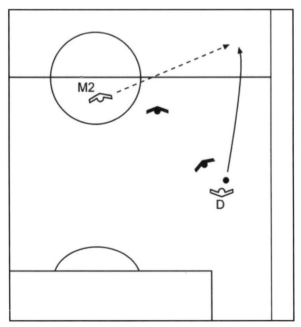

Diagram 121
Blind side run

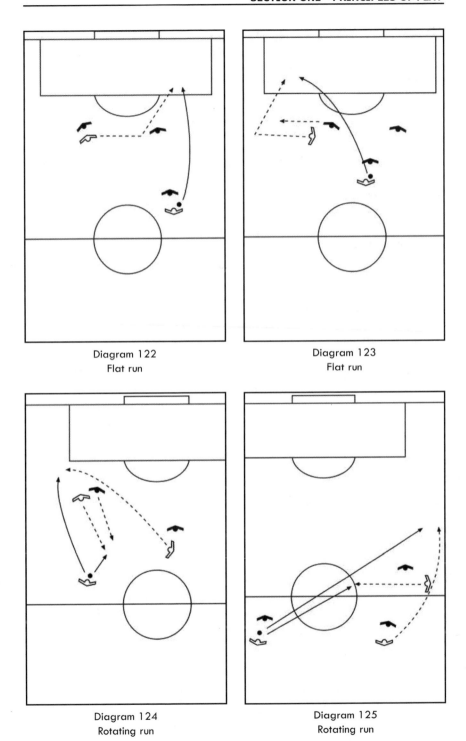

Diagram 122
Flat run

Diagram 123
Flat run

Diagram 124
Rotating run

Diagram 125
Rotating run

The flat run: Often it is necessary for an attacker to delay his forward run to avoid running into off-side. The attacker can start off with a flat run that keeps him on-side and change direction the instant the ball is played. Diagrams 122 and 123 illustrate examples of flat runs.

Rotating runs: Rotating runs essentially mean that players are interchanging positions and confusing the opponents. Diagram 124 shows a forward and a midfielder rotating positions, with the forward running into midfield and the midfielder attacking the space created. Diagram 125 shows a wide midfielder moving inside, allowing the inside midfielder to go wide. In both situations, the ball can be passed to either player, depending on the reaction of the opponents. The Dutch Total Football style, made famous in the 1970's, relied a lot on players interchanging positions with such runs. Player interchange is now a regular feature of modern soccer.

Third Man Running: The principle here is that while two players are inter-passing and drawing everyone's attention, a third player runs, usually from behind the ball, into the space behind opponents to receive the through ball. Obviously, the run needs to be well timed to avoid getting caught off-side. Often, the 'third man' is the one initiating the passing sequence by making a forward pass and embarking on a forward sprint into space and ends up with the ball two or three passes later. Diagram 126 shows how midfielder M2 makes a third man run to penetrate behind the defense.

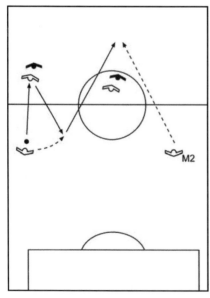

Diagram 126
Third man running

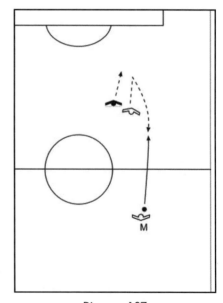

Diagram 127
Dummy run

Dummy runs: Good attackers never remain static and always try to make their runs unpredictable. Attackers are constantly looking to fool defenders by making dummy runs in an attempt to send the defender the wrong way and create space for themselves. They do this by moving off in one direction and darting back into another to receive the ball. This kind of movement is the bread and butter of top level forwards. Some coaches describe the run to create space for oneself as "One run for the defender and one run for oneself". Most coaches describe it as a 'dummy' run followed by the real run. The dummy run can be very short, even a step or two, just enough to send the defender the wrong way. The timing of the dummy run is crucial. Too early, and the defender has time to recover. Too late, and the ball might be played into the wrong space. Diagrams 127 through 131 show variations of dummy runs.

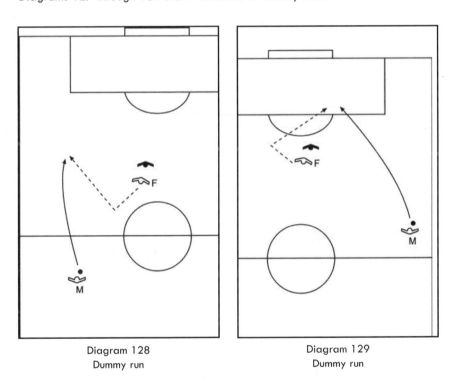

Diagram 128
Dummy run

Diagram 129
Dummy run

Diagram 127: here the attacker makes a dummy run forward as if he is trying to get into the space behind the defender but then checks back towards the ball to receive a pass to feet. **Diagram 128:** this time, the forward makes a dummy run towards the ball and then spins away to attack the space down the wing. **Diagram 129:** F makes a dummy run away from the center and cuts back to attack the central area behind the defense. **Diagram 130:** The timing of the dummy run is important. Here, the wide midfielder makes his dummy run towards his own half while D1 is receiving the ball. The moment D1 has the ball under control and is looking up to find his teammates, the midfielder spins and sprints down the wing asking for the ball. **Diagram 131:** In this example, the wide midfielder shakes off his marker by running up the wing and, as soon as D3 is ready to pass the ball, he checks back at speed to receive the ball to feet.

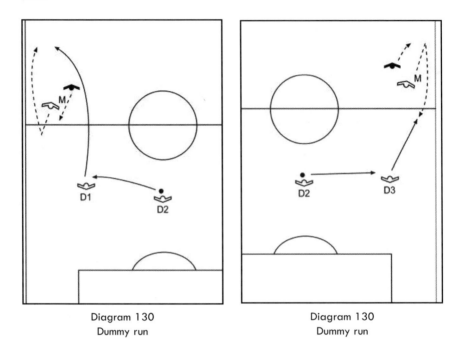

Diagram 130
Dummy run

Diagram 130
Dummy run

ATTACKING PRINCIPLE: PENETRATION

The obvious implication of the term penetration is: playing the ball forward. But penetration means more than that. Since the objective of the game is to score goals, penetration is not just about going forward, but also getting the ball into areas behind opponents. It means attacking the spaces behind opposing defenders to create goal chances. A team can keep possession of the ball for a long time, but if it cannot penetrate into goal scoring areas, it will not win many games. Penetration can be accomplished in many ways: An individual dribbling past a defender, a combination play between two players such as a wall pass, a crossover or an overlap, or a long pass into space behind opponents.

Penetration can be achieved methodically, with patience, using a succession of short and medium passes, or it can take the form of a quick counterattack. It all depends on how well organized the opponents are. But for penetration to occur, the two most important elements are: 1) players must be willing to run into spaces behind defenders, and 2) the ball carrier must recognize early any opportunity to penetrate, whether by dribbling or passing the ball forward, before defenders have time to regroup and adjust.

Diagram 132 illustrates examples of penetration: Pass 1 achieves penetration by playing the ball around a defender into a winger's run. Pass 2 achieves penetration by playing the ball behind the opposing midfield into the forward's feet. Pass 3 achieves penetration by playing the ball into space behind defenders. Passes 4 and 5 are an example of a wall pass combination to get in behind the pressurizing defender.

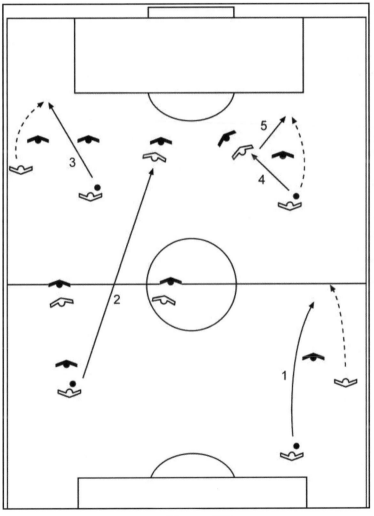

Diagram 132
Penetration

ATTACKING PRINCIPLE: CREATIVITY AND DECEPTION

Coaching attacking play is a delicate balancing act. It's about teaching the principles of play, but not at the expense of stifling the players' freedom to express themselves. Soccer is part science and part art, and how much of each is open to debate. As mentioned in the introduction, observations of top level soccer clearly demonstrate that the most successful teams find that often elusive balance between rehearsed movement and spontaneous instinctive play. Good coaches learn quickly that it's individuals who win games, not tactics, and that every system can be beaten by an individual play. The notion that goals are scored as a result of avoidable human mistakes doesn't diminish the fact that it takes individual creativity to exploit those defensive mistakes. When a team is fortunate to have players with the ability and initiative to make things happen on their own, goals will come. When a team has players who always look to surprise opponents, and who can think for themselves, goals will come. Defending systems are designed to stop the expected. No system can handle the unexpected if it is allied with skill, speed of thought, and deception.

Soccer is a player-centered sport. Once the players enter the field, they are the decision makers and the coach is relegated for the most part to a spectator's role. It is therefore not enough to teach the principles of play. The principles of play are just the tools. The players must learn how and when to use these tools. At the youth level, it means that coaches should allow and encourage their players to solve their own problems on the field, and only provide guidance when necessary. Young players' individual creativity and sense of adventure should not be suppressed. Good coaches understand the power of learning through trial and error and allow for the fact that their players will make mistakes as they explore the limits of their own ability. It won't always work, but in the long run, it will pay off!

PRINCIPLES OF DEFENSE

The moment a team loses possession of the ball, the entire team must react quickly and collectively to win the ball back. If at all possible, pressing the ball to *win it back immediately* should be the first priority. If that is not possible, the next best option is to pressure the ball and mark players to *prevent a counterattack*. Team formation is irrelevant here. It's the principles of defense that dictate players' actions. Regardless of team formation, the following principles must govern the movement and decisions of the players, if they are to regain the ball:

Pressure
Recovery
Cover
Balance
Compactness.

DEFENDING PRINCIPLE: PRESSURE

Pressure means to deny an opponent both the time and space in which to play the ball and to prevent him from passing or dribbling the ball forward. As soon as the ball is lost, a player from the team that has just lost possession must apply immediate pressure. The purpose of immediate pressure on the ball is, firstly, to try to regain possession. If it's not possible to regain possession, then the next objective of immediate pressure is to prevent opponents from playing the ball forward and mount a counterattack. By delaying the opponent's attack, immediate pressure allows teammates to recover goal-side of the ball and get organized.

As mentioned earlier, applying pressure starts the moment the ball is lost. But pressure must continue unrelenting until the ball is won back, or at least until the ball is pushed back into the other team's half. Immediate pressure on the ball is a must in the defensive third and the middle third. The decision on whether to apply pressure on the ball in the attacking third depends on the strategy imposed by the coach, i.e. whether to apply full-field pressure or retreat back upon loss of possession.

Constant pressure is achieved by closing down on the ball as it is played from one player to the next. It requires alertness, anticipation and tenacity since success depends on the players' ability to close the distance while the ball is in flight. Otherwise, opponents will have enough time on the ball to play it forward. The ultimate pressure produces an interception, the most desirable way to regain the ball. A clean interception avoids unnecessary fouls and presents a golden opportunity to counter. If interception is not possible, then the next best thing is to arrive at the same time as the ball and force the opponent into a mistake.

Properly applied pressure hurries opponents into mistakes or, at the very least, forces the play sideways or backwards. Loose pressure allows an opponent to play the ball anywhere he wishes, giving him the time to measure a good forward pass. Since one of the main objectives of pressure is to prevent the ball from going forward, pressure should come, whenever possible, from a player who is goal-side of the ball. Diagram 133 illustrates proper pressure applied by midfielder M2 who started from a goal-side position (M2 was between the ball and his own goal). Midfielder M4 could have applied pressure as well but was not goal-side of the ball and might not have been as successful in preventing the opponent from playing forward. Diagram 134 shows what happens when the pressure is not applied early, or is too loose, allowing the attacker to play the ball forward into dangerous areas.

Lastly, care must be taken by the pressurizing player to avoid rush challenges. A good defender stays on his feet and waits for the attacker to make a mistake or show enough of the ball to warrant a tackle. Calculating on the side of caution is better than lunging into reckless tackles. Good defenders concede very few free kicks in dangerous areas and only tackle when they have cover behind them. Bad defenders allow their eagerness to get the better of them and too often miss-time their tackle. The result is either a dangerous free kick, or a beaten defender, on his backside and unable to recover.

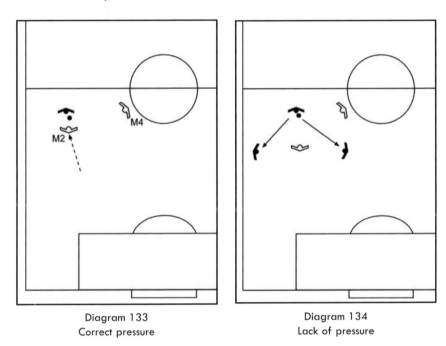

Diagram 133	Diagram 134
Correct pressure	Lack of pressure

DEFENDING PRINCIPLE: RECOVERY

As soon as possession of the ball is lost, and as one player is applying immediate pressure on the ball, all the other players must fall back and recover to a position both goal-side of the ball and goal-side of the opponents. The objective of these recovery runs is to get the whole team between the ball and the goal (goal-side of the ball) and create 'numbers up' around the ball as well as in the back. Recovery runs usually fall under one of three general purposes: 1) to apply pressure on the ball; 2) to get goal-side of an opponent in order to mark him; or 3) to get goal-side of the ball and cover space behind teammates.

Diagram 135 demonstrates these recovery runs. In diagram 135, opponent 2 has the ball, F1 is recovering towards the ball to apply pressure, M3 is getting goal-side of the ball in order to provide cover for F1, M1 is chasing opponent 1, and M5 is falling back goal-side of the ball to take up a covering position in midfield. Notice that even though opponent 4 is running wide, away from the ball, M5 is not following him closely but is retreating into a more central position from where he can cover his midfielders and still keep an eye on player 4.

As can be seen, all the players are expected to recover and defend, including the forwards. Of course the forwards cannot be asked to chase the ball all over the field. In Diagram 135, once opponent 2 passes the ball forward, F1 cannot do anything else defensively. As long as he applies pressure on player 2, tries to win the ball and hurries him into making a bad pass, he has done his job. Depending on the coach's instructions, F1 might be required to track opponent 2, or any other defender who runs into midfield to join the attack. F1 and F2 will most likely be given instructions to pressure the ball in a certain way that forces it into a pre-determined area, but more on that later in the book.

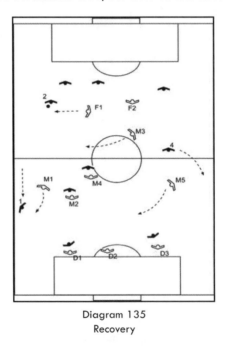

Diagram 135
Recovery

DEFENDING PRINCIPLE: COVER

Cover in defense refers to the help given to the pressuring player by a teammate or teammates positioned close behind him. If the pressuring player is beat by a dribble, the covering player can apply immediate pressure. Hence, cover provides the extra safety against penetration and allows the beaten defender to recover and the defense to reorganize.

Of prime importance are both the distance and angle of the covering player. He should be close enough so that he can apply immediate pressure if the challenging player is beaten. However, he should not be so close that a quick attacker can beat both players by playing the ball past both of them and accelerating. Diagram 136 illustrates a covering player's positioning relative to the ball and the goal. In diagram 136, covering player D2 communicates to his teammate D1 to channel the ball down the side (D1's left) and tackle at the right moment. D1 can tackle with the knowledge that even if he does not succeed, D2 is right behind him to provide cover.

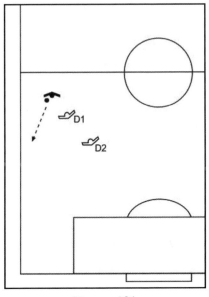

Diagram 136
Cover in defense

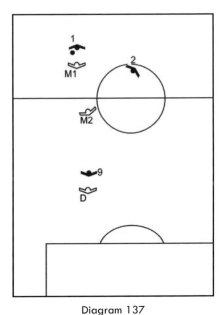

Diagram 137
Covering, marking and blocking lane

Ideally, the defending team should have numbers up around the ball, which means that the covering player is the extra player and, therefore, doesn't have to mark anyone. However, many times it's a 2v2 or 3v3 situation around the ball and the covering player is also forced to mark. Diagram 137 shows how midfielder M2 positions himself to both provide cover for M1 and mark 2. From his position, M2 can see both the ball and his mark, 2. Notice also that M2's excellent positioning enables him to block the passing lane from 1 to forward 9 as well.

If 1 were to pass the ball to 2, M2 would immediately close down on the ball and M1 would drop back behind M2 to become the covering player. Such coordinated movement ensures that pressure is always applied quickly and frontally and saves M1 from running back and forth between the two opponents. This also serves to illustrate that players' roles are constantly changing as the ball is passed around. In our example, M2's role switches from covering to pressuring and M1's role reverses as well.

DEFENDING PRINCIPLE: BALANCE

Balance addresses the defensive needs in the areas away from the ball. Whereas pressure and cover are narrowly focused on the ball, balance takes care of the rest of the field. Defenders who are far from the ball and on the other side of the field are the ones who must provide balance. A team with good balance has players who are positioned to apply quick pressure on the ball if it's switched to the other side of the field. A team with balance also has players who are positioned to cover the dangerous space in front of the goal. Diagram 138 shows how defenders D3 and D4 provide proper balance. If the ball is switched to opponents 3 or 4, D3 and D4 can apply immediate pressure by closing the distance while the ball is in flight. If the ball is played into the space behind them, the dangerous scoring area, it is obvious from the diagram that D3 and D4 will be first to the ball. Diagram 139 shows how vulnerable the defense could be to a cross-field pass if D3 and D4 are drawn too close to the ball, destroying the team's balance.

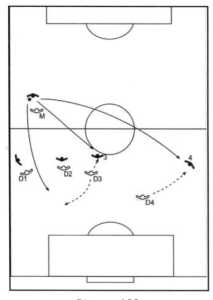

Diagram 138
Balance in defense

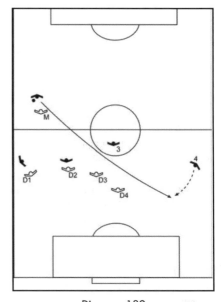

Diagram 139
Lack of balance

DEFENDING PRINCIPLE: COMPACTNESS

If there is one principle that is best associated with modern defensive tactics, it is the principle of compactness. Compactness means that the whole team squeezes together both vertically and laterally in order to reduce the spaces between them, cover for each other, and create numbers up around the ball. Top teams have become so adept at squeezing spaces that the effective playing area is often reduced to a third or even a quarter of the field. Compactness is the ultimate solution to the danger of the 'hole'. When defenders are pushed up against the midfield, the hole shrinks and the opposing midfielders' favorite hang out can no longer be exploited.

To stay compact, defenders must push up as their team is going forward to reduce the gap between them and their own midfield. Likewise, the space between the midfield and the forwards can be reduced, either by the forwards retreating when the ball is lost or by the midfielders pushing up behind the forwards. As soon as the ball is lost, the wide players on the far side of the field must pinch inside in order to reduce the spaces in midfield. The end result is shown in diagram 141.

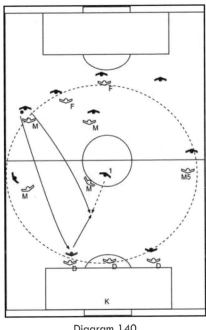

Diagram 140
No compactness

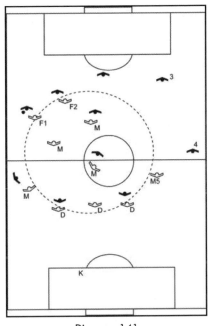

Diagram 141
Good compactness

Diagrams 140 and 141 illustrate the contrast between no compactness and good compactness. In diagram 140 the defending team is too spread out. Notice how 1 can exploit the open space between the defense and the midfield by receiving the ball, turning and attacking the defense. Diagram 141 shows a team with proper compactness, essentially reducing the playing area that needs to be defended (the area defined by the dotted line). Notice how, in Diagram 141, the defenders have pushed up to reduce the gaps in midfield. Also notice how M5 pinches inside to improve compactness and provide additional cover for the defense. It is imperative that forwards F1 and F2 do not allow the ball to be switched to O3 or O4, otherwise the whole team will have to sprint across the field to re-apply pressure.

More and more teams are playing with flat defenses and no sweeper. With teams playing in a more compact fashion and defenders pushing up without the safety of a sweeper behind them, the keeper's role has evolved to that of a sweeper-keeper. Gone are the days when a keeper could remain in his six-yard box and just play his line. Modern keepers are required to come out and control an area as big as the whole defensive third and are expected to intercept through balls played behind their back line. A team that has speedy defenders and a quick, mobile keeper can afford to push up to the half way line and stay there even when they lose the ball. But if the keeper or the defenders are too slow, the only safe way to achieve compactness is by having the whole team retreat back when possession is lost, in order to reduce the space between the defenders and the keeper.

TEAM SHAPE AND PRINCIPLES OF PLAY

Coaches often make a reference to 'team shape'. By that they are referring to the positioning of the players relative to each other at any point during the game. A team exhibits a good shape in attack when its players are spread out, making the effective playing area big, and positioned to provide width, depth (ahead and behind the ball), and good support angles around the ball. Obviously, maintaining a good shape when in possession enables a team to keep the ball and penetrate into scoring positions. Conversely, a good defensive shape has all or most players goal-side of the ball, with one or two players applying pressure on the ball and the rest providing cover, balance and compactness in order to make the effective playing area small.

Shape is the key to successful tactics and good soccer. Shape is everything! When players move according to the principles of play, the correct shape will likely be sustained. Team shape is more important to maintain than team formation. Team formation is just a frame of reference, a blue print of the players' responsibilities. Team shape is the actual physical location of the players on the field at any given moment. It's the shape that will determine success or failure, not the formation.

TEAM SHAPE IN ATTACK

Every time a team wins possession of the ball, its players should be spreading out quickly into new positions that enable the team to penetrate while keeping possession. In Diagram 142 the left defender has the ball and his teammates demonstrate a good attacking shape within a 3-5-2 formation.

The qualities of a good attacking shape are all apparent in diagram 142. Forwards F1 and F2 have pushed up high to provide **DEPTH** ahead of the ball. Defenders D2 and D3 have adopted **SUPPORTING** positions behind the ball in case D1 cannot play the ball forward and needs to relieve pressure by playing the ball back. Midfielders M1 and M5 provide team **WIDTH** to stretch the opponents. Notice the positions of M2, M3, and M4. The central midfielders hold the key in creating an effective attacking shape. Each one of them is deeper than the next. Yet, they can all receive a pass from D1 while keeping clear of the passing lane to the forwards.

This shape provides D1 with a variety of passing options for **PENETRATION**. Also, if M4 receives a pass, M3 is in a position to **SUPPORT** him from behind, and M2 supports M3 in the same way. The ability of the midfielders to support each other from behind is extremely important in modern soccer. The battle for control of the midfield is fierce, punctuated with tight marking and squeezed spaces. Midfielders often receive the ball while facing their own goal and under pressure. Modern midfielders need immediate support behind them in order to pass the ball back in the direction they are facing, instead of turning into pressure. In diagram 142, if the ball goes from D1 to M4 and back to M3, penetration into midfield is achieved without losing possession and with the added advantage of M3 facing up field and having several passing options for further penetration. In contrast, diagram 143 shows how difficult it would be to penetrate if all three central midfielders destroy the midfield shape by moving towards the ball. Not only do they all present the same passing option for D1, they will all have to risk turning into pressure or play it back to a defender without achieving any penetration. The midfielders in diagram 143 are too flat.

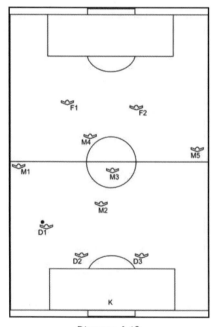

Diagram 142
Good attacking shape - triangulations

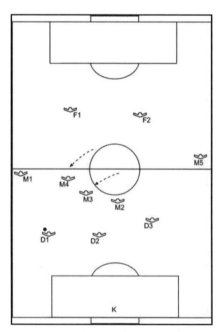

Diagram 143
Poor attacking shape - flat lines

Notice also that, in diagram 142, every player is either slightly ahead or slightly behind the other players around him. In other words, the players are not 'flat' relative to each other. This creates a multitude of support and passing 'triangles', which helps the team maintain possession. Some examples of these triangles are the D1/D2/M2 triangle, the M1/M4/F1 triangle, the M2/M3/M4 triangle, or the M4/F1/F2 triangle. As you can see, the permutations are limitless. And it all stems from the intelligent positioning of the players relative to each other. These triangles provide many proper **SUPPORT ANGLES** and allow for more diagonal passes which are more effective than straight horizontal or vertical passes. Contrast that with the flatness exhibited in diagram 143. Not only are the midfielders flat relative to each other, but the three defenders are flat as well. If the defenders are put under pressure, D1 will have no choice but to play the ball back to the keeper. Playing the ball back to the keeper is fine as a last resort but it also concedes any territory previously gained and essentially forces the team to restart the attack from deep, making it harder to play out of the back. The angled support positions of D2 and D3 in diagram 142, behind D1, facilitate a switch to the right side without the need to play it all the way back to the keeper.

Diagram 144
Poor shape - straight lines

Diagram 145
Good shape - staggered lines

Good shape has other features worth noting. The team shape shown in diagram 144 has decent depth and width, but central midfielders M3 and M4 are in a straight line, together with F2, making it difficult for D2 to pass to M4 or F2. Diagram 145 shows how staggered positions allow passes to skip lines and facilitate penetration.

The safety versus risk equation has a profound impact on the team shape and player movement. Diagram 146 reveals a very stretched team, well spread out both vertically and horizontally, with M2 in possession. Is this a good shape? The team is too stretched, which could lead to a number of problems. When players are too spread out, it encourages long passes, which could be intercepted. It is difficult to provide quick support to teammates or create a numerical advantage around the ball. But, above all, it leaves the team dangerously vulnerable to the counterattack if possession is lost. The shape in Diagram 147 is more defensively sound while still providing width and depth. In diagram 147, the defenders stepped up to stay connected to the midfield and are tucked inside more to provide cover and close support. With M1 and M5 already providing width, there is no need for the defenders to get wide at this particular moment. As the attack progresses up field, the defenders should move up as well to maintain compactness and a constant distance of 40-50 yards between themselves and the forwards.

Diagram 146
Poor shape - too spread out

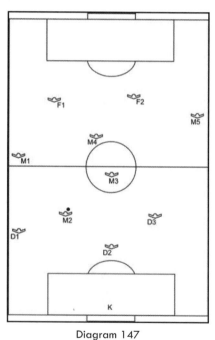

Diagram 147
Good shape - better support

As mentioned before, a good attacking shape should provide the player on the ball a variety of short and long passing options while securing a quick support following a long pass. Refer to diagram 148 and note that if midfielder M3 elects to switch play using a long pass to M5, the team could lose possession. M5 could be double challenged by 1 and 2 and lose the ball since no one is in a good position to offer him quick support. Defender D3 is the closest player but he will hesitate to abandon his position to support M5 since he is the last man. Diagram 149 shows a better team shape where either M2 or D3 can provide a quick support for M5 following a long switch. Notice also that in diagram 149 the ball can be switched from M3 to M5 by either one long pass or a couple of medium passes through M2.

Another feature of a good attacking shape is the ability to apply immediate pressure on the ball if it is lost. In diagram 149, if M5 is stripped of the ball, D3 can step up and apply immediate pressure to prevent a quick counterattack. But in diagram 148, if M5 loses the ball, there is no one to stop the other team from mounting a quick counterattack.

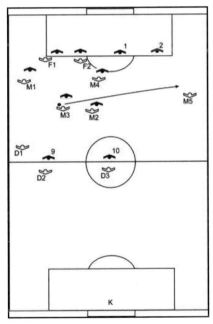

Diagram 148
Poor shape - M5 is too isolated

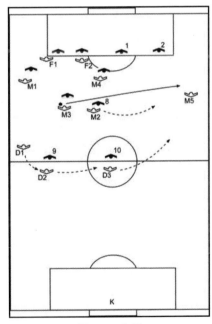

Diagram 149
Good shape - support for both flanks

To summarize, a good attacking shape should have the following features:

1) Provide depth, width and good support angles.
2) Provide support behind the ball.
3) Create maximum triangulation and many options for angled passes.
4) Provide a variety of short and long passing options.
5) Allow a switch from one side of the field to the other, using both one long pass or a couple of medium passes.
6) Staggered arrangement that allows passes to skip lines.
7) Allow the ball to be played from the back to the front using either one long pass or a combination of forward passes followed by short drop passes to supporting players.
8) Provide enough players around the ball such that if the ball is lost, immediate pressure can be applied.
9) Provide immediate support following a long pass.

TEAM SHAPE IN DEFENSE

Up to now, the discussion of team shape focused on the attacking side. Let us now examine the defensive aspects of team shape. Obviously, a team that adheres to the defensive principles of pressure-cover-balance-compactness when possession is lost will automatically adopt a good defensive team shape. Diagram 150 illustrates a good defensive shape by the white team. All the features of solid defending are easily apparent: Immediate pressure on the ball. Defenders outnumber attackers 6 to 5 and all the defenders are goal-side of the ball. The opposing striker is tightly marked and double marked because he is in the dangerous scoring area. The other opponents are loosely marked since they are outside the dangerous area and pose no immediate scoring threat. The marking distance is dictated by the proximity to the ball and the area of the field, and the further from goal, the looser the marking. At the same time, the marking is such that each defender can easily close the distance and apply immediate pressure should his mark receive a pass. Notice that the positioning of the six defenders prevents penetration and invites square passes to wide players, thus keeping the ball in front of the defenders. It is clear that any ball played into the space behind the defense will likely be given away.

But even before a team loses possession, the positioning of the players needs to reflect some balance between attack and defense. For starters, it's always defensively sound to maintain 'numbers-up' in the back. This simply means that defenders should outnumber opposing forwards by at least one player at all times, even when their own team has possession, otherwise they can be vulnerable to the counterattack. So, if the defending team leaves two forwards lurking on top, the team engaged in attack should keep at least three defenders in the back. This is clearly illustrated in Diagram 149, where defenders D1, D2 and D3 are staying back to mark 9 and 10. In contrast, Diagram 148 shows how vulnerable the team is to the counterattack. If the opponents were to win the ball, it could easily spring a 2v2 counterattack, pitting 9 and 10 versus D2 and D3.

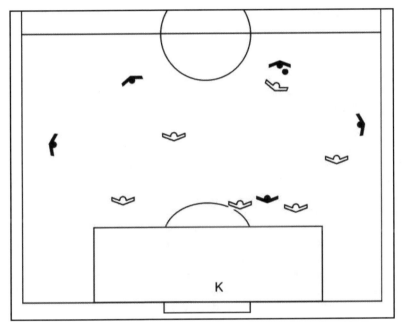

Diagram 150
Good defensive shape

Notice also in Diagram 149 how midfielder M2 is adopting a 'holding' position in front of the three defenders. The holding midfielder has a vital role in maintaining a defensive balance within the team shape. From his holding position, M2 can apply immediate pressure on any opponents who break out into midfield on a counterattack. M2 is also able to block passes to 10 as well as challenge any clearances. If M2 decided to run ahead of the ball and join the attack, he would leave his team naked should a turnover occur. It is easy to see that if the opponents win the ball while M2 is out of position, 8 could sprint and join the forwards to make it a very dangerous 3v3 counterattack. Of course, there are times when a team is forced to throw caution to the wind, take chances and not worry about keeping numbers up in the back. These include when a team is a goal or two behind in the second half, or any other time when a goal is urgently needed.

The modern game demands that defenders overlap into attack, which means that, in order to maintain numbers-up in the back, midfielders must be trained to cover for the overlapping defenders. This creates a whirl of player movements, as defenders interchange with midfielders and midfielders interchange with forwards, all the while looking to maintain a balance between the number of players positioned behind the ball to those in front of the ball. Even at the top level, this delicate balance between attacking and defensive shape can be momentarily lost, resulting in 1v1 or 2v2 attacks. The best teams are the ones who manage to keep a balanced team shape the longest, with the least number of breakdowns.

TEAM SHAPE AND TRANSITION

The term transition is used in soccer to describe the moment a team loses the ball. Soccer is a fluid game with frequent give-a-ways, interceptions and tackles, where the ball changes possession on the fly. Analysis of soccer reveals that the ball changes possession between 200-400 times in a game. The moment teams lose the ball they are very vulnerable to the quick counterattack since most of the players are committed to an attacking shape. Indeed, many goals are scored immediately following a dispossession. This magnifies the impact of transition on the outcome of the contest. The team that reacts more quickly on transition from attack to defense, as well as from defense to attack, will enjoy a significant advantage and will likely dominate the game.

Transition has always presented a 'catch-22' dilemma for coaches. Everyone understands the benefits of spreading out when in possession. The less technically skilled the players, the more space they need to prevent losing the ball. But, on the flip side, the more spread-out, the more vulnerable a team is to the quick counterattack. The trouble is, players who are technically weak are likely to lose the ball often, even if they do a good job of spreading out and making space. Therein lies the problem. Teaching players to adopt an attacking shape by spreading out can result in frustration if the players keep losing the ball and conceding goals. Good coaches understand the limitations of their players and know how to maintain the fine balance between attacking shape and cover at the back. Diagram 146 shows the dangers of spreading out too much, should M2 lose the ball. Diagram 147 shows a safer team shape in attack, with the three defenders closer together and able to cover for M2.

At the youth and developmental levels, where results are not important, coaches should still emphasize the sound principles of attack and teach their players to spread out and play good soccer. At the senior and professional level, where the result is the only thing that really matters, coaches must work out a team shape and a game plan that take into account their players' technical limitations and does not leave them exposed on transition.   One way to minimize the risk of counterattacks is to continue to emphasize depth within the team shape but sacrifice some width. Depth is simply too vital for penetration and must be maintained. But width can be sacrificed to some extent, meaning that the play-ers don't have to spread out from sideline to sideline when in possession. (Note: section 3 in this book has a chapter on 'shadow play' which contains an exam-ple of a practice session that teaches the team's midfield how to stay compact as they possess the ball and play it from side to side).

Teams that traditionally boast technically exceptional players, such as Brazil and Holland, tend to worry less about the counterattack threat from spreading out. Their players have such confidence on the ball and are such great passers that they are not afraid to spread out and stretch the game as much as possi-ble. Their game plan is based on patient possession and forcing the other team to do all the chasing. By contrast, many 'Latin' teams, such as the Central and South American teams, and European teams such as Italy, tend to pack the mid-field area and try to play through the middle. They are more inclined to sacri-fice width in the name of safety. They don't open up the game as much and are more cautious as they push up in attack. Italy is especially known as a cau-tious team that doesn't commit too many players to attack. The Italian psyche is fixated on safety first and counter to score. Generally speaking, the skill level of 'Latin' midfielders is very high, which allows them to concede some width and still maintain possession. They are used to playing in tight spaces and are not afraid to receive and hold the ball under pressure. If they have to, they can rely on individual ability to escape from pressure.

Either way, coaches should train their team to deal with the moments of transi-tion and teach the players how to maintain a team shape that strikes the right balance between attack and transition to defend.

TEAM SHAPE AND YOUTH SOCCER

Young players are drawn like magnets to the ball and do not easily understand the concepts of shape and angles. Teaching inexperienced players to maintain a proper team shape is one of the most challenging tasks of the coach. But it is an extremely important concept and is well worth the effort. In order for coaches to teach shape, they have to get into the habit of taking their eyes off the ball and constantly survey the field. Coaches must monitor the positions of all the players relative to the ball, and should be continually asking themselves: Who is providing depth? Who is providing width? Who is providing support behind the ball? Are there many support triangles near the ball? Do we have enough players behind the ball?, etc. Many inexperienced coaches tend to fix their eyes on the ball and follow it as it moves from player to player. By staying focused only on the ball, they cannot judge team shape and, thus, cannot teach team shape. A coach who cannot teach shape cannot teach tactics. It's as simple as that!

COACHING THE PRINCIPLES TO YOUTH PLAYERS

Tactics are defined as the decisions made by players in the course of the game. Players are constantly making decisions on where to run, when to run and what to do with the ball. As explained before, these decisions should be based on the sound principles of attack and defense. This implies that teams who are well versed in the principles of play and who adhere to these principles are more likely to win games when playing against teams who are not properly coached. All else being equal, teams who are well coached will find more success against poorly coached opponents.

However, the reality of youth is such that it's quite common to see games played between two teams of uneven strengths. Varying rates of physical and technical maturity in young players often result in mismatched opponents. When a mismatch occurs, the physically superior team will likely create many scoring chances without the need to apply the sound principles of play discussed herein. A simple long pass through the middle to a rushing forward who is bigger and faster than everyone else might be all that is needed to create a breakaway opportunity. Although the object of the game is to score more goals than your opponent, youth coaches should always emphasize and teach their players to play with skill, flair, good technique and, above all, using the sound principles of play. The manner of the win is just as important as the win itself, if the long-term goals of player development are to be achieved.

Youth coaches should evaluate their team's performance objectively and look beyond the game result in the process of match analysis. If a team's play exhibits the sound principles of attack and defense and the players work hard but still lose to a physically or technically superior opponent, the coach should take heart in his team's performance and be satisfied that his coaching is influencing his players. He should congratulate them on a good game. By the same token, if his team plays without applying the principles but still wins through physical domination or through sheer luck, the coach should not get carried away by the result and should not ignore the evident shortcomings. He will be doing his players a disservice if he does not address the tactical deficiencies. An over-reliance on physical play will back fire in the long run when opponents will start to catch up in physical maturity.

Whether the game is played in Brazil, China, or America, the tactical principles would still hold true. The concepts of support, depth, pressure, etc. are universal, transcending time and place. These principles have withstood the test of time and will continue so in the future. The differences in the way the game is played around the world have more to do with local tradition, history, culture, weather, and style. In other words, the manner in which these principles are applied and interpreted will change from coach to coach, from country to country. But no team will find consistent success if it fails to apply the sound principles of play.

The principles of play discussed above form the sound foundation of tactics regardless of the number of players on the field. These principles are just as applicable in a 4v4 game as they are in an 11v11 game. Teaching tactics in small-sided games is therefore the preferred method for introducing the principles of play to young players. The high level of repetition associated with small-sided games and the simpler environment are more appropriate for young players. Small-sided games can assist players in assimilating the concepts, applying the principles, and ingraining the associated good habits.

But the youth coach must not forget to link the good habits learned in small-sided games to the 11-a-side game. It becomes a matter of showing the players how the principles taught in the small-sided games apply to the big game. This can be done in many ways: Watching top level games together with the players and drawing their attention to the proper execution of the principles by top level professionals is one way. Chalk talk, pre-game and halftime talks can help, depending on the attention span of the players. Exhibition games obviously present ideal opportunities for applying the principles to the big game.

At some point though, coaching sessions will have to be conducted to address the demands of the full-size, eleven-a-side conditions, in order to maximize the transfer of learning from the practice to the game. Ideally, the coach would need 22 players for practice but in reality, most youth teams only have small rosters of 15 to 18 players. It is however possible to replicate 11-v-11 scenarios in practice with less than 22 players and still coach realistic, big game situations. Later on in the book, practice methods for replicating game situations using less than 22 players are introduced and explained.

SECTION TWO

SYSTEMS OF PLAY

DEFENDING SYSTEMS

Previously, we noted how all the movement of attackers was essentially intended to either **create space** or **run into space**. When it comes to defending, all the positioning and movement of defenders is basically intended to either **mark players** or **mark space**. Coaches use one of the three basic approaches in organizing their teams defensively. They either rely on the **man-to-man marking system** or the **zonal defending system**, or a **combination of the two**. Regardless of the defending system used, every player engaged in defending must either be marking a player or marking space. This concept never changes. But each system has its own guidelines that tell players when they should be marking a player and when they should mark space, and how to shift between the two. Let us first examine the basic features and mechanism of each system:

MAN-TO-MAN MARKING

In this system, players are matched up against specific opponents and are assigned to mark them for the whole game. For example, each defender marks the same forward, following him wherever he goes, while the defensive midfielder is marking the attacking midfielder from the opposing team, throughout the game.

Not all the players are assigned a specific opponent to mark. Teams that play man-to-man usually employ a sweeper behind the man markers who does not have any marking responsibility. The sweeper's role is to cover for his defenders and patrol the dangerous space in front of the goal. The sweeper is the extra protection needed with the man-to-man system. The inherent weakness of the man-to-man marking system is that defenders and midfielders can be pulled out of position and stretched all over the field by the opponents' movement off the ball. This can create dangerous gaps in the back, which can be exploited. The sweeper's job is to close those dangerous gaps, as well as provide cover for his defenders in case any of them gets beaten. Other players who would normally not be expected to mark a specific opponent are the attacking midfielders and the forwards.

Diagram 201 illustrates a typical man-to-man system as employed by team X against Black. The formation of the X team is 3-5-2. Notice that the sweeper

(X1), the attacking midfielder (X2), and the two forwards (X3, X4) are not marking anyone specific. Of course, these four players will still be required to help their team defend. For example, the forwards will be instructed to track down any overlapping defenders. In diagram 201, all the players given a marking assignment are denoted as 'Xm' and will basically follow their assigned opponents wherever they go, especially in the defensive half. The man-to-man marking system will not necessarily be used all over the field since the overriding consideration, regardless of system used, is to maintain a compact defensive shape. Obviously, the pressure-cover-balance-compactness principles of defense must still be applied within the man-to-man marking scheme. So, if an opponent drifts back into his own half, the player assigned to mark him might let him go and just wait for him in the defensive half. In Diagram 202, 3 has the ball and is challenged by his marker, midfielder M3. Notice how all the other midfielders slide back-and-in to provide cover and compactness in case M3 is beaten. M2 is still marking 2 but is also covering for M3. M1 and M4 are still responsible for 1 and 4, but they are also tucked inside, to maintain cover and compactness. The positions taken by M1, M2, and M4 allow them to keep both the ball and their mark within their vision. This is very important, because if 1, 2, or 4 tries to sneak into the dangerous space behind the defense, they must be picked up by whoever is responsible for marking him. Also, if the ball is played to midfielder 4, M4 will immediately close him down, while the rest of the team will adjust their positions to maintain cover-balance-compactness.

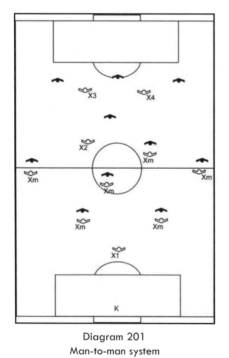

Diagram 201
Man-to-man system

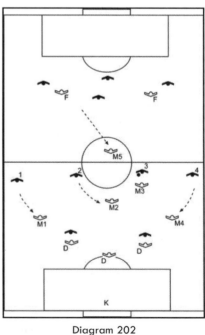

Diagram 202
Defensive principles within man-to-man

For man-to-man marking to be successful, the players must be strong in one-ver-sus-one duels. The match-ups have to be carefully chosen in such a way as to maximize the chances of success in all those one-versus-one duels because if the players get beaten too often, the system will break down. The players have to match their mark's speed, stamina, and strength in order to keep up the tight marking and not be overrun. It is also important to keep the opponents from stretching the defense and opening gaps between the units. The sweeper should be in charge of maintaining team compactness by keeping the defense close to the midfield and organizing the off-side line when applicable.

ZONAL DEFENDING

Zonal defending means that each defender is assigned a zone to defend. The idea here is to place the defenders in a horizontal line, commonly called the back line. The defenders react to the location of the ball by moving up, down and laterally together as a unit, as if they are connected to each other with a string. As they move, they remain within the same relationship, meaning they don't interchange positions. When one leaves the line to pressure the ball, the others slide laterally to close the gap created and maintain compactness. The term 'flat-back-four' is coined by coaches to describe zonal defending with four defenders in a line. Although the traditional way to play a zonal system is to employ four defenders in the back, more and more teams are switching to just three defenders, essentially playing a 'flat-back-three'.

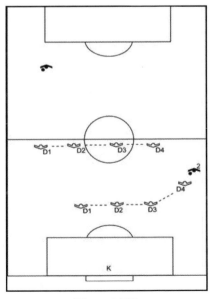

Diagram 203

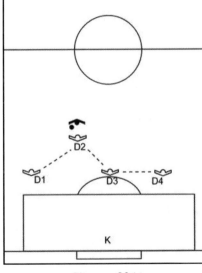

Diagram 204

Diagrams 203 and 204 depict the typical movement of a zonal back line. Diagram 203 shows the back line when opponents have possession in their own half and how they would adjust when the ball is switched to 2. If defender D4 leaves the line to apply pressure on the ball, the other defenders slide across to the right and slightly behind D4, to provide cover and compactness. In diagram 204, D2 applies pressure and the other defenders slide inside to cover. Furthermore, the distance between the defenders depends on how far they, and the ball, are from their own goal. The closer they are to their own goal, the more compact they become and the smaller the gaps between them. This becomes quite clear when comparing their spacing in diagram 203 to diagram 204.

Within this arrangement and movement, each defender is responsible for defending his zone, meaning the area between him and his adjacent partners. Each defender picks up and marks whoever enters his zone and 'hands him over' to the adjoining defender when he leaves his zone. The advantage of zonal defending is that players can remain in the area of the field where they are most comfortable, they do not have to do as much chasing as in man-to-man systems, and team shape and compactness can be more easily maintained.

Diagram 205
Zonal defending system

Diagram 206
Defending principles within zonal system

Diagrams 203 and 204 illustrated how the zonal defending concept is executed by the back line. Diagrams 205 and 206 show how the whole team would defend within the context of zonal defending. In diagram 205, the team's basic formation of 4-4-2, arranged in zones, is depicted. The defenders are denoted as D1 to D4, the midfielders are M1 to M4 and the forwards are F1 and F2. The midfielders shown in the diagram are also arranged in a zonal defending shape, but that is not necessarily required. Some coaches arrange their midfield in zones, with the two central midfielders positioned side by side and slightly behind the outside midfielders, as shown in diagram 205. In such an arrangement, the two central midfielders share the duties of holding and a distributing. But most 4-4-2 formations use a defensive midfielder behind an attacking midfielder in the center (the 4-4-2 formation is more thoroughly discussed in the next chapter on team formation).

Diagram 206 shows how the team would adjust to the ball being played to the right fullback (1). Notice how F1 and F2 slide across to apply pressure on the ball. Notice also how D3 and D4 slide towards the center to close the gaps and how M4 drops inside to provide balance. The result of all this movement is a compact team shape that will be hard to penetrate. Notice also that although players are moving, the overall team orientation and symmetry is maintained. That is, D2 and D3 are still inside, flanked by D1 and D4.

Although this chapter provides a general concept of zonal defending, a more in-depth discussion is needed to help the reader fully understand the mechanics of this system. A more comprehensive explanation can be found in the chapter on functional training in section three, where a complete step-by-step progression for teaching zonal defending is presented.

Both the man-to-man marking and the zonal defending systems are simply a method of organizing the team defensively and getting all the players on the same page. A good defense must start with organization, clearly defined roles for each player, and a sufficient overlap of responsibilities so that each player can cover for teammate's mistakes. One method of defending is not necessarily better than the other. The choice of the system depends to a large extent on the players' strengths and weaknesses and the philosophy of the coach. The most important thing is to actually have a system and to make sure that all the players understand it and buy into it.

It is important to emphasize again that the players must not follow the system like robots, at the expense of the basic principles. It's the principles of defense, not the system, that dictate players' actions. All the system does is give each player a main role and provide some guidelines on how to switch from marking to covering. Regardless of the system used, there must always be immediate pressure on the ball in the defensive half and every opponent who enters the dangerous scoring areas in the defensive third must be tightly marked. Otherwise, the system fails.

It is also worth remembering that soccer is a fluid game with constantly shifting conditions. No two situations are exactly alike. Many times, situations will occur that do not fit neatly into the system. Whenever the defensive system doesn't quite solve the problem, or whenever the system breaks down, the players must react quickly and solve the problems on their own, even if it means departing for a short time from the agreed system. For example, the team in diagram 207 is defending man-to-man. How should the players adjust if 1, who is supposed to be marked by X5, manages to get in behind X5 and receives a pass? Someone must apply immediate pressure on 1 before he bears down on goal. Normally, the sweeper's role is to cover for such lapses by his defenders, but in this case sweeper X1 is too far from 1 to apply immediate pressure. The closest defender to the ball is X2, so he must leave his mark (9) and apply pressure on the ball. At the same time, someone else must quickly pick up 9, before he gets the ball from 1. That could be done by either X4 or by sweeper X1. In the meantime, X5, X8 and X7 should be recovering towards their goal to provide cover and numbers up in the dangerous scoring area.

Another example where the situation will require a temporary departure from the system is shown in diagram 208. This time, we are looking at how the four defenders, marking zonally, react to the opposing forwards' runs. Forward 9 starts a run towards the ball, so D2 must follow him to stop him from receiving and turning. Meanwhile, forward 10 runs into the space created by 9. Defender D3 must follow 10 because D2 has left the area and D1 is too preoccupied with opponent 2. So, the need to track down players and not let them receive and turn overrides the zonal marking and the defense has temporarily lost its zonal shape.

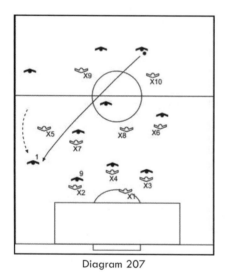 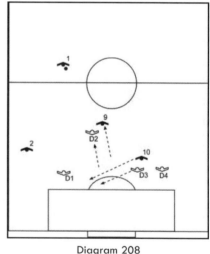

Diagram 207   Diagram 208

The point of these examples is that, regardless of the system, the players will often be required to react quickly to a breakdown and solve the problem on their own. Then, once the ball is regained or goes out of bounds, the players can resume their basic shape and assigned roles within the system.

HOW TO DECIDE ON A MARKING SYSTEM

As mentioned before, the decision regarding which marking system to employ depends mainly on the players available. Generally speaking, younger players encounter difficulties in learning to play zonal marking since it takes a high level of tactical awareness, ability to read the game, and constant communication on the part of all the defenders as they 'hand over' opponents to each other. As youth coaches can attest, it's hard to find many young players who readily talk on the field. Man-to-man marking is easier to teach since the markers' roles are simple to understand and only one leader (the sweeper) is required to make it work. That's not to say that young players cannot play zonal defending. It will just take them longer to learn. It can also be argued that learning to defend in zones will make them better defenders in the long run since, in zonal defending, they cannot rely on a sweeper to clean up after them. So, the long term goals of the coach and player development issues might also impact the decision on which marking system to use. But to help coaches decide, advantages and disadvantages of each system are discussed below.

One advantage of man-to-man marking, already stated previously, is that it is easier to teach than zonal defending because it is tactically simpler. Each defender is given an opponent to mark, with a single focus of preventing that opponent from receiving the ball and doing anything dangerous with it. Therefore, if there is insufficient time available to prepare a team before an important competition, man-to-man marking could be the answer. Another advantage of man-to-man marking is that it's possible to apply tighter pressure on opponents, making it harder for them to receive and turn in dangerous areas. That's because, with a sweeper positioned behind them for cover, the man markers can afford to stay tight on their mark and make his life difficult. The markers can follow their opponent closely and try to intercept passes to feet, knowing that their sweeper will cover the passes played into space behind them.

Man-to-man marking is most effective when a team has many players who are fit, tenacious, and strong in one-versus-one situations and are physically able to match, or beat, their opponents speed for speed and strength for strength. It's also effective when the opposing team has attackers with a 'bad first touch', who tend to give the ball away under pressure. Man-to-man marking can be potent against certain styles of attack. When an opposing team is known to be direct in attack, with a tendency to get the ball to the forwards early, or when the attack relies heavily on the target man up front for its build up, marking the forwards man-to-man can disrupt the attack and yield many turnovers.

But there are also disadvantages to man-to-man marking. Opponents can pull defenders out of position and create spaces that can be exploited by midfielders running through from deep. It is difficult for the sweeper to cover simultaneously for every defensive blunder and it can be dangerous when a defender gets beat without any cover behind him. The sweeper can also be pulled away from good covering positions by an intelligent passing game. For example, in diagram 209, forward 1 receives the ball and holds it, drawing the sweeper (S) closer into a covering position. The forward then plays it back to a supporting midfielder who immediately sends it through into the empty flank.

A team marking man-to-man can easily lose its shape. Opponents who make lots of interchanging runs can drag defenders into areas of the field where they feel less comfortable. When the team finally wins the ball, it might not be in an ideal shape to start a counterattack, with the players a bit disoriented. If team shape is hard to maintain, it also makes it difficult to rehearse counterattacking moves or general attacking patterns in practice since the coach is not sure if, for example, his left defender will still be in his usual position when the ball is won.

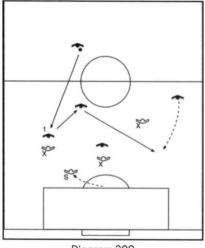
Diagram 209

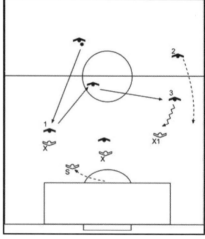
Diagram 210

In a man-to-man system, it is hard to create numerical superiority around the ball since defenders are more concerned with following their assigned opponent rather than overloading the area around the ball. This can make a team vulnerable in the flanks, where defenders could be isolated 1v1 without cover. Worse still, an overlapping opponent could create a 2v1 situation in the flanks before help arrives. This weakness is illustrated in diagram 210. As in diagram 209, the sweeper is drawn towards forward 1. The ball is then played wide to opponent 3 who dribbles at the isolated defender while opponent 2 is creating a 2v1 with an overlapping run.

The deeper position of the sweeper makes it harder to play an offside trap. For this reason, the modern sweepers tend to play a lot closer to their man markers in order to keep the defense compact and shepherd it up closer to the midfield. Some sweepers play almost in line with their defense, but what they gain in compactness they lose in covering range.

And now to zonal defense. When properly executed, a zonal back line is hard to break and acts like a solid barrier across the field. Indeed, attacking against a zonal defense can virtually feel like 'running into a wall'. The advantage of zonal defending is that the defenders do not have to cover as much ground chasing around, since they pass opponents to each other while remaining in their zone. Hence, zonal defending is better to use if the players are not as fit as the opponents. In zonal defending, team shape and symmetry is maintained - the left defender is always on the left side and the right defender is always on the right. And since defenders don't chase forwards all over the place, the back line remains intact and gaps are not as easily created in dangerous areas as they are in man-to-man marking. It is easier for a team defending zonally to keep the defenders pressed up behind the midfield, thus maintaining compactness and squeezing the spaces between the units. It is also easier to overload the area around the ball and double-team opponents. With a relatively flat back line, it is easier to play the offside trap. And lastly, it is easier to counterattack from a zonal defense, and rehearsing attacking patterns in practice is more productive since most of the players remain in their areas and team shape is intact.

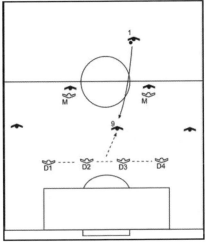

Diagram 211

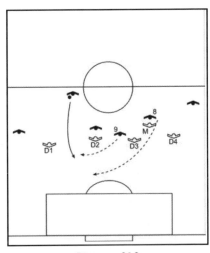

Diagram 212

But there are also disadvantages to zonal defending. Defenders need to switch their mindset back and forth from defending space to marking players as opponents move into and out of their zone. This can create moments when opponents, in transition between zones, are not marked tightly by anyone - a dangerous situation if close to goal. Sometimes, forwards who drop into the midfield are left unmarked to receive the ball and turn since defenders are usually reluctant to abandon the back line. This problem is illustrated in diagram 211, where forward 9 drops into midfield to receive a pass and is allowed to turn because D3 did not stick to him tightly.

Zonal defending is susceptible to diagonal runs into the spaces behind the back line, especially diagonal runs that traverse zones. Refer to diagram 212 and notice how either forward 9 or midfielder 8 can sneak into the space behind the back line for a through pass while D2, D3, and M are caught ball watching and are slow to figure out who should mark whom. Even if D3 is alert and follows 9, we still have a very dangerous 1v1 situation in front of goal with no immediate cover. Defenders marking zonally in a flat back line are usually coached to 'hold their line' and let the forwards run into off-side. Defender D3 in diagram 212 might elect to 'hold the line', meaning stay in line with his other defenders, and let 9 run alone into off-side. But if the forward times his run properly, he could beat the off-side trap. Also, opposing midfielders can beat the offside line by running through from deep positions. Playing flat with zonal defending could be living dangerously since any mistakes at the back will prove costly with no sweeper to provide cover.

As can be seen, zonal defending requires constant communication, quick decisions, and alert minds. It can present tactical demands beyond the ability of inexperienced players. Coaches who employ a zonal defending system need to be fluent in the system, understand its strengths and weaknesses and allow their team enough time to learn it properly.

COMBINATION OF MAN-TO-MAN AND ZONAL DEFENDING

Given that both man-to-man and zonal defending have inherent weaknesses, many coaches find creative ways to blend the two systems in order to minimize these weaknesses. For example, how should a team that normally plays zonal defending adjust if their next opponents have an attacking midfielder who is very creative and is known to be adept at timing his runs from deep into spaces behind the flat back line. One solution is to maintain a zonal back line but assign someone to mark the dangerous midfielder man-to-man for the whole game in order to neutralize him.

Some coaches play a sweeper behind a zonal marking defense. The logic here is to provide the extra safety of the sweeper, who would pick up any runners coming through from midfield. The sweeper could also step into midfield to help defend the area in front of his defenders. Whatever system is used, the bottom line is that players must react to the game, not to the game plan. Players must learn to solve tactical problems instantaneously, individually and collectively. This will require shifting back and forth from marking space to marking players to making tackles to covering teammates, regardless of the system used.

PRESSING SYSTEMS

In addition to deciding whether the team will defend man-to-man or zonally, coaches need to determine in which areas of the field they want their team to start applying pressure on the ball. Terms such as full field pressure, high pressure, and low pressure are typically used by coaches to explain their chosen strategy. Pressing tactics are in vogue now. Many high level coaches train their teams to flood the area around the ball the minute they lose it and try to win it back before the other team has time to settle and keep it. The logic of instant pressing is sound. When teams win the ball, they are usually not in an ideal shape to protect it and need a few seconds to transition from a defensive shape into a possession shape. If a team can commit players into pressing the ball the instant they lose it, the chances of regaining it are high.

To succeed in pressing, the players have to be in top physical shape and trained to react quickly and decisively. But even with highly trained top players, it is extremely demanding physically to play a pressing game for ninety minutes and do it all over the field. Also, players at the highest levels are technically and tactically so sharp that applying pressing tactics all over the field could easily backfire. For this reason, most coaches will have a predetermined strategy of when, where and how to press, and this strategy might vary from game to game, depending on the opponents and on whether it is a home or an away game. The pressing strategy could also change during the game, based on the score, how much time is left, and the flow of the game.

High Pressure
High pressure means that the team will try to win back the ball everywhere, including deep inside the opponent's half. Full-field-pressure is another term used to describe high pressure all over the field. It means that the opponents will not be allowed the time and space to settle and possess the ball and build up from the back. In a perfectly executed pressing maneuver, the instant the ball is lost, the closest player to the ball applies immediate pressure to try to win the ball, another player provides close cover, essentially double teaming the ball, while the rest of the players push up and tightly mark all the opponents

who can potentially receive a pass. The pressure on the ball must be applied in such a way as to limit the outlet options. By selecting the correct angle of approach, even if he doesn't win the ball, the pressing player can force the ball carrier to concede a corner or a throw in. The pressing player can also approach the ball in such a way as to steer the ball into a more favorable area where his teammates are outnumbering the opponents and are likely to win the ball.

The 2002 Men's World Cup tournament saw very little high pressing. Most teams retreated into their own half when possession was lost. This was due to many factors. The excessive heat made a prolonged high press strategy unwise. Playing seven games in one month at that intensity was impossible. Modern international level defenders are technically and tactically better equipped to solve pressure. And many players arrived at the pre-World Cup camps tired from a long European season. Only Japan and South Korea were physically able to press the ball for long periods in the game and even they run out of steam at the later stages of the tournament.

High pressure is more popular and effective in the women's game. The top national women's teams, such as the U.S.A., Norway, Germany and China, have an athletic superiority that allows them to press opponents and physically domi-nate them. In the United States, some of the more successful college women programs rely on high pressure tactics using three, and even four, forwards. The University of North Carolina has set the standard in aggressive, all-out pressure and has won countless collegiate national championships. High pressure is effective in the women's game because female players have not yet acquired the passing range of the men's game. Very few female defenders possess the technique and power to break pressure with long accurate passes and teams with superior athletes take advantage of this weakness. But many programs worldwide are focusing on improving the training, fitness, and technique in the women's game, which will inevitably bring with it more sophisticated tactics and less reliance on sheer athleticism alone.

Teams that play a full field pressing game usually play with three forwards. It would be very difficult to high press with only two forwards. In addition, for high pressure to be effective, the whole team must maintain compactness when in possession in the opponent's half. This means that, as the team is attacking, its defense must push up and stay close to the midfield and the midfield in turn must stay close to the forwards. Hence, when the ball is deep in the other team's half, the defenders are pushed all the way up to the half way line. This way, if the ball is lost, everyone is close to each other and in a good position to apply pressure on the ball in numbers, to 'hunt in packs'.

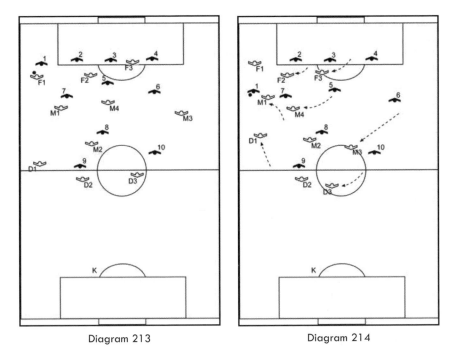

Diagram 213   Diagram 214

Diagram 213 shows how compactness is preserved as the ball is played into the opponents' half by a team playing a 3-4-3 formation. Winger F1 has possession while practically the whole team bar the keeper is in the attacking half. Diagram 214 depicts a possible scenario where F1 tries to dribble the ball but ends up losing it to 1. Now, how would a team playing high pressure react? In diagram 214, F1 is not in a position to apply immediate pressure on 1. It then becomes the job of M1 to put 1 under pressure. M1 leaves 7 and closes down on 1 at an angle that prevents a pass to 7 and forces 1 down the flank. Simultaneously, M4 leaves 5 and closes down on 7, while F2 closes the outlet back pass and F3 closes the outlet square ball to 5 or 3. D1 pushes up to provide cover for M1, M2 stays close to 8, D2 stays tight on 9 and D3 and M3 slide inside to provide cover. If all this pressing movement is coordinated quickly and decisively, 1 would be surrounded by F1, M1, and D1, while all the potential outlet targets would be tightly marked, increasing the likelihood of a turn over. 1 would have to be incredibly quick of mind and skillful to switch the ball to the other side, where 4 and 6 are, before M1 closes him down. Even if 1 succeeds in switching the ball, the danger to the pressing team is not imminent since it's all happening so far away from their own goal and they have enough time to slide across and apply renewed pressure. Notice also that the pressing team's goalkeeper takes up a position at the top of his penalty box, from where he can reach any through balls played behind the defense.

Playing high pressure can pay dividends if the opponents are not very skillful and are likely to give the ball away. Many teams have defenders who are not comfortable on the ball, even at the professional level, and are therefore susceptible to high pressure. Also, if the opponents are known to not relish playing against high pressure, or are athletically inferior, pressing them could put them off their game and cause turnovers. But, as mentioned before, it's very tiring to play high pressure for the entire game. It's also a high-risk tactic and can backfire if not executed properly. If pressure on the ball is not effectively applied, one pass can beat all the players who are rushing towards the ball and lead to a dangerous counterattack. Also, teams who play high pressure are pushing everyone up and, thus, leave large spaces behind, which can be exploited by quick forwards. It is very risky for teams who lack speed at the back to play high pressure because they are vulnerable to the pass over the top into these spaces. This problem is exacerbated if the keeper is too slow, restricting him from covering the large area.

For this reason, many coaches prefer to limit using high pressure to certain strategic situations. For example, some coaches choose to apply high pressure for the first 10 minutes of the game to gain the initiative, unsettle the other team early on and maybe even score an early goal. Others apply high pressure when certain players who are technically suspect have the ball, or when behind late in the match.

Some coaches train their teams to intentionally create situations in which high pressure is most effective. For example, playing the ball deep into the corners and sending two or three players to chase, with the rest of the team pushing forward in concert to win any clearances. This ploy can often win the ball or force a throw in or a corner kick. The much maligned but sometimes effective, so called British style of pumping endless crosses into the penalty area is another high pressure tactic that can wear down opponents and produce scoring chances. The success of these crosses relies on the forwards to aggressively attack the cross, in tandem with a midfield arranged around the box and trained to win the 'second balls', meaning the knock downs or clearances.

Regardless of the exact method used, the main objective of high pressure is to keep the ball in the other team's half and to pressure them into coughing it up close to their own goal. The logic here is simple - if you win the ball close to the other goal, you don't have to go far to score. If you win the ball in your own half, you have to penetrate past a lot more opponents to get to the other goal.

Low Pressure

The strategy of low pressure generally means that whenever the team loses the ball in the attacking half, they retreat back towards their own half and wait. A low pressing team will have a pre-planned idea of how far they would allow the other team to progress before they start applying pressure. The opponents would be allowed to possess the ball deep in their own half, but as soon as the ball is played into a pre-determined area the defending team immediately applies aggressive pressure. Typically, a team that plays low pressure would have its forwards backtrack to a line somewhere between the half line and around 10 yards into the opponents' half. Diagram 215 illustrates the area into which a team, playing low pressure within a 4-4-2 formation, would generally retreat and wait.

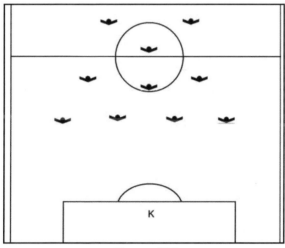

Diagram 215
Italy's low pressure shape

This is exactly how Italy defended in the 1994 World Cup when they reached the Finals, losing to Brazil on penalty kicks. Notice how compact the team shape is, with every unit pressed against the one above. This made it very hard to play through the midfield, while Italy's back four and keeper had plenty of speed, experience and aggression to deal with any balls played over the top.

The advantages of playing low pressure are that it is physically less demanding, it is easier to maintain compactness, and easier to create numerical superiority around the ball. It is also a better system for teams who do not have a quick, mobile goalkeeper. By retreating back into a low pressure stance, the keeper has a smaller area to patrol. Another advantage is that it invites opponents to push forward and attack, leaving spaces behind, which can play right into the hands of a team that is effective at quick counter attacks.

How far back a team should retreat depends on the speed and mobility of the back line and the keeper. The danger of backtracking too much is that the team is constantly defending in its own half and any mistakes are taking place too close to goal for comfort with no chance to regroup. It's also harder to get out of the half from such a deep position once the ball is won. Diagram 215 shows an ideal trade-off between playing low pressure without retreating too deep into one's own half.

It should be noted that regardless of the strategy used, low pressure or high pressure, no team can afford to allow opponents to receive the ball and turn freely inside the defending half. Immediate pressure must be applied anywhere in one's own half. The principles of pressing, that is flooding the area around the ball, can be used within both high pressure and low pressure systems. It's really a question of deciding where to start pressing.

CHANNELING THE BALL

Another important aspect of team defending that needs to be integrated into the overall game plan is to pre-determine which way to steer the ball in certain areas of the field. Simply put, players pressuring the ball need to know whether to force the ball towards the flank or towards the center of the field. The decision on which way to channel the ball depends on the team formation, the defensive strengths of the players, the opponents' tendencies and strengths, and the location on the field.

The strategy of channeling might vary from game to game, or even vary within the same game, for example, forcing the ball one way in certain parts of the field and another way in other parts. If the team formation contains strong ball winning midfielders in the center, the coach might want his players to force the ball inside, towards the center of midfield, where his players are primed to win the ball. If the team's defensive qualities are on the flanks, or if the coach likes to squeeze play against the side lines, he might instruct his players to force the ball wide.

Forcing The Ball Down The Line
Italy in the 1990's, under the coaching of Arrigo Sacchi, was considered the ultimate defensive machine. Diagram 215 shows how Italy lined up defensively. Their forwards allowed the other team to build from the back, but as soon as the ball was played to the wide backs, the forwards were instructed to close down the ball and force it down the flank. Diagram 216 demonstrates how the Italian system is based on the ability of the forwards to close the ball in such an angle that forces the opposing wide back to play it down the line. This makes the wide back's pass predictable and allows the Italian midfielders to cheat

and slide to the right in order to pounce on the pass with numbers. The three unmarked opponents on the Italians' blind (left) side are not likely to get the ball if the forwards press the ball from the inside.

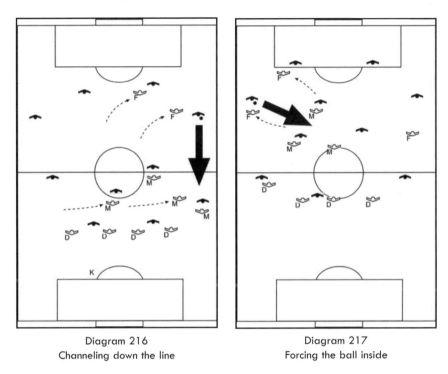

Diagram 216
Channeling down the line

Diagram 217
Forcing the ball inside

Forcing The Ball Inside

The US Women's National Team that won the 1999 Women's World Cup played a high pressing 4-3-3 formation, in which their forwards channeled the ball inside. Diagram 217 illustrates how the American left winger blocked the outside pass and forced the ball into the middle, where the three American mid-fielders were waiting in a close-knit triangle. Notice how the center forward blocked the square pass to the central defender and how the right winger positioned herself to intercept or pressure any balls switched across.

The advantages of this strategy were numerous. First of all, the right back was forced to shift the ball to her weaker (left) foot to keep it from being tackled, which inhibited her passing range and increased the likelihood of a poor pass. Secondly, the American midfield triangle was compacted in the middle and had physically dominating players, such as Michelle Akers, waiting to win the ball. Thirdly, winning the ball in the central area was ideal for launching a counterat-tack in any number of ways.

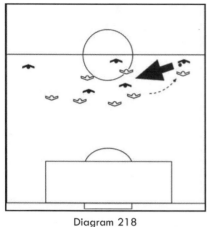

| Diagram 218 | Diagram 219 |
| Showing the ball inside | Showing the ball outside |

Since the modern game is all about compactness in the center and open space on the flanks, many coaches feel that the best ploy is to steer the ball inside, right into the massed and crowded midfield. Some coaches use the following strategy: When the ball is in the middle third, pressure on the ball is applied to force the ball inside, as shown in Diagram 218. But when the ball is in the defensive third, it is more prudent to force the ball to the outside, as shown in Diagram 219, since it is too dangerous to let the ball be dribbled inside, within shooting range on goal.

In addition to an overall game plan, special situations might warrant specific solutions. For example, if playing against a wide attacker who specializes in dribbling around the outside and crossing, forcing him inside might be the right approach. When a wide attacker switches position to the opposite wing in order to dribble inside and shoot with his strong foot, the pressing defender should force him to the outside. Any time a player is known to be uncomfortable handling the ball with his weaker foot, forcing the ball to his weaker side might prevent a shot on goal. Clearly, any advance knowledge of opponents' strengths and tendencies is useful for deciding how to channel play.

At the top level, coaches usually scout their opponents and use the information to plan their defensive strategy. The objective is to steer the ball into areas where opponents are not as effective, or into areas that maximize the odds of winning the individual duels. When it comes to channeling, the most successful teams are those that come prepared with a collective plan for specific areas of the field, but with a flexibility to adjust to special situations. However, a word of caution is necessary here. At the lower levels and the youth level, opponents are often an unknown quantity. Youth coaches should not confuse their players with too many channeling variations and should keep the game plan simple and easy to execute.

TEAM FORMATIONS

System of play refers to the roles assigned to the players. A good starting point for discussing systems of play is to look at the team formation, which is usually denoted by three digits. These three digits represent the number of players who are assigned the role of defenders, midfielders, and forwards within the system. This chapter describes some of the most common formations, as well as the modern variations of these basic formations. Each formation is analyzed in terms of its strengths and weaknesses. The discussion also includes suggestions on how to get the most out of the formation, in attack and in defense.

THE 4-4-2 FORMATION

The 4-4-2 formation usually utilizes a four man zonal defense without a sweeper, four midfielders, at least one of whom is a defensive midfielder (M2 in diagram 220), and two forwards who work closely together up the middle. Diagram 220 shows a traditional 4-4-2 formation.

Diagram 220	Diagram 221
Traditional 4-4-2 formation	Brazilian interpretation of 4-4-2

The 4-4-2 defense is comprised of two central defenders and two wide defenders, the wide backs, who are individually described as the 'left back' or the 'right back'. Refer to the section on defensive systems for a more detailed explanation of the zonal marking system. When a 4-4-2 team has possession, the wide backs join the attack often by overlapping, thus providing width and flank penetration. This is especially possible when a 4-4-2 team plays against only one or two forwards. With no wingers to mark, the wide backs have more freedom to join the attack

The organization of the midfield quartet in the 4-4-2 formation has many variations. The two most common are the diamond shape and the box shape. The diamond shape midfield consists of a defensive midfielder, two wide midfielders and an attacking midfielder as in diagram 220. The **box shape** midfield has two defensive midfielders behind two attacking midfielders, which gives the team a 4-2-2-2 look (Diagram 221). Brazilian teams use the 4-2-2-2 formation to great effect, allowing the wide backs to overlap and attack at will while the two central defenders and the two defensive midfielders rarely venture up field, staying back to provide cover.

The two forwards usually take up central starting positions, staying close to each other and leaving the flanks for the wide midfielders. From their central position, the forwards serve as the focal point for the attack, working hard to make themselves available for probing penetrating passes. Sometimes they are required to make diagonal runs from their central positions into the flank areas behind the defense to provide an outlet passing option. The most typical front line combination has one forward staying high while the second forward is slightly withdrawn. The high forward provides depth for the team by pushing up and stretching the field as much as possible. The high forward also acts as a target player. He is usually physically strong, can receive and control long passes, can hold the ball under pressure with his back to goal and lay it off to his partner or to other midfielders. The withdrawn forward is usually more mobile, covering a wider area, and is allowed to roam freely and feed off the target player. In some teams, the withdrawn forward is almost like a fifth midfielder. The old classic British forward combination in the traditional 4-4-2 formation had a 'big-man-little-man' tandem, with the 'big' man playing the high target role, and the 'little' one playing off him. But the two-forward system doesn't have to be a 'big and small' combination. Brazil's '94 World Cup winning team had Romario and Bebeto up front, neither of whom was 'big'. Romario, however, stayed high and central while Bebeto did all the hard running, and the result was 6 goals for Romario and the World Cup for Brazil.

The 4-4-2 formation is used increasingly at the top level because it has a number of important advantages. In addition to the advantages of playing zonal defending at the back as discussed previously, the 4-4-2 has nice symmetry and a lot of flexibility in the way the wide midfielders and wide backs are utilized.

The wide midfielders can be used either to help with flank play by pushing them wide, or to bolster the center of the midfield by tucking them inside. In the old days, the wide midfielders in a 4-4-2 system tended to stay wide most of the time and, working in tandem with the overlapping wide backs, provided effective penetration in the flanks. But with the wide midfielders playing mostly wide, the center of the midfield was vulnerable, with only one defending midfielder in front of the back four. Opponents exploited this weakness by flooding the center of the midfield (for example, using 3-5-2 or 4-5-1), controlling possession in midfield and starving the wide players of the ball. Coaches who still wanted to play 4-4-2 corrected the weakness in the middle by tucking the wide midfielders inside when possession was lost to bolster the center of the midfield. When the ball was regained, team width could be re-established quickly by either the wide backs stepping up or the wide midfielders getting wide again.

Having 4 players in the back makes it easier and safer for a defender to step up and join the attack since that still leaves three covering at the back. A team that employs only three defenders (i.e. 3-5-2 or 3-4-3) will require a more complicated adjustment by its midfielders in order to cover for an overlapping defender or risk leaving just two at the back.

Another positive feature of the 4-4-2 is the readily available option to relieve pressure on the ball by playing it out to one of the wide backs. The wide backs are usually free and, therefore, have more time and space to hold the ball. From there, they can start a counterattack down the flank. Playing the ball to the wide back buys the team valuable time to transition from a defensive mode to an attacking mode. In other words, to re-gain the attacking shape necessary for launching an attack. In fact, whenever the ball is won in the central midfield area and the option to play it forward is not on, the chances are the ball will find its way to one of the wide backs. It will either be played 'square' directly to the wide back, or be played back to a central defender who will then pass it out to the wide back. Either way, the wide defenders in a 4-4-2 formation see a lot of the ball since they are often used to maintain possession as well as a springboard to attack.

As mentioned before, it is important for a team playing 4-4-2 to solve the numbers game in midfield and not get outnumbered in the central area. One way to accomplish this is to tuck the wide midfielders inside and give the wide backs the responsibility of marking the opposing wide midfielders. Diagram 222 shows how defensive midfielder M2 is outnumbered in the center because wide midfielder M3 is marking the opposing wide midfielder who has the ball. Even if M1 slides inside to help M2, the other team can quickly switch the ball to opponent 5, resulting in M1, M2, and M3 expending a lot of energy chasing the ball in midfield and essentially playing 3 versus 4, while at the back we have the unnecessary ratio of four defenders marking only two forwards.

Diagram 223 illustrates a better use of the wide backs. Defender D4 is responsible for pressuring the ball when it's played to the wide midfielder. The starting position of D4 is inside, close to D3, but as soon as the ball is played wide, he closes down the ball quickly. If the ball is switched to opponent 5, full-back D1 would pressure the ball and D4 will resume the original covering position beside D3. This creates a 'numbers-up' situation in the center of the midfield and still provides the cover of an extra defender at the back. In diagram 223, M2 ends up being the extra midfielder. He is free to defend in a number of ways. He can double up on a forward should that forward receive a pass (diagram 224). He could send M3 to double up with D4 on opponent 1 by picking up opponent 3 (diagram 225). Or he could stay put and provide cover for the midfield and the central defenders. As can be seen in diagram 223, the 4-4-2 can be used in a way that makes the spine of the team, the center, strong and well protected while still maintaining the flexibility of pushing the wide midfielders outside if so desired, as in diagram 225. The key to success here depends on the ability of the wide backs to close down the ball quickly and hold their own against the opposing wide midfielders.

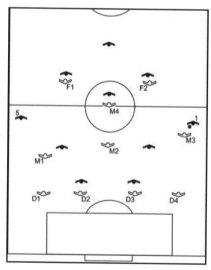

Diagram 222
Outnumbered in the center

Diagram 223
Better use of wide backs

Another advantage of the 4-4-2 system is that the responsibility for creating width in attack and penetration down the flanks is shared by two players, the wide back and the wide midfielder. For example, in diagram 223, if M1 was working hard at marking and chasing in the midfield, he might not have the energy or the time to sprint wide to a winger's position when his team finally wins the ball. Instead, D1 can step up, provide width, and overlap into attack, while M1 rests. Some systems, such as the 3-5-2, lack this flexibility and have only one wide player on whose shoulders fall most of the burden to both defend and attack on the flanks.

The two forwards in a 4-4-2 formation have to work together as a unit in both attack and defense. In attack, it's important for the forwards to assume a central starting position, with at least one of them as high as possible, and stay close to each other. They can stay high and central, and be the focal point of the attack, or they could make runs in any direction, as needed. They could also make lateral runs away from the center, pulling their markers with them, and creating space for the attacking midfielders to slice through the middle. Whatever they do, they should be aware of each other's movement, work in tandem and make complementary runs. For example, if one forward shows for the ball (runs towards the ball), the other forward should look to run away from the ball into the space behind the defense. Diagram 226 illustrates these complementary runs. M2 has the ball and F1 shows for the ball while F2 runs into the space behind the defense. This combination of movement provides M2 with a passing option to the feet of F1 or to the space attacked by F2. In diagram 226, M2 elects to pass to F2 and, as soon as the pass is made, F1 spins to his left and sprints towards the penalty area to help F2. Diagram 227 shows how the two forwards can create space for midfielder M4 by pulling their markers away from the central area.

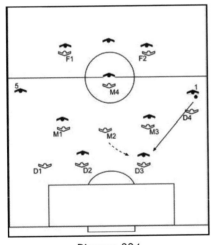

Diagram 224
Double up on the forward

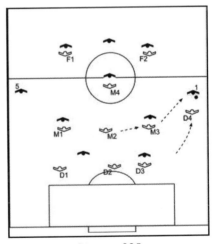

Diagram 225
Double up on the wide player

Whenever possible, the two forwards should try to receive the ball inside the central areas, denoted by the shaded area in diagram 226. There are a few reasons for this. First of all, the forwards are most dangerous when in possession in the areas closer to goal. Secondly, they leave the flanks open for penetrating runs by the wide players. Thirdly, more passing options and combinations are possible from a central position, making their next move unpredictable.

In diagram 226, F2 managed to receive the ball in the central area. From there, he can pass the ball to M1 who can either hit an early cross for F1 and M4, or take on the defender and cross from the end line. Diagram 228 shows what happens if F2 received the ball in a wide position. Receiving the ball by the touch line, with his back to the field, limits F2's vision and options, and gives him very little room to maneuver the ball. F2 can try to turn on the defender, which is difficult to do, or pass it back to M1, which is what the opponents would want him to do. Another problem with relying too often on balls sent wide, as in diagram 228, is that good defenses, anticipating this pass, will send two defenders to chase F2 and double team him against the touch line.

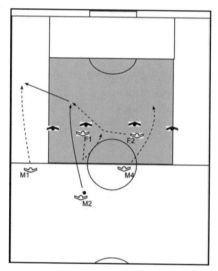

Diagram 226
Forwards making complementary runs

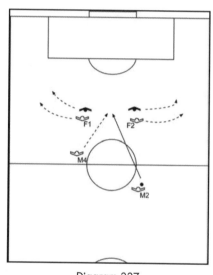

Diagram 227
Forwards creating space in the middle

One of the disadvantages with the 4-4-2 system is that the forwards can get isolated up high. This occurs when the midfielders and defenders are defending in a tight, eight-player block and allow a big gap to form between them and the forwards. When this happens, the forwards are disconnected from the rest of the team and a counterattack is hard to execute. A long ball to the forwards is easily intercepted or tackled away before the midfielders have time to join and support the attack. To prevent this from causing turnovers, one of the forwards needs to drop deeper and stay closer to the midfield. Alternatively, the counterattacks could break out on the flanks, utilizing the wide midfielders in combination with the forwards.

In defending, the two forwards in a 4-4-2 formation will be expected to apply the first pressure on the ball, whenever the opposing defenders are in possession. The two forwards will usually try to force the ball towards the flank area and keep it down on that flank to make the next pass predictable. Diagram 229 illustrates a classic 4-4-2 defending. As the ball is passed to opponent 4, forward F1 challenges at an angle of approach that encourages 4 to play it down the flank, and F2 closes down on 3 to prevent the ball from going around the back to the other flank. This type of pressure on the ball by the forwards makes it easy for the rest of the team because 4's options are limited and pre-dictable. Now D1 can close down the wide midfielder in anticipation and M3 can slide inside since 8 will not be able to get the ball from 4. Midfielder M1 is now free to double team on 7 or 9 or 5, depending on where the ball is passed. M3 can double team with M2 on 6, or on 10. All these permutations are possible because the forwards applied the first pressure and forced the ball to one side. With play condensed to a small area and the players so close to each other, the ball is essentially pushed into a 'dead end' and possession is easier to gain.

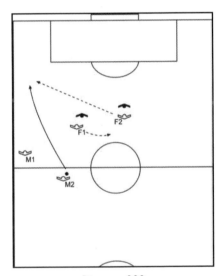

Diagram 228
Forward receiving balls wide

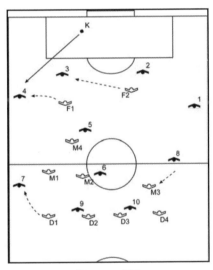

Diagram 229
Forwards defend and channel ball

To summarize, the 4-4-2 formation provides a good balance between defense and attack. It has a built-in flexibility for playing against a variety of systems. We already discussed the flexibility inherent in the midfield, where the four midfielders can be arranged in a wide diamond shape, a tight central diamond, four across, or in a close knit box formation. Having four in the back provides a stable platform for defending against almost any attacking alignment. Four defenders can handle one forward, two forwards or three. It is easy for the defenders to adjust to the number of forwards without needing to make major alteration to the system. If the opposing team uses only one forward, the wide backs should be comfortable enough to step up into the midfield area as need-ed, since they are routinely doing it in the 4-4-2 system. And if the other team uses three forwards, the four defenders should be able to cope without needing extra help from the midfielders. Teams that play with only three at the back would require a bigger adjustment if they find themselves facing a team with three forwards and such adjustments could disrupt their rhythm.

THE 3-5-2 FORMATION

The 3-5-2 formation is typically comprised of a three man back line, five midfielders and two forwards. The back line is traditionally made up of two man-markers and a sweeper, although recent trends see some teams adopting a flat, zonal three. Most coaches who play 3-5-2 instruct their wide midfielders to drop back in line with their defenders when possession is lost, essentially reverting to a 5-3-2 formation whenever necessary.

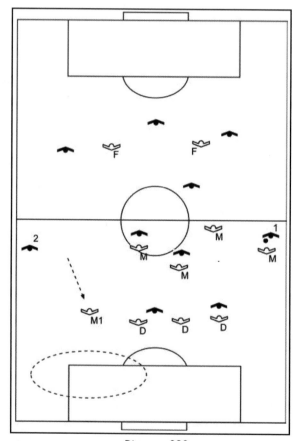

Diagram 230

The conventional back line of two markers and a sweeper operates as explained in more detail in the section on defensive systems. The markers rarely venture up the field. Their role is limited to marking tightly the opposing forwards and covering for everyone else. Even when their team has possession, the markers need to be defensively disciplined and stay close to their mark, in case of a turnover and a quick counterattack. The sweeper has more freedom and is allowed more mobility based on the needs of the moment, sometimes stepping into midfield, but most times roaming behind his defense to pick up loose balls or through balls. German teams are traditionally adept at using the sweeper to initiate attacks and act as a distributor. The famous Franz Beckenbaur redefined the role of the sweeper with his play in the German teams of the seventies by adding a creative dimension to the role of the sweeper. Beckenbaur's passing and vision was the foundation of the German attacks. He spent just as much time in front of his defenders as behind them, choosing the moments to make effective forays into the midfield and beyond. Since then, the idea of an attacking sweeper became vogue at the top level. Many German teams play 3-5-2 with an attacking minded sweeper. Whenever a German sweeper steps up into the midfield, the defensive midfielder drops back to cover for him to maintain three at the back. This rotation allows the sweeper to pop up unmarked, making him difficult to contain.

If the three defenders use a flat zonal marking system, they would use similar principles to the flat four. The main difference between a flat four and a flat three is that the three defenders would not attempt to defend the whole width because they would be too spread out and leave too many gaps. Instead, the three would hold the line by staying close to each other, and leave the weak side flank for the wide midfielder to cover. Diagram 230 illustrates the role of the wide midfielder in covering the weak side and giving the team defensive balance. In Diagram 230, opponent 1 has possession. The three defenders (D), playing zonally, slide across and stay close to each other while the wide midfielder M1 drops back to provide the defensive balance on the weak side. His positioning gives him a head start in a foot race and allows him to be first to any balls played behind the defense into the dangerous dotted area. By facing up field, he can anticipate and intercept square passes to opponent 2 and start a counterattack. Notice how M1's position makes the system look essentially similar to four at the back.

The whole purpose of the 3-5-2 is to create numerical superiority in the vital midfield area. The rationale is that there is no need to play with four at the back if opponents employ only two strikers. Better to throw one more player into midfield to clog up the center, improve possession and dictate the game. A five-man midfield provides a better connection to the forwards, especially if two central attacking midfielders are used. The attacking midfielders can quickly support the forwards whenever they show for the ball.

The other advantage of playing five in midfield is the ability to spring an extra midfielder into attack. Defenders are always wary of midfielders who make runs from deep, especially if they are good at losing their marker. Whereas the 4-4-2 has one such midfielder, the 3-5-2 has two, which makes for double the problem and double the element of surprise. Teams that have an abundance of midfielders who are both skillful and mobile can cause havoc with their runs from midfield if they play with five. Their skill allows them to keep possession in the middle third and wait for the right moment to spring someone in behind the opponents' defense. English teams playing the conventional 4-4-2 have always had problems with continental teams who employed five in midfield. The five midfielders outnumber and suffocate the four and keep the ball for long periods until defensive breakdowns present the moment to strike. Portugal and Romania did exactly that to England in Euro 2000.

Some teams overload the center even further by dropping one of the forwards into midfield and playing 3-6-1. The lone forward stretches the field to create space and the six midfielders are hard to contain when you don't know which of them will make attacking runs. Argentina in 1986, with Valdano the only recognized forward and the majestic Maradona one of those six midfielders, played the 3-6-1 to perfection, winning the World Cup. Argentina displayed a patient possession game, combined with unpredictable movement of the six midfielders who popped up anywhere and everywhere in a swirling improvisation that was hard to keep in check.

The midfield arrangement can vary widely. The most common has a defensive midfielder in a 'holding' position in front of the defense, two attacking midfielders in front of him, and two midfielders who are positioned very wide. The three central midfielders form a close triangle that provides plenty of bodies in the center. On top of them, the two forwards are positioned centrally, one higher than the other, similar to the striking duo of the 4-4-2 formation. Diagram 231 illustrates this arrangement. Some coaches prefer the extra security of a second defensive midfielder and invert the triangle in the center, as shown in diagram 232. Others still prefer to split the central midfielders' duties into a holding midfielder, an attacking midfielder, and a midfield organizer, who demands the ball, distributes and orchestrates the attack. Zidane is the quintessential midfield organizer in the French midfield, always available for the ball and usually involved in most of the French attacks. His absence in the key first round games at the 2002 World Cup cost France dearly and demonstrated both his value to the team and the danger of relying too much on one player.

The 3-5-2 formation makes for a strong spine, with three central midfielders providing plenty of numbers in the middle and making it easier to control this key area. The potential weakness of the 3-5-2 is on the flanks, where there is too much open space that opponents can exploit. The wide midfielder must be strong in one-versus-one duels and have the speed and tackling ability to dominate his opponent since he is often isolated on the flank. If he gets beat, there is no fullback behind him to cover, as would be the case in the 4-4-2 formation. When the team is attacking, the wide midfielder gets forward and provides flank penetration and when the team loses the ball, he must drop back to help the three defenders. This means that the wide midfielders are expected to shuttle on their own, from penalty area to penalty area. Obviously, this is a lung-busting role requiring supremely fit athletes. This creates an imbalance of workload in the team, where the system asks too much of the wide midfielder compared to the central midfielders.

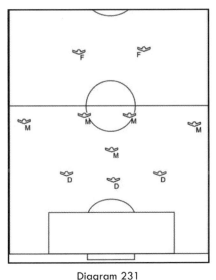

Diagram 231
3-5-2 with two attacking midfielders

Diagram 232
3-5-2 with two defending midfielders

Given the scope and energy required of wide midfielders in the 3-5-2, coaches must be careful to select the right player for the wide position or else he could turn out to be the weak link. In addition, the central midfielders and the two forwards would need to chip in with their share of flank penetration by making diagonal runs from inside to outside whenever the wide midfielder is too deep or too tired to get wide himself. Diagram 233 illustrates this point, showing how wide midfielder M1, having adopted a covering position when his team was defending, is now too deep to turn and sprint up the flank if his team wins the ball. Midfielder M3 or forward F can make a diagonal run in order to sustain the momentum of a counterattack and not have to wait for M1 to join the attack.

In any case, the 3-5-2 system demands flexibility, versatility and mobility from the five midfielders. They need to understand how and when to switch from midfielder to attacker to wide player to extra defender. The system requires players who are tactically sharp and physically fit enough to continuously inter-

change positions. The midfield mobility is crucial in this system. If the midfielders are too static or do not make enough forward runs, the attack will lack penetration and most passes will be of the harmless square variety. Furthermore, if
the three central midfielders stay too close to each other, they would 'step on
each other's toes' and lose possession by making unnecessary 5-10 yard passes
to each other in a clogged midfield. At least one of the three central midfielders should be looking to make attacking runs to open up the game

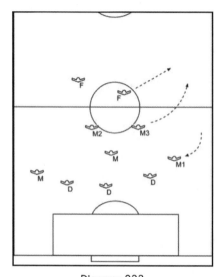

Diagram 233	Diagram 234
Attackers sharing the flank workload	Forwards channeling the ball inside

One more thought regarding the midfield: It is not advisable to put a player
into a wide midfield position if he lacks speed. Without speed, he cannot offer
his team flank penetration. However, if a coach is forced to use a slow player
out wide in a 3-5-2 system, that player's role becomes more of a distributor
than a runner. This means that he helps the midfield possess the ball, offers an
easy outlet target in a wide position, and delivers through balls for other players to run onto.

The forwards in a 3-5-2 operate similarly to the twin strikers of the 4-4-2 formation by starting high and central, working off each other, and making complementary runs. Just as in any system, one of them must provide depth and act
as a target player, pushing up as high as possible and playing with his back to
goal, while the other is more mobile and flexible.

Defensively, the forwards would be required to close the defenders when the
other team has possession. Whereas in the 4-4-2 system, the forwards would
most likely be asked to channel the ball to the flanks and force it down the line,

in the 3-5-2 the flanks are the weak link, making it wiser to force the ball inside where the three central midfielders await. This means that when the opponents are building up the attack from the back, the forwards' starting position is wide and their line of approach invite a pass inside as opposed to down the line, as shown in diagram 234.

The 3-5-2 system is defensively suitable to playing against two strikers. It is generally too risky to play with only three at the back against a team with three forwards. When this happens, one solution is to drop the defensive mid-fielder back into the center of the defense and play with four at the back. The sweeper can remain a true sweeper, playing behind the three man markers. If the coach wants to maintain five in midfield, he can pull a forward back and play 4-5-1. It all depends on how dangerous the other team is and on whether the emphasis of the game needs to be defensive or offensive.

We already discussed the flank dilemma in the 3-5-2. Playing against two markers and a sweeper, coaches try to exploit the spaces on the flanks by ask-ing their two forwards to stay central and close to each other. This creates huge open spaces on either side of the defense into which attacking midfielders can run and receive balls. It is for this reason that teams playing 3-5-2 require their wide midfielders to drop into these spaces and essentially adopt a 5-3-2 defensive formation. It all boils down to how quickly a 3-5-2 can transition to a 5-3-2 and how often they are required to transition. The success of this system depends on it.

THE 4-3-3 FORMATION

The 4-3-3 formation has four defenders playing zonally, three midfielders, and three forwards. The defense operates in the conventional zonal marking system, which is thoroughly explained in a previous section. The midfield is arranged in a central triangle, either with one holding and two attacking, or two holding and one attacking midfielders, depending on the players available and the strategy of the coach. The forwards are usually in the form of a central striker and two wingers. Diagram 235 shows a 4-3-3 arrangement, with one holding defensive midfielder.

It is important to note that the midfield is arranged in a compact triangle at the center. It is not advisable to spread the three midfielders across the width of the field since that would leave the central midfielder isolated and outnum-bered, rendering the center too weak. The wingers already provide the width necessary for attack and the outside defenders are also available to step up into midfield and overlap on the flanks. Therefore, there is no need for the midfielders to spread out. Another feature of note is the positioning of the for-wards relative to each other. The center forward would normally push as high as possible to create depth while the wingers would usually start off slightly below so as not to be flat with the striker. If all three forwards are high and flat, it is easy for the other team to play them off-side by quickly stepping up. If the wingers start off deeper than their striker, they can time their forward runs without getting caught off-side. They can also receive a pass to feet easier if they drop off their marker and open their body to the field.

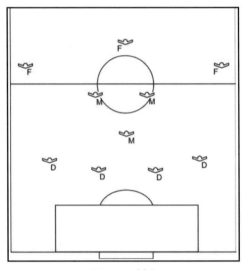

Diagram 235
Conventional 4-3-3

The 4-3-3 appeals to coaches who like their teams to play open, attacking soccer. The three forwards give the system many exciting attacking possibilities by stretching the other team's defense. It also enables the team to play high pressure and win balls in the attacking third. Additionally, it forces opponents to adjust their formation if they normally play with only three defenders and any opportunity to force an adjustment upon the opposing team is advantageous since it can break their rhythm.

The 4-3-3 has probably the most balanced distribution of workload among the players. No one is required to sprint long distances in transition from defense to attack or vice versa since the players are evenly spread out over the field. The fact that the workload is evenly distributed and every player's role is more sharply defined makes this system suitable for youth teams who are newly exposed to 11-a-side tactics. Young players don't have the stamina for repeated long sprints and need to be given simplified roles in their formative years.

Systems that employ three forwards are very popular with women and girls teams. The effectiveness of high pressure defending in the women's game has already been discussed in a previous chapter. Female defenders have difficulties dealing with the aggressive pressing game that is possible with three forwards. Another reason for the popularity of the three-striker attack in women's soccer is the improved odds of scoring goals. The quality of crosses and finishing in the women's game still lags behind the men's. With more players attacking crosses and pouncing on poor clearances, the probabilities of scoring rise accordingly.

Regardless of age, gender or maturity level, the key to success with the 4-3-3 is having two wingers who have the skill and speed to be dangerous and effective in one-on-one duels. Coaches who are lucky enough to find two such players, in addition to the center forward, can use this system to great effect. Without wingers who have the pace to get in behind defenses, either by dribbling or by making runs, the 4-3-3 formation will not be as potent. The modern game can only afford the luxury of sticking a player out wide if he does the business on a regular basis by getting behind his opponent and contributing to team penetration. Otherwise, it's a waste of a player. Marc Overmars, the Dutch winger who played for Ajax and Arsenal in his prime, was the archetypal winger. His speed and close control meant that few defenders could handle him and he also contributed his share of important goals for club and country. Overmars was one among a number of Dutch wingers in the eighties and nineties that were instrumental in the success enjoyed by Dutch teams famous for employing three forwards.

One drawback of the 4-3-3 is that spreading three forwards over the width of the field makes it difficult for them to interchange. The element of surprise and off-the-ball movement is sometimes missing from this system because there are only three midfielders and they are unlikely to make many runs into spaces ahead of the forwards. If the three forwards restrict their movement to vertical runs with little lateral or diagonal runs and the midfielders stay behind them, the whole attack becomes too static and predictable, making the opponents' marking assignments easy to sustain. Even if the three forwards try to interchange on the fly, team shape will likely suffer from chaotic movement and the attacking rhythm will stutter. With three forwards, it is actually better for the forwards to stick more rigidly to their positions and allow the built-in advantages of the system to take care of penetration.

In attack, the striker in the 4-3-3 provides depth and acts as the target player. He normally pushes as high as possible and plays with his back to goal, making himself available for long probing passes from the defense or midfield. The striker should limit his range of movement to the central zone and leave the flanks for the wingers to exploit. If he keeps running wide, he would bring his marker along and interfere with the wingers' runs. When their team has possession in their own half, the wingers should stay wide and 'hug the line' to help in the build-up of the attack. The winger's body position should be open to the field so he can see everything and judge his next move. This is a crucial point for the winger, which is often overlooked at the youth level. The art of wing play in terms of positioning and movement off the ball does not receive the attention it needs by youth coaches. If a team is going to play with three forwards, the coach must spend considerable time teaching his wingers the positioning necessary to make the system work. The basic fundamentals of body position and starting position are illustrated in diagrams 236 and 237.

Diagram 236 shows the wingers adopting the correct stance and position to support the ball. Here, a midfielder has the ball and is 'faced up' with the ability to play it forward. Since the ball is still in their team's half, the first priority for the wingers is to help bring the ball out. Hence, they both adopt very wide positions, hugging the line, and facing inside. With this open stance, they can see the whole field and can better judge whether to stay put and receive a pass to feet, or run behind opponents to receive a pass into space. For example, the right winger can decide, based on how tight opponent 4 is to him, whether to stay and get a pass to feet (pass 1) or sprint behind 4 for a through ball (pass 4). If the ball is played to the striker, the right winger might feel that he can outrun opponent 4 and get a through ball from the striker (pass 2). The left winger decides to stay deep and be available for a switch (pass 3) because his vision tells him intuitively that opponent 1 will likely beat him to any through ball into space. These decisions can only be made if the wingers' body is open as shown in diagram 236.

Diagram 237 shows an incorrect stance, where the forwards are not using the width, and are all playing with their backs to goal. Their collective positioning does not offer the ball carrier any options other than a pass to feet. There is no variety and no possibility to penetrate behind the defense. It is clear that if the ball is played behind the defense, the opponents will get to it first. In diagram 237, the attackers are playing right into the hands of the opponents, making it easier for them to mark tight and simpler for them to defend.

Once the ball is played into the attacking third, the winger without the ball should sprint into the penalty area to meet the cross and try to score. For example, in diagram 236, if the right winger manages to latch on to pass 2 or 4, the left winger does not need to stay wide any more and should sprint into the penalty area to score.

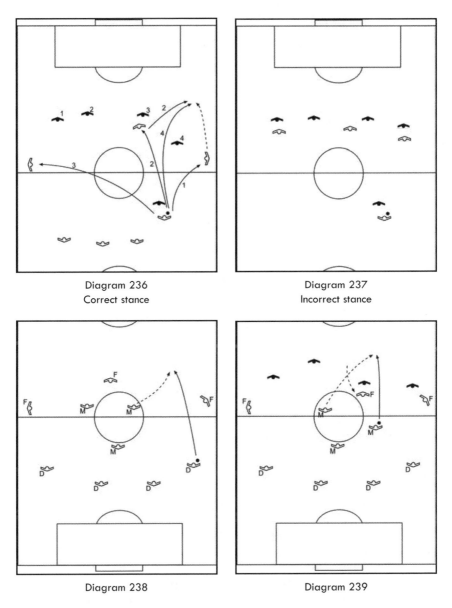

Diagram 236
Correct stance

Diagram 237
Incorrect stance

Diagram 238

Diagram 239

It was mentioned earlier that the 4-3-3 can be predictable in attack. The midfielders can add a surprise element and variety to the attack by making runs
behind the opposing defense. They can do it with a run between the forwards,
as shown in diagram 238, or they can interchange with the striker, as shown in
diagram 239.

The two wide backs can also add another dimension to the attack by overlapping and creating a 2 versus 1 on the flanks. As long as the three units of

defense, attack and midfield don't remain static and interchange intelligently, the 4-3-3 can be devastatingly hard to stop.

When the ball is lost, the forwards are expected to be the first line of defense. When the strategy calls for high pressure, the forwards push up against the defenders and try to win the ball early. If the game plan is to retreat, the wingers are expected to drop into midfield to help redress the numerical balance in this crucial area, giving the team a 4-5-1 look. Regardless of the strategy, the wingers will be required to track overlapping runs by the opposing wide backs.

Diagram 240

Diagram 240 illustrates one dilemma with this formation. The wide midfield areas between the defenders and the wingers are of some concern since they represent empty pockets that can be exploited by opponents. Coaches who employ the 4-3-3 need to work out how and who should close down the ball in these wide zones. The wide backs are an obvious first choice to step up and challenge the ball, as illustrated in the section on the 4-4-2 formation, since the most likely opponent to receive the ball there would be the outside midfielder. If the other team plays with three forwards, then one of the midfielders will have to close down the ball. In any case, the prevalent thought of coaches who like to use 4-3-3 is that an opponent with the ball in these wide areas poses no immediate danger, as long as either a defender or a midfielder quickly enters the zone to put pressure on the ball and as long as the winger follows the overlapping defender from the other team.

THE 3-4-3 FORMATION

This formation, shown in diagram 241, is used by coaches who believe in the attacking potential of three forwards but still prefer to play with four midfielders. As long as the team has three very capable defenders who can handle any two forwards, this system has the best of both worlds: numbers in attack and numbers in midfield. The midfield has great flexibility. It is usually arranged in a diamond shape, with a defensive 'holding' midfielder behind two wide ones and one attacking midfielder underneath the forwards. The shape and movement in midfield can vary to suit the situation. The wide midfielders can spread out and combine with the wingers to penetrate on the flanks or they can tuck inside to create a compact diamond and numerical advantage in midfield, since the wingers already provide a built-in width. Having four midfielders facilitates runs out of midfield since there is adequate cover should one make a penetrating run ahead of the forwards. All this makes for an exciting formation with many attacking options.

Diagram 241
3-4-3 formation

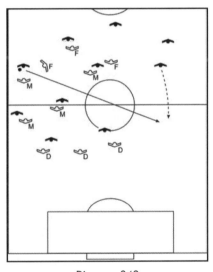

Diagram 242
Diagonal pass beating a high press

The responsibilities of the forwards in attack and defense are similar to any system that utilizes three forwards and is already elaborated on in the section on 4-3-3. The midfielders' roles are also previously covered with many similarities to the 4-4-2 midfield. The three defenders would normally work as two man markers and a sweeper, similar to the 3-5-2, although some teams use a flat zonal marking system with the three defenders. With only three at the back, the defenders would have to be very disciplined and not over commit to attack. They would tend to build up quickly from the back by distributing the ball early and then supporting the attack from behind the ball, rarely overlapping. With so many other players committed to attack, there is no need for the three defenders to make runs. It is more prudent for them to stay and cover.

Just like the 4-3-3, this system is very attack oriented and is geared to putting pressure on opponents early. With such an accent on attack, the 3-4-3 lends itself to playing high pressure defense. But committing to high pressure tactics with only three defenders in the back does have its risks. Teams can be vulnerable to quick counter attacks on the flanks since the three defenders cannot cover the whole width. A long accurate diagonal pass from the back line to the opposite flank can punish a high press. This weakness is illustrated in diagram 242. It's obvious from diagram 242 that a back line of four would be better able to deal with such diagonal passes.

The 3-4-3 is geared towards possession play in advanced areas. This is the system made famous by Ajax of Amsterdam, who used it religiously over the past 20-30 years. It worked for them because they had the best players in Holland and they trained them from an early age to play within this system. With three forwards and four midfielders empowered to attack and every player technically accomplished, Ajax was able to keep possession in the other team's half and turn the screws slowly and methodically until the right defense-splitting pass presented itself. When you have superior players, as Ajax did, who win the majority of their individual duels and don't give the ball away easily, you can afford to play with three forwards and only three defenders. Ajax was able to dictate the game and most of the play was taking place in the other team's half.

This formation is obviously more suited to playing against teams with two forwards. If opponents play with three forwards, either the defensive midfielder adjusts by dropping into a central defender position, essentially switching to 4-3-3, or the three defenders would have to cope with a 'numbers-even' situation in the back.

VARIATIONS OF TRADITIONAL FORMATIONS

In the previous chapter, the most common formations were described, namely the 4-4-2, the 3-5-2, the 4-3-3 and the 3-4-3, with the discussion mainly focusing on the traditional application of these formations. But the modern game is undergoing tactical trends that combine the true and trusted conventional systems with clever variations. Coaches at the highest level often tinker with the basic formations, tweaking them to suit the opponents or maximize their own players' strengths. The modern game is experiencing an evolution of innovative formations that are basically derivatives or spin-offs of the traditional configuration, as coaches are forever trying to outmaneuver each other.

As is often stressed in this book, the principles of play should always be the core that dictates players' movement. A team formation is just a numerical 'code' that provides each player with an indication of his primary role. The principles are eternal and will never change. What is changing, however, is the players' increasing ability to perform multiple roles. The modern player is fitter, physically and mentally quicker, technically more accomplished, and tactically more sophisticated. Advances in science, fitness training and coaching methods are responsible for the emergence of a new breed of player. The prototype new-age player is a very mobile, tough 'human machine' with energy and stamina, a player who can press the ball, tackle the ball, create chances and score goals. Whereas in the past, players could only handle one role, the modern player is much more versatile. The game is so fluid and quick that it's often hard to discern which formation is being used.

With such versatility at their disposal, coaches are quick to fiddle with the basic formations to gain advantage. The evolution of the attacking midfielder's role is a case in point. Attacking midfielders had it good in the past. They stayed high, just behind the forwards, their only concern was to get the ball, keep it away from the defensive midfielder assigned to mark them, and carve out scoring chances. The defensive midfielders were content with just marking and covering. But as soon as coaches started to teach their defensive midfielders to step up and be more creative, the role of the attacking midfielders had to change in response. Now, the shoe was on the other foot as the attacking midfielder had to learn to chase his chaser. The same happened when defenders started to attack, forcing forwards to track them down. The better these defenders were at creating chances, the more vital it became for attackers to increase their defensive contribution.

The most important tactical battles are fought in midfield. Regardless of formation used, the objective for each team is to find a way to control the midfield. Whoever has control of the midfield is in a better position to penetrate and create chances. When two teams are equally skilled and evenly balanced, the team that can create a numerical advantage in midfield around the ball will dominate this vital area. This coveted numerical advantage can be accomplished with movement. For example, forwards dropping into midfield and/or defenders stepping up at the appropriate moments. This movement off the ball is both synchronized through rehearsed training and improvised by individuals solving the demands of the game.

Coaches can also achieve midfield dominance by tweaking the basic formations. Some examples of how coaches manipulate the formation were already mentioned in the previous chapter. A coach can take the basic 4-4-2 and modify it to 4-4-1-1 or 4-5-1 by dropping a forward deeper. Similarly, a 3-5-2 can be converted to a 3-6-1, a ploy famously used by Steve Sampson's American team in the 1998 World Cup. The fact that Sampson's strategy didn't work is more a reflection of the players' shortcomings than any fault of the system per se and goes to show that a system is only as good as the players. Another example is with the back four system, where usually the wide backs are the ones expected to step up and tip the numbers scale in midfield, but sometimes the central defenders can step up as well. This chapter describes some of the variations used by modern coaches to gain the coveted midfield advantage over opponents.

Italy in Euro 2000 - No Attacking Midfielder

In the beginning of the book, the importance of getting the ball into the space in front of the defense, often called the 'hole', was emphasized. Most decent teams can possess the ball in their own half without too much difficulty. The hard part is to keep the ball for long periods in the other team's half. The ability to possess the ball high is a clear indication of midfield dominance. Teams that can string passes at will in the attacking half will have more success at working the ball into the hole. From there, penetration is possible using dribbling, combination plays and defense-splitting killer passes. The traditional approach is to plug one or two attacking midfielders in the formation, whose duty is to find ways to penetrate into the hole. Some coaches take a different approach. They play without a recognized attacking midfielder and leave it up to the players to figure out how to exploit the hole.

Italy, under Dino Zoff, played some games in Euro 2000 without an attacking midfielder. Italy played 4-4-2 with the four midfielders strung across the field, using two defensive midfielders (Di Biagio and Dino Baggio) playing side-by-

side and flanked by two wide midfielders, as shown in diagram 243.
The forwards took turns dropping into the hole to receive and spin or one of the
defensive midfielders would step into the hole. The advantages of this system
were obvious. Having two hard working ball winners in the center of the midfield gave the team a solid defensive cover and allowed the wide backs and
wide midfielders more freedom to overlap. Secondly, if one of the defensive
midfielders moved forward into attack, the other one would stay home to cover.
And thirdly, the element of surprise, with opponents not sure who will pop up in
the hole, made it unpredictable. The disadvantage was that there was no place
for a genuine creative flair player in midfield in a system more suited for hard
working ball winners. Was it successful? Italy reached the Final, were 1:0 up
and a few seconds away from winning the whole thing. They conceded a late
goal and eventually finished second to France. The purists might bemoan their
lack of flair, but obviously it was a successful system for them.

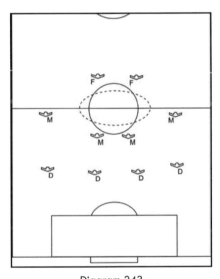

Diagram 243
Italy's 4-4-2 with no attacking midfielder

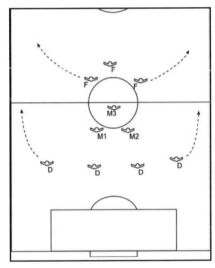

Diagram 244
France's version of 4-3-3

France in 1998 - Compact Version of 4-3-3

In the previous discussion of the 4-3-3 formation, it was noted that the traditional application of this system tended to be too static and predictable. The
French team that won the 1998 World Cup played a modern version of 4-3-3
that was very compact defensively, yet rendered it unpredictable and harder to
defend against. France strengthened the defense by playing with two defensive midfielders. The attacking midfielder was, of course, Zidane (M3 in
Diagram 244), who had a free role. The two defensive midfielders, Petit and
Deschamps, were very effective ball winners whose disciplined play enabled

not only Zidane to roam freely but also allowed the two wide defenders to overlap into attack with frequency. But the unique feature of the French formation was the way they employed the three forwards, with one high and two tucked inside right behind him. They called it 4-3-3, but it looked more like 4-2-1-2-1, or could even be described as 4-5-1. How one called it was irrelevant. The end result was that when France defended, they were very compact and hard to penetrate, but when they won the ball, they broke out in an unpredictable way, with the two withdrawn forwards making diagonal runs into wide spaces and the two wide backs overlapping on the flanks. Unlike the conventional 4-3-3, where the wingers provide a built-in width, the French interpretation did not have true wingers and relied on the wide backs and the withdrawn forwards to create width, using intelligent and improvised movement. The French version was a lot more sophisticated and required tactical awareness of the highest order. Players had to think quickly on transition from defending shape to attacking shape in order to establish width. But the system was fluid and hard to contain and brought France untold success in the form of the World Cup trophy, as well as the Euro 2000 Championship.

Tempting as it is, youth coaches must be cautious when trying to copy systems used by the top teams. The French system that was so effective in winning the World Cup is probably too sophisticated for most youth teams or school teams. The traditional 4-3-3, as shown in diagram 235, is more appropriate at the lower levels, provided the team has speedy wingers.

Playing With Only One Forward

Although the system was denoted as 4-3-3, the French team that won the World Cup played with a high forward, supported by the two attackers underneath, as shown in diagram 244. Playing with only one target player up front is becoming more common in modern soccer. It only requires a single player to stretch opponents and give the team depth. The rest of the attacking players can concentrate on flooding the midfield and winning control of this vital area, from where they can make forward, slashing runs to support the lone striker. It is difficult to defend against such an attacking ploy, provided you have a target player capable of holding the ball on his own and willing to run a lot to make himself available.

Playing with only one forward can be especially effective against a flat back four. The four defenders are usually reluctant to break their line and end up marking only one player. This creates a numbers-up advantage in midfield, allowing the midfielders behind the lone forward plenty of possession in the center of the park, and enabling them to exploit the hole in front of the back four. When Manchester United, who uses the flat back four, played against

European teams that employ two withdrawn strikers underneath a lone target player, they had a tough time coping with the withdrawn strikers running at them from the midfield.

Diagram 245 shows the dilemma defenders face in this situation. With the defensive midfielder already marking the opposing attacking midfielder and the back line defenders reluctant to be pulled into midfield, the withdrawn forwards can find space to receive and turn with the ball and attack the back line. Playing just one up front requires mobile midfielders who can support the attack very quickly. The attacker must be very adept at receiving balls with his back to goal and protecting the ball until help arrives. The build up of attack must go through the midfield since long balls to a single attacker would not work well.

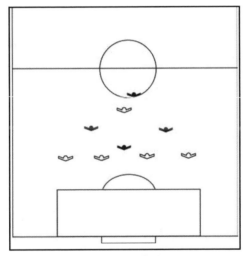

Diagram 245

Playing With Two Defensive Midfielders

Employing two defensive midfielders is becoming the vogue. Teams such as France, Italy and Brazil showed how two ball winners in midfield can bring success. On the face of it, the system sounds very negative. But in reality, the safety of having two defensive anchors in midfield allows the defenders and the other midfielders more freedom to attack. It also clogs up the vital space in front of the defense, making it hard for opponents to penetrate into the hole. The key is to have ball winners who can also play and create. Petit, one of the two French ball winners in midfield, scored the third goal in the 1998 final against Brazil. Davids does the same for Juventus and Holland. These players embody the modern anchoring midfielder: a perpetual motion all rounder who is powerful and strong on the tackle, mentally and tactically disciplined, but possessing passing and scoring ability to boot.

Romania in Euro 2000 - Back Four plus Sweeper

An interesting formation was used by Romania at Euro 2000. Romania has always favored playing a deep, defensive game with quick counter attacks. In the nineties, they had relative success relying on the counter attacking potential of their great playmaker, Hagi. Their system in Euro 2000 had a sweeper behind a back four, two defensive midfielders in the hole, Hagi, the brilliant attacking midfielder who had the freedom to roam with no defensive duties, and two forwards. Diagram 246 illustrates Romania's formation, best described as a 1-4-3-2 or a 1-4-2-1-2. If Romania fell behind, they would switch to a 3-5-2 by pushing the wide backs up into wide midfield as shown in diagram 247.

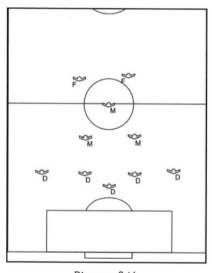

Diagram 246
Romania's 1-4-3-2

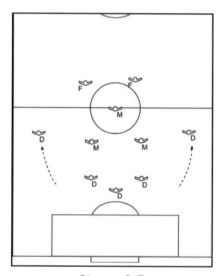

Diagram 247
Romania switching to 3-5-2

Brazilian System 1982 to 1998 - The 4-2-2-2

For close to twenty years, Brazilian teams have developed their own interpretation of the 4-4-2, using a box midfield, which makes it really a 4-2-2-2. Brazilian soccer has managed to combine individual flair with a tactically sound system that has served Brazilian teams well over the years. Just about every team in Brazil plays this system. It is therefore quite amazing that, even though everyone plays the same way, teams still manage to serve up exciting attacking soccer, without falling into the tactical stalemate one would expect from teams playing identically.

Brazilian soccer is a wide open game that flows end to end. The main reason is that Brazilian teams do not squeeze the units together and play compactly, which creates much more space in midfield than in European games. It is much easier to play through the midfield in Brazil because the first coordinated resistance encountered is in the attacking third. The players are also extremely skillful, their range of passing and receiving is exceptional, and they revel in one-versus-one duels.

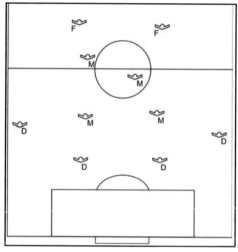

Diagram 248

As mentioned before, the Brazilian 4-4-2 is really a 4-2-2-2 formation, where the midfielders are organized in a box formation, with two defensive midfielders behind two attacking midfielders. This leaves the flanks open for the right back and the left back to attack at will. See diagram 248 for the standard Brazilian formation.

Unlike in Europe, where only one wide back attacks at a time while the other one slides inside to cover, in Brazil both wide backs attack simultaneously. Diagram 249 illustrates this feature, where both the right and the left backs are moving up in wide positions. The defensive holding midfielders rarely attack and provide cover for the overlapping defenders. In diagram 249, the defensive midfielder would either slot into the vacated area (a) or drop in between the central defenders (b).

Another feature of Brazilian soccer is the way they use their forwards. The Brazilian forwards do not combine with each other in the way that European forwards do. The two forwards in the European teams stay close together and play off each other. The Brazilian forwards for the most part stay apart and look to combine with the midfielders and overlapping wide backs. Diagram 250 illustrates the typical movement off the ball by the forwards when the right back has the ball. The right forward would either show for the ball to feet or run behind the defense for a through ball and the attacking midfield would support him. Between the three of them, the overlapping defender, the midfielder and the forward would look for ways to combine and penetrate on the right flank. Notice how the left back stays wide and waits for a possible switch. While this is happening, the second forward would move away from the ball to the blind side and wait there. By moving away from the ball, the second forward is providing the option of a long switch that can unbalance the other team and create a 1v1 situation in a very dangerous area close to goal. Brazilian forwards relish the chance to go 1v1 near goal. Also, if the ball is switched to the left back, he can immediately combine with the second forward down the left wing.

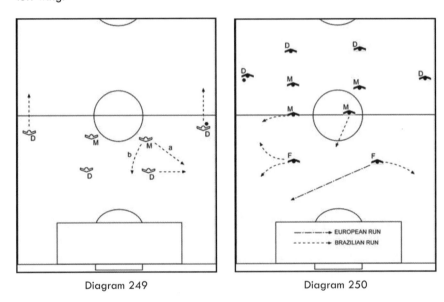

Diagram 249   Diagram 250

The other advantage of the second forward's sliding movement away is that it puts him in a position from which he can attack a through ball by running towards goal as opposed to the traditional diagonal runs towards the corner flags, made by European forwards. The forwards' movement in opposite direction also opens up a gap straight down the middle through which one of the attacking midfielders can make a run.

Diagram 251 shows the options for penetration that are available to an attacking midfielder if he receives the ball. Option 1 is a through ball to the right forward or to the overlapping defender. Option 2 is a switch to the feet of the second forward who can then take on his marker 1v1 to goal. Option 3 is a through ball into space behind the defense. Option 4 is a pass for a second midfielder running through the middle.

Brazilian teams like to switch the point of attack with long passes. Switching the point of attack is obviously not unique to Brazilian soccer, but they do have a penchant for playing the ball from side to side more often than other countries, and their wide backs are ideally positioned to stretch the opponents with long passes. Brazilian players can hit long accurate passes with great ease and will readily switch play with one single pass.

A typical Brazilian passing pattern involves a pass into the flank, followed by a drop pass to a supporting player, followed by a long diagonal pass to the wide back or forward on the opposite flank. The long pass would be played into feet or into space, depending on the situation. Diagram 252 illustrates a typical passing sequence. Brazilian forwards are comfortable receiving the ball on the flanks with their backs to the field. Their skill and the readily available support make them hard to dispossess.

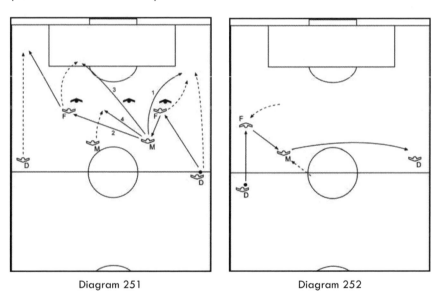

Diagram 251　　　　　　　　　　　　Diagram 252

Rigid Defensive Block Behind Flexible Attack

If there is one defining modern tactical trend, it must surely be the melding of a rigid, zonal defensive block with a flexible, free flowing attack. The two contrasting concepts form the foundation of modern systems. Coaches recognize that a very flexible, slippery, unpredictable attacking style is required to break down modern defenses, and that likewise, a compact, zonal defensive block is the best antidote against flexible attacks.

Many top teams have found a way to merge the two concepts into their formation. Portugal is one of the teams that featured this combination in their 'dream team' of the late 1990's. In Euro 2000, Portugal played a very attractive and creative brand of soccer, which was based on a six man defensive block supporting a flexible attacking midfield that had the license to interchange freely and go anywhere they pleased. The six man block consisted of a zonal flat four plus two midfield anchors. In front of them were three very skillful and mobile midfielders, one of whom was the excellent Figo. The three midfielders were devastating in one-on-one against defenders. The lone forward stayed high and kept the opposing central defenders occupied. This ploy isolated the wide defenders, creating the one-on-one duels the Portuguese midfielders craved. Figo was especially good at starting outside on the wing and running inside with and without the ball. He favored starting on the right wing, but was not averse to switching to the left. With the ball at his feet, he could beat the defender on the outside and cross, or he could cut inside and shoot. Without the ball, he would lurk wide, wait for the space in front of the defense to open up, and ghost inside into the dangerous 'hole' to receive a ball and dribble at the heart of the defense.

In 2000, Portugal reached the European Championships Semi-Finals. Unfortunately, the 2002 World Cup is best forgotten as far as Portugal is concerned. The unlucky coincidence of a loss of form for a number of key players meant that Portugal never got off the starting blocks and were eliminated in the first round. Diagram 253 depicts the Portuguese line up with the three attacking midfielders stretching the defense.

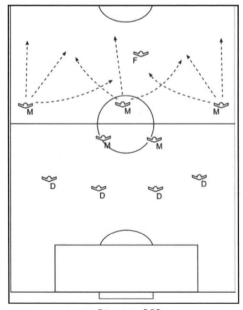

Diagram 253
Portugal 4-2-3-1 formation

Three at The Back - Defending Zonally

Over the last ten years, teams have increasingly applied the principles of zonal defending with only three defenders. The reason was simple: The traditional two-marker-plus-sweeper system was too easily pulled apart with intelligent movement by the forwards. Coaches who still preferred to play with only three at the back switched to zonal defending to plug the holes, using three central defenders. This essentially combined the best features of two systems. It allowed teams to benefit from the economy of just three defenders AND keep it compact by defending zonally. Now the central defenders presented a solid three-man wall, which moved as a unit and couldn't be pulled apart. It also meant that the traditional wide defender was no longer needed and could be replaced by wide midfielders. As long as the wide midfielders were able to drop back and defend the flanks when needed, this system was efficient. In fact, the 2002 edition of the Brazilian National Team departed from tradition and employed a three man zonal defense with great success. See below.

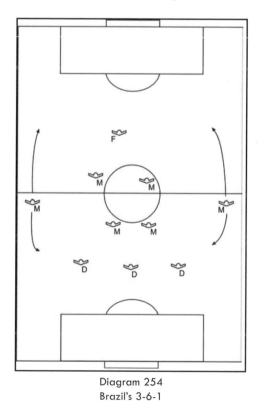

Diagram 254
Brazil's 3-6-1

Brazil in 2002 - 3-6-1 With Zonal Defending

After almost twenty years of playing their unique blend of 4-2-2-2, the Brazilian team broke with tradition and played a very fluid 3-6-1 that brought them their fifth World Cup triumph. Diagram 254 shows the Brazilian alignment that coach Scolari used in the final against Germany. A flat back line, comprising three central defenders (Roque Junior, Edmilson, and Lucio) and protected by two defensive midfielders (Gilberto silva and Kleberson) formed the defensive core of the team. Cafu and Roberto Carlos provided flank penetration in midfield, Ronaldo stayed high and central as the lone striker, and Ronaldinho and Rivaldo were the creative attacking midfielders who had the license to pop anywhere they wanted.

This was a very flexible system that was designed to oscillate from 5-4-1 when defending to 3-6-1 when building up in midfield, to 3-2-5 when penetrating into the attacking third. The system asked Cafu and Roberto Carlos, the right and left wide midfielders, to drop into a wide defender's position when defending and transform into wingers when attacking. It was a measure of their supreme fitness and tactical maturity that they performed their role to perfection, maintaining a fine balance between wing play and defensive cover.

Brazil actually started the tournament playing a 3-5-2 system, with only one defensive midfielder (Gilberto Silva) and two attacking midfielders (Juninho and Rivaldo) in the center of midfield. But this formation proved defensively fragile against good teams. Scolari adjusted the formation by switching to two defensive midfielders, dropping Juninho and replacing him with the more defensive Kleberson. The result was a more compact shape and better cover in midfield. Brazil won the 2002 World Cup partly because everyone on the team was willing to work hard for each other. Even Rivaldo, Ronaldo and Ronaldinho, who were on the team for their attacking flair, maintained a work ethic and dropped back to chase and tackle. But the main reason why Brazil won the tournament was the superior individual skills of the Brazilian players. Systems don't win games. What the system did accomplish was utilize the best attributes of each player in a way that contributed towards a well oiled machine. But ultimately, players win games. Brazil didn't win the tournament because they played 3-6-1. Brazil won it because it had the best players.

POSITIONS AND THEIR ROLE

In order to be effective, **ALL** formations, regardless of how original or sophisticated they are, will have to include one or more players in each of the following seven basic positions:

1) Central defender and/or a sweeper
2) Wide defender
3) Defensive midfielder
4) Attacking midfielder
5) Wide midfielder or winger
6) Forward
7) Goalkeeper.

For a team to be successful, it must have players who are capable of slotting into these generic positions within the framework of whatever formation is used. No formation by itself can bring success if the players cannot adequately perform the roles inherent in these positions. In order to help coaches place their players into a position that fits their ability, a brief description of the role of each one of the above mentioned positions is warranted.

The Role of the Central Defender

The central defender usually marks the opposing forward, especially the forward who acts as the target player. His first task is to prevent the forward from receiving the ball, or at least prevent him from turning and going to goal. Central defenders are usually physically big and strong, good in the air, and are good tacklers. Speed is an important asset, especially if there is no sweeper behind. In a formation without a sweeper, one of the central defenders is also the leader of the defense who reads the game well, organizes the defense, organizes the off-side trap, and initiates counterattacks with intelligent passes out of the back. Offensively, a central defender will sometimes need to step up into the midfield area in order to help his team in possession or to start an attack, but he rarely ventures too far up the field unless it is for a set play such as a corner kick or a free kick. Central defenders are very disciplined players who take few risks and play it simple and safe, since one mistake at the back or one bad pass could prove costly.

The Role of the Sweeper

If a sweeper is used behind the defense, the central defenders become pure man-markers, leaving the job of organizing to the sweeper. The sweeper is the leader of the defense and many times of the entire team. He does not have a specific marking assignment but is there to organize and cover his defense, marshal the space behind his defense, intercept any through balls, and initiate counterattacks. As with any defensive position, speed is an asset. Sweepers are usually intelligent, versatile players who can tackle the ball as well as pass it over long distance. Since he is a free player not burdened by a marking assignment, the sweeper goes wherever he thinks he is needed. His starting position is usually a central one, right behind his defense. But from there, he might chase after a through ball, or sprint wide to cover a defender and create a 2 v 1 situation, or step up to pressure the ball. Offensively, since he is not marked by an opponent, the modern sweeper is tactically adept at taking advantage of his freedom by joining the attack whenever he feels it is safe to do so.

The Role of the Wide Defender

The main defensive job of the wide defender is to stop opponents from penetrating down his flank. The wide defender also provides cover for the central defenders and balance for the team. The modern wide defender does quite a lot of attacking as well. Since there are very few teams who engage true wingers, the wide defender is not shackled by a marking assignment and is often free to overlap into attack. Many teams use the wide defenders as an outlet to relieve pressure on the ball, maintain possession, and act as the springboard to attack. Wide defenders must be capable tacklers, with both speed and stamina to run from penalty area to penalty area. Their attacking duties dictate that they must have great passing and crossing ability.

The Role of the Defensive Midfielder

Simply put, the main role of the defensive midfielder is to protect the defense. The defensive midfielder plays what is known as a 'holding' role, meaning that he doesn't usually make attacking runs but rather stays in the 'hole' - the all important space in front of his central defenders. Regardless of the midfield formation, the key duties of the defensive midfielder are to win the ball in midfield, to mark the opposition's attacking midfielder, to organize the other midfielders, and to snuff out counterattacks when possession is lost. The defensive midfielder is therefore a disciplined player who is tenacious in the tackle, with good stamina. When his team has possession, the defensive midfielder supports the attacking midfielders from behind, and helps them switch the point of attack. Since the defensive midfielder operates just in front of the defense, he has to be secure in possession and a good distributor of the ball. One rarely sees a defensive midfielder taking many touches of the ball, or taking any risk for that matter. A typical defensive midfielder plays it simple, receiving and releasing balls with one or two touches, using his first touch to turn away from pressure, and usually choosing a safe pass to maintain possession.

The Role of the Attacking Midfielder

The attacking midfielder is expected to do it all: Create goals, score some himself, link the defense with the forwards using passes, combination plays and individualism, and defend a bit as well. The way the attacking midfielder goes about his business depends on the midfield permutation used and the range of his talents. Some attacking midfielders like to go to the ball, demanding it from their defenders and launching attacks with quality passes. Other attacking midfielders like to roam higher up, making runs into spaces created by the forwards in order to penetrate and score. The best midfielders are versatile and skillful enough to do both, which makes it hard to contain them. Attacking midfielders are often coined 'half-midfield-half-forward', emphasizing their dual role as creators and scorers. The term 'speed of play' is used often in evaluating attacking midfielders because they must be very comfortable receiving balls in crowded areas, have instant control, size up situations quickly and pass accurately with both feet. They are the most creative players on the team as well as the natural leaders.

The Role of the Wide Midfielder

The wide midfielders provide width in attack and penetration down the flanks. When a team has possession, the wide midfielders will usually move out towards the side lines and try to get behind the opposing wide backs, just like wingers. Wide midfielders are also expected to try to get on the end of crosses and score. For example, when the ball is crossed from the left flank, the right midfielder is expected to run into the penalty area to meet the cross. When their team loses possession, the wide midfielders will be required to recover back into midfield and pick up an opponent. The modern wide midfielder probably covers more yardage than any other player and therefore must have tremendous stamina as well as speed. He must be a good passer, a good crosser and dribbler and is expected to contribute his share of goals.

The Role of the Forward

The most obvious role of the forward is to score goals. But forwards are expected to do a lot more than just score goals. They provide depth in attack by pushing up and stretching the other team's defense, they create space for the midfielders with intelligent movement off the ball, and they play an important part in the build up by acting as target players available for penetrating passes. When their team loses the ball, the forwards become the first line of defense by closing down the ball in the opponent's half to try to win it or, at least, contain it and buy their teammates time to recover back in defense. Forwards must be able to receive balls under pressure with their backs to goal or on the run. They must be good finishers with both feet and with headers, and not be afraid to give it a go from anywhere. Speed off the mark, agility, dribbling, confidence and deception are the trademarks of a good forward.

The Role of the Goal Keeper

The modern keeper's role has expanded in scope. Aside from the reflex shot stopping and handling crosses, the modern keeper acts like a sweeper, coming off his line to intercept through balls, and initiate counterattacks with his distribution. Good keepers communicate effectively to their players and organize the defense in order to snuff out potential danger before it happens. Through proper positioning, awareness, and constant specific and clear communication, the keeper helps his team prevent goal chances from developing. Keepers have become better at playing with their feet and it is now a pre-requisite for top-level keepers to be good passers over short and long distances. The modern keeper is the last line of defense and the first line of attack.

SELECTING A SYSTEM OF PLAY

The first step in coaching tactics is to evaluate the players' abilities, strengths and weaknesses in order to decide on the most appropriate formation and playing system. It is important to select a formation that is suitable for your players and avoid trying to copy a system simply because it was successfully used by others. At the highest level of the game, coaches can search and acquire players that specifically fit their vision of a system. But at the youth level, most coaches do not have the luxury of picking players to suit their preferred system. Generally speaking, at the lower echelons of the game and at the youth level, coaches must do with the cards that are dealt to them and select the formation that best suits the players at their disposal.

In order to select the appropriate system, a sound understanding of the basic systems and the type of players required for each position to make the system work is a pre-requisite. Previous chapters dealt with the most common systems of play, such as the 4-4-2, the 4-3-3, the 3-5-2, and the 3-4-3, as well as the roles and requirements of each position. Using that as a guideline, coaches can evaluate their playing staff.

Of course, the decision on which system to play at the youth level could also be based on player development consideration or a club's philosophy and training priorities for each age group. If the overall master plan for the club is to teach all the teams a certain playing system at a certain age, this philosophy might override the need to consider a system that fits the players. For example, the 4-3-3 formation might be the best place to start for young teams who are newly exposed to the 11-a-side game and whose players are embarking on the long road to tactical awareness. In the author's opinion, the 4-3-3 system is probably the easiest one to introduce to young players because each position has a clear role and a distinct area of operation with a minimum overlap. In the 4-3-3 formation, players don't have to fulfill multiple roles as they would in a 4-4-2 or 3-5-2 formation. They are strictly defenders, or midfielders, or attackers and their tasks are sharply defined. The 4-3-3 system also spreads the players evenly over the field and is physically less taxing for young players. The workload in a 4-3-3 is evenly distributed. Another advantage of 4-3-3 for young teams is the fact that three players are learning to play as attackers from a young age. This would have the long-term benefits of producing more players who are comfortable going forward, regardless of where they might end up playing later on.

Coaches will rely heavily on their previous experiences, their beliefs and biases, past successes and failures and intuition, to decide on a playing system. But whatever their experiences, most coaches should mull over the following important considerations in the decision process:

How Many Players Are Available for Each Unit?

The first step would be to figure out how many players in the squad have the attributes for each line. In other words, how many players can play defense, how many could play in midfield, and how many could do a job up front. This information alone could become the main consideration in deciding on a playing system. For example, if a coach finds that he has an abundance of midfielders and only a few defenders, this fact could sway him to play a system that can accommodate many midfield types, such as a 3-5-2 formation. As another example, coaches who contemplate using four at the back, within a 4-4-2 or a 4-3-3 system, will need a left footed defender to make it work properly. Using a right footed defender on the left will hinder penetration on the left flank for a few reasons. The right footed defender's first touch and body orientation will likely be inward and result in play directed towards the crowded center. Also, it is easier to block a forward pass coming from the right foot on the left side. And lastly, a true left footer can bend long in-swinging passes down the left flank, which are preferable to chasing out-swingers coming from the right foot.

The Basic Strategy - Attack or Counterattack?

Another key decision that needs to be made early in the process, while taking stock of the players, is which basic strategy is most suited for the available personnel. Should the team play an aggressive attacking style and try to impose its game on the opponents or should it play a more cautious defensive game, let the other team come at them and counterattack. In other words, where will the game be played most of the time, in their half or in your half?

In order to play an attacking style, all the players must be physically fit and must have an aggressive mentality. A team playing an attacking style must be able to play high pressure defending since it is not consistent to commit a large number of players to attack but then turn and sprint back to one's half to defend when the ball is lost. And since there will be acres of space behind the back line, a team playing an attacking style must have speed in the back.

On the other hand, teams that are physically unfit, or lacking overall team speed, might be better off playing a defensive game that conserves energy, and choose their moments to attack wisely. It all boils down to the one-versus-one duels. If a coach is not confident that his players can win the individual duels, he might want to rein his players in so they can cover for each other and not be isolated one-on-one. Also, a team that doesn't have speed in the back, but has quick skillful forwards might be more suited to playing a counterattacking game. By dropping back into their half whenever the ball is lost, a team without speed in the back can eliminate the dangerous space behind the defense, stay compact, and use their quick forwards to counterattack.

Where to Play the Best Players?

Coaches have long struggled with the dilemma of where to play their best players. As a guideline, and this might sound like a cliché, but the spine of the team is of paramount importance. The five positions with the most influence on the team's performance are unquestionably those along the center: the goalkeeper, the central defender/sweeper, the defensive midfielder, the attacking midfielder, and the target player. Care must be taken to plug players into these five key positions who can perform the required tasks. A coach that has only a few players with speed should first insert speed in the back line and in the front line before anywhere else. This will give the team some safety in the back and penetration on top. A back line and a front line without speed will have very little chance of coping with good opponents.

Next, and of particular importance, is the role of the defensive midfield. Inexperienced coaches neglect to appreciate the impact of the defensive midfielder and often plug the wrong person in this key position. The main responsibility of the defensive midfielder is to protect the defense. He is like a sweeper in front of the defense. He must stay in the hole most of the time, be able to win balls, organize the midfield and play a very disciplined simple game. When coaches put an attacking minded player in this position, the balance in midfield is usually undermined and the defense is left exposed.

Determine the Arrangement in Each Line.

Once the coach has decided on the basic strategy/style of the team and where to place his key players, he should analyze each line, starting with the defense, and decide the best arrangement within each unit. The strengths and weaknesses of all his potential defenders should provide clues as to the best alignment. Should they play man-to-man with a sweeper or a zonal defending system? There is a trend currently at the top level towards zonal defending. Could your team defend zonally? If the team has the following attributes, a zonal system might be appropriate:

1.   Defenders with intelligence and ability to read situations quickly.

2.   At least one, and preferably two defenders who are vocal and willing to lead and are capable of playing in the middle of the defense.

3.   A keeper who is comfortable playing outside the six yards box and has the speed and range to fulfill the role of a sweeper-keeper.

4.   Wide defenders with speed and at least one central defender with speed. Speed in the back is always important, regardless of system used. But the point here is that slow defenders will make it impossible to play a flat zonal defense since there is no sweeper to provide cover.

Once the coach decides on a defending system, he can proceed to his midfield. Is the midfield alignment compatible with the back line? For example, if the coach is confident in his back line, he might choose a midfield arrangement with an accent on attack. If, on the other hand, the coach is worried about the defense, he might use a more defensive formation in midfield, such as employing two defensive midfielders that can better protect the back line, or using wide midfielders whose role is slanted more towards defensive cover than offensive thrust. Either way, a well functioning, balanced midfield must have players who can win the ball, players who can pass the ball, and players who can score. If a coach is lucky enough to have a few midfield players, each of whom can do all of the above, all the better. But chances are, the coach will have to find the best combination of players who can complement each other to produce a balanced midfield. The expression "the sum of the whole is greater than the sum of the parts" comes to mind when constructing a midfield.

The midfield formation must also be in harmony with the forward line. For example, a three-man front line needs a midfield unit that is especially adept at passing the ball than one that is good at carrying the ball. If quality balls are consistently delivered to the three forwards, both into space and to feet, they can then take care of penetration and finishing. On the other hand, a front line with only one or two forwards needs physically fit midfielders who are good at making penetrating runs and supporting runs from midfield, can take players on, and can score their share of goals as well.

The Principle of Continuity

Once a system is chosen, it is very important to stick to it long enough for the players to become well versed in it. A common mistake coaches make is to change the system often, either because of poor results or to counter the opponents' system. This tends to complicate matters for the players, especially inexperienced ones. Moving players around into different positions from one game to the next not only has questionable benefits for getting results in the short term, but is also likely to retard player development in the long run. It is better to emphasize stability than variety when it comes to introducing young players to the intricacies of systems. Coaches must have patience and a belief in their own initial intuition.

With a few exceptions, the best long-term approach with youth teams is to keep to the same system for the whole season or year, and allow the players to develop an understanding of the formation. This is especially wise if the season is just a prelude to the more important play-offs or cup games. Keeping a stable, constant formation, with little chopping and changing will contribute towards achieving peak performance at the most desirable time, the play-offs. Once the players become adept with a certain formation, they can switch to learning another formation in the following season.

The principle of continuity can be just as valid with more mature teams. When a coach does not panic and change the formation of his team after every bad performance, he sends a clear message to the players that he has faith in the system and in the players. The players in turn will respond positively to this approach and will grow in confidence. It's true that at the highest international levels teams increasingly change their line up and system from game to game, depending on the opponent. Real Madrid switched systems from game to game in their triumphant march to the 2002 UEFA Champions Leagues, in order to adapt to opponents or due to injury absence of players such as Figo. Real Madrid interchanged between 4-2-3-1 and 5-2-1-2 away from home to 4-1-3-2 or 4-2-2-2 at home and got the results needed to win the trophy. But even with all these changes, upon closer scrutiny one can still detect a healthy degree of commitment to continuity by the Real Madrid coach. Real Madrid relied on a core of eight key players who always played in the same position. These players were Cesar in goal, Salgado, Helguera, Hierro and Roberto Carlos in the back, Makelele always as the holding midfield, Zidane as the roving attacking midfield and Raul as the target player up front. Had Figo been healthy, it would have been a stable core of nine.

Top teams can switch systems because they employ the very best players. Top level players can handle playing to different systems. They represent the 'finished product', meaning they are technically and tactically so advanced, they can adapt to varying roles from game to game. The most successful top teams are also engaged in many competitions and end up playing an excessive amount of games. This requires maintaining a large player pool and using a squad rotation system to rest players and avoid burn out.

System constancy should not be confused with tactical adjustments that are sometimes necessary in the course of a game. There are many instances when a team needs to make a tactical change in the middle of the game. The obvious cases are when a team is trailing and needs to increase its offensive punch by switching to a more attacking formation, or when a team is trying to protect a lead and adds a defender, or when a team is playing short. Field conditions, weather, and other outside factors can also influence a tactical adjustment.

The principle of continuity preached here has to do more with the deliberate, methodical approach to the tactical development of a team, where players are given time to learn one system properly before moving on to another. To reach peak performance, a team should have a basic system that everyone under-stands and which is used most of the time. It doesn't mean that coaches should never make changes. Good coaches know when and how to make tactical adjustments. Inexperienced coaches make changes too frequently, often under the misplaced and overblown conviction that they can influence the course of the game merely by moving players like pieces on a chessboard.

Players Must Learn Their Own Main Tasks First

When coaches select a system, they must also have a clear idea as to which players are responsible for certain key functions and clearly communicate their expectations. For example, which players are expected to provide penetration and which ones are expected to distribute the passes. Which player will be the main target for outlet passes up front and which players are responsible for giving the team width as it transitions from defense to attack. Which players are given the license to roam freely and which ones are expected to stay disci-plined and cover. This doesn't mean that players are shackled into rigid roles. But for a team to function efficiently, each position carries a distinct main responsibility that must be understood by the player filling it. Players should be capable of executing their own main task before they can perform other peo-ples' tasks. Developing versatility in players is desirable, but is a long process that must start with learning a basic role first.

Patience Breeds Confidence

As mentioned before, young players should be allowed enough time to learn a specific position. Each player should be assigned a main position, one that he can handle and allowed to occupy most of the time. A word of caution here. When inexperienced players are taught a position, they are likely to look ten-tative in the first couple of games. This is only natural, since they are probably thinking too much, trying to do what they believe their coach wants, and going through the trial and error process. Veteran coaches understand the learning process and anticipate the hesitant performance in the early stages. Seasoned coaches don't reach premature conclusions about players and let the players pass through the steep part of the learning curve before passing judgment. In due course, players will settle down, gain in confidence and start listening to their own instincts. Once a player becomes comfortable in a position, he can be taught another position. It might take a few games or a whole year before a player is deemed ready for another role. This approach builds a sound foundation of tactical awareness, and is a solid platform for the development of rounded, confident players, ones who are comfortable in any area of the field.

SECTION THREE

METHODS OF COACHING

PLANNING A PRACTICE SESSION

At the very beginning of the book, it was mentioned that the four components of soccer training are technique, tactics, fitness and psychology. Although this book is mainly concerned with tactical training, we need to keep in mind that modern coaching methods are based on the premise that the best training activities are those incorporating as many of the four components as possible. Furthermore, all activities should replicate the game, meaning that the activities chosen should mimic as closely as possible the demands of the game. This is called the principle of sport specificity.

Training must be specific to the sport. The design of the activities should replicate the demands of the sport, otherwise the transfer of learning from training to the game is not optimal. For example, practicing crosses using a stationary ball, from only 20 yards out, does not prepare the players to successfully execute crosses in a game since, on a regulation size field, the crosses will originate from further out, hence the pace and flight of the ball and the timing of the runs are different and the ball is rarely stationary in open play. As another example, receiving balls at the edge of the penalty area and taking a leisurely five or six touches to turn and get set for a shot does not prepare a forward for the demands of his position since, in a real game, he will not be allowed so much time and space on the ball that close to goal.

Reproducing game conditions in training is necessary with regard to all the components, including the environmental and physical aspects of the upcoming games. Even details such as the length of the grass, inflation of the ball, size of the field, hardness of the playing surface, time of day and the temperature will need to be similar to game conditions for best training results. Training in 70 degree heat does not prepare the players to play when the temperature is 80 degrees. Obviously, many teams do not have the means or facilities to replicate exactly the conditions of the next game, but coaches must be cognizant of the principle of specificity and plan the practices to reproduce as much of the match conditions as possible.

Coaches do, however, have control over the practice plan and choice of activities. Care must be taken to put the players through game-related activities that incorporate the components of soccer. For example, running laps around the field only addresses stamina, which is a fitness component, but fails to improve anything else. If balls are introduced and the players are dribbling around the field instead of just running, the technical dribbling component is now added. But dribbling in a straight line at a constant speed doesn't really imitate real game situations. Moving the players into the field and having them dribble in a restricted area, using fakes to change directions and accelerate with the ball brings the activity even closer to the real game since we now have both a fitness and a technical component and they both incorporate soccer specific movement patterns. Having players dribble randomly in a grid is fine as a warm up activity, but the tactical and psychological components are still missing since, without opponents, there are no decisions to be made. If we place the players in 1 v 1 or 2 v 2 situations in a grid just outside the penalty area, add a keeper, and ask them to find ways to get shots on goal, we now have some tactical elements to the practice. If we add a second goal and a keeper, we have added the important tactical element of transition. And if we keep score or attach some form of reward for success, we have also added a psychological edge to the activity. Now it finally looks like soccer, feels like soccer, and prepares the players for the game of soccer.

A practice session will not necessarily have a tactical focus. The main objective of a practice depends on how it fits within the annual master plan, whether it is in the off-season, pre-season, or in-season, and how it fits into the weekly cycle. For example, in the off-season, the main training goals will likely be to improve technique and physical strength, while during the season tactical training will assume a higher priority. The fact that a particular practice has an objective narrowly focused on one component doesn't contradict the need to incorporate as many components as possible into every activity. Coaches simply manipulate the activity to fit the training objective and provide feedback to the players specific to that objective. An activity that was used to work on technique can be modified to focus on fitness by adjusting the work-to-rest ratio or by increasing the tempo. A small-sided practice game can be used to work on technique by focusing on and correcting technical mistakes, or it can be used to teach a tactical concept if the coach so desires. The attention of the coach might be concentrated on one component as he monitors an activity and interacts with the players, but all the four components of soccer are nevertheless present in that activity.

It also follows that every activity should involve the ball. Aside from the fact that players enjoy working with the ball, it is obviously impossible to replicate the game without a ball. The ball-to-player ratio will depend on the topic. If the focus is technical, players should work in smaller groups, with more balls, to increase the technical repetitions. If the topic is tactical, only one ball is needed on the field, but ample balls should be strategically placed around the field or grid to maintain a flow and not waste valuable time chasing miss-kicked balls.

Before we move on to the main focus of this section, namely methods of coaching tactics, one last thought regarding the general aspects of practice planning. No matter what the topic is, at some point in the practice the emphasis must shift to the 'application to the game', i.e. tactical considerations. For example, a practice devoted to a technical topic such as 'passing' would undoubtedly involve many repetitions of passing drills. But the practice would not be complete without a final activity where passing solutions are applied to game-like situations. It is not enough to work on technique in isolation. Working on technique-on-demand is paramount. And technique-on-demand implies making decisions, which is the essence of tactics.

Let us now examine the aspects of planning a practice specifically geared to a tactical topic. Whenever a coach is designing a tactical session, the topic selection and the associated activities will depend on the following factors:

1.   The developmental needs of the players
2.   The game analysis
3.   The players' abilities

The Developmental Needs of the Players

This factor is more applicable to youth teams. Age-specific tactical priorities might dictate the topic over other considerations. For instance, a tactical practice for 10 to 12 year-olds should address decisions on the ball within individual and small-group situations. The most appropriate activities should range from 1 v 1 games to 4 v 4 games. The focus of coaching should be fixed on individual attacking and defending, as well as on combination plays involving two and three players, such as wall-passes, takeovers and overlaps.

At these young ages, it would be pre-mature to work on aspects such as zonal back four defending or long diagonal switches, or spend too much time on set plays. Even if 10 to 12-year-olds are already playing their official games on large fields within 8v8 or 11v11 formats, the training environment must concentrate on the player with the ball and his immediate surroundings. Coaches who try to skip developmental steps, or 'fast track' their players into large group activities are doing their players an injustice. It is far more important to ingrain good individual habits and develop comfort on the ball with young players. Without a solid individual technical and tactical foundation, the game's individual duels, which, as was stated earlier, are so crucial for team success, will be lost. Gradually, as the players get older, tactical topics can shift towards the large group and team tactics.

Depending on the age and ability of the players, tactical activities might need to be preceded by a thorough technical warm up that prepares the players technically for that activity. The success of a tactical activity depends to a large extent on the technical proficiency of the players and, in some instances, a good 30 minutes of solid technical work might be required to get the players ready for the tactical session. Mature professionals will require less time for technical preparation than young novices, but all players will need brushing up on technique on a regular basis. Many coaches overlook this point and wind up frustrated when the session is spoiled by frequent technical breakdowns.

The Game Analysis

The second factor, match analysis, is another key indicator of what needs to be covered in training. Weaknesses detected in the previous game provide ample clues as to what needs fixing before the next game. The 'team development' cycle of observing the team play - analyzing the game - designing practices to work on deficiencies - and observing the next game to evaluate the effectiveness of the training is the cornerstone of coaching methodology. At the higher levels, scouting reports of opponents are used extensively to draw the weekly training plan, with activities designed to prepare the team to deal specifically with that opponent.

Extracting information from games is such an important observation skill in tactical preparation. This is where the coach's ability to 'read the game' is crucial. Good coaches can observe a match and figure out the problem areas. Experience is needed to pin down the real cause for breakdowns because the answer might not always be found near the ball, or not necessarily at the exact moment of the breakdown. To illustrate this point, observations of a recently played local game are used. In the game, a team playing 4-4-2 was having problems getting out of its own half after winning possession. Every time the wide defender passed the ball forward, usually towards one of the two strikers, the striker would lose the ball under pressure from his marker. This scenario, which kept repeating itself, is shown in diagram 301.

Certainly, the forwards' inability to control long passes with their back to goal was a contributing factor to the frequent turnovers. Designing a practice to work on the forward's receiving technique would probably be a good idea. But, from a tactical point of view, the problem originated before the pass was even made. Whenever the ball was won in midfield by the team in question, the back line was slow to react and did not drop back quickly to adopt a shape for possession. Because they did not drop and offer the midfielders an easy and safe passing outlet, the defenders were under immediate pressure from opposing forwards whenever receiving the ball from the midfield. This resulted in rushed attempts to play the ball forward away from the dangerous and crowded areas. And since no one at the back had time on the ball and passes were rushed, the midfielders and forwards had no time to transition into a good open shape for possession. The wide midfielders had no time to give the team width and offer good angled support, which forced the strikers to sprint towards the sidelines to show for the ball and provide an outlet. When forwards are sprinting to receive long passes and are running into the sidelines under pressure, turnovers are the likely outcome.

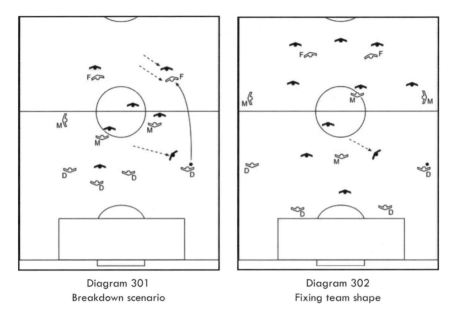

Diagram 301
Breakdown scenario

Diagram 302
Fixing team shape

An experienced coach would identify the key problem as a combination of technical deficiencies on the part of the forwards, and a tactical failure to transition quickly and effectively from a defensive shape to an attacking shape. In this example, there isn't much anyone can do to improve the technical deficiencies for that game, but the tactical aspects can be addressed at half-time by showing the defenders how to back-pedal and adopt a good shape for possession in the back. This will allow the team to keep the ball in the back, catch their breath, and give enough time to the rest of the players to spread out and prepare for the build up. If the half-time talk fixes the tactical problem, team shape should look more like that shown in Diagram 302, where it is quite obvious that the wide back has much more time on the ball and the wide players can receive the ball facing the field rather than facing the sidelines. If the half-time talk does not correct the problem, a tactical practice session that recreates the moment of transition from defense to attack in one's half would be desperately needed.

The Ability of the Players

The third factor in practice planning is based on the coach's ability to match the complexity of the session with the level of the players. Sounds simple enough, but it takes an experienced eye and keen observations to ensure that the activities are challenging and appropriate. Too easy and players get bored. Too difficult and the players get restless or lose interest. Skillful manipulation of grid size and the number of players is necessary to make the activity technically and tactically challenging, but not to the extent that success is unachievable. The safest approach is to start by erring on the easy side, allowing the players to achieve success, and quickly progressing to more game like and challenging situations. One of the most rewarding aspects of coaching is when a coach can successfully influence players' performances in an activity through actual 'coaching'. Anyone can achieve success by making the activity easy. The true coach can stretch his players' abilities, create real game problems for them to solve and, through interaction and feedback, help the players solve and succeed.

TACTICAL COACHING FEEDBACK

Observational skills and **feedback** are the 'bread and butter' tools used by coaches to interact with players and improve performance. It is commonly accepted that the main opportunities to provide meaningful feedback to the players and influence their performance come during practices, at the pre-game and halftime talks and, to a lesser extent, while the game is in progress. Although player performance can improve even without any coaching, simply from the sheer volume of practicing and playing, quality coaching can guide players and teams to higher levels more quickly. The objective for the coach is twofold: To speed up the rate of improvement and impose his ideas on the players. Effective coaches are able to convey concepts to their players and create a team in their own vision. If the feedback is technically sound and the instructions are clear, concise, specific and positive, the players are more likely to respond. Ineffective coaches have little impact on performance. Typical symptoms of ineffective coaching include inconsistent performances, a lack of team cohesion, and an over-reliance on individual plays to get results. Let us now examine how coaches can provide effective tactical feedback.

PROVIDING FEEDBACK IN PRACTICE SESSIONS

In the practice environment, once a coach explains and/or demonstrates the activity to his players, he steps back and allows them to start. The first thing the coach should observe is whether the players understand the objective of the activity. For example, if the players look confused or are taking up the wrong starting positions or are passing in the wrong sequence, it might be necessary to stop and explain more clearly the organization of the activity. The next pur-pose of observation is making sure the activity replicates the situation the coach had in mind when planning the practice. Once the coach is satisfied that the activity is simulating the desired scenarios, he can proceed to provide coaching feedback.

The sequence of the feedback is crucial. The recommended sequence for mak-ing tactical corrections is as follows:

1.   First correct the **shape,**
2.   Then, correct the **movement off the ball,**
3.   And finally, correct the **decisions on the ball**.

There is no point in correcting a wrong passing decision if the team shape was poor in the first place. If the shape is not right, the decisions on the ball are moot. Coaches need to observe the positions of all the players without the ball and, if necessary, fix this aspect first. Once the shape is right, the player on the ball will have better support and a variety of passing options.

Next, the coach should focus on the behavior of the players without the ball. Just adopting a good shape is not enough. The coach should observe how players ask for the ball. Are the players making themselves available for a pass? Which players should be making runs to receive the ball? Do the runs complement each other, or are they getting in each other's way? Verbal communication and/or a sudden checking run are some of the more common cues players use to ask for the ball. If play is too static or the players don't give good early signals to the ball carrier, play can easily break down. Coaching feedback might be needed here.

Once the desired shape and movement off the ball are achieved, it is time to observe and correct the decisions on the ball. Are the players making the right choices from among passing, dribbling, shooting or crossing? Are they making the correct passing choices? Do they see all their options? Are the possession-versus-penetration decisions in sync with the risk versus safety considerations?

It really doesn't matter which topic is being addressed in the session. Virtually all tactical topics, be it Defending, Possession, Penetration, Counterattacking, Switching the point of attack, or any other topic, would require a specific team shape and player movement before a correct decision on the ball can be made.

Good coaches don't just tell players what to do. They also explain to the players why. The ultimate objective is to render the players less dependent on the coach, to create problem solvers, not robots. Soliciting feedback from the players is always useful. Allowing players to find solutions and express opinions is a vital part in the process of nurturing intelligence and independence. If the volume of coaching feedback at the end of the season needs to be as much as it was at the beginning of the season, the coach has not succeeded in developing a team.

PROVIDING FEEDBACK IN GAMES

Coaches should always have objectives in mind to accomplish at every game. Just as a practice is seen as a learning opportunity with specific goals aimed at improving performance, games should be approached with the same philosophy. The main difference, of course, is that a winning result is always one of the objectives when a game is involved. Some games you win, and some games you lose, but every game should be regarded by the coach as another tactical fine-tuning step in the ongoing process of team building. Otherwise, the game is a wasted opportunity.

The tactical objectives of the game should relate to the content of the practice sessions preceding it. For instance, if the team focused during the week on flank play, then this attacking aspect should receive special attention and figure prominently in the pre-game and halftime talks. Good coaches can reconcile the need to win the next game with the long-term tactical team building goals. Game by game, the building blocks of the team's core strategy and system of play are laid, with pre-determined calendar milestones for reaching peak performance.

The pre-game talk should be short and specific, and should focus on the two or three key objectives. All the tactical information should be given AFTER the starting line up is announced. Players will listen more intently if they are receiving information pertaining specifically to their position. If the tactical instructions are explained before players know which positions they will occupy, the information will lose its effectiveness. Ideally, the players should be told the line up, then the tactical game plan, and then sent out to warm up. A quick, upbeat, no-more-than-ten-second long reminder of the key objectives could be delivered just before kick-off.

As stated many times before, shape is everything, and more often than not, breakdowns in games are caused by poor team shape. Coaches should be constantly monitoring the team shape and how their team transitions from attacking to defending shape and vice versa. To effectively assess team shape, coaches should develop the habit of surveying the field and not keep their eyes fixed only on the ball.

Team shape can be corrected while the game is in progress, using short 'buzz' words directed at specific players. Buzz words, such as "stretch!", "drop!", "tuck in!", can convey meaningful instructions to players, provided these words were used by the coach in practice and the players can therefore relate them to concepts previously taught. Otherwise, these words are merely 'coaching jargon' that don't mean anything specific to the players.

Top coaches earn their money at the halftime talk. At the top level, halftime is the last chance to regroup and get a result from the game. At the developmental levels, it is a chance to provide guidance towards solving the problems encountered in the first half. Halftime talks make or break coaches. The key is to zero in on the two or three most important points and give specific instructions that players have control over and can execute. Vague clichés, such as "we need to defend better!" or outcome-oriented demands, such as "we need to score two goals!" are ineffective. The first one is too abstract and doesn't tell the players HOW they could defend better, and the second one focuses too much on the outcome instead of the process and puts added pressure on the players. The halftime talk should be positive, focusing on what needs to be done in the second half to solve the problems, and NOT recount what was done wrong in the first half. Once again, any substitutions should be announced before the tactical information is given, so that players can benefit from feedback specific to their position.

To summarize, a methodical approach to ingraining a team's tactical identity is highly recommended. This is especially important with newly created teams or squads with a large influx of new players. Both the practice sessions and the games should be used in the tactical team building process. A reactive, off-the-cuff approach to providing feedback in games might be enough to win the game itself, but will it help the team reach peak performance down the road? If no thought is given to specific objectives for each game, especially those against weaker opponents, many of the games will end up as wasted opportunities to get more than just the win points. The next chapter provides suggestions on how to use a methodical approach to coaching tactics.

THE 'SITUATIONAL' APPROACH TO COACHING TACTICS

With twenty two players on a large field and a round ball that can be made to land anywhere, inexperienced players can get bewildered by the seemingly endless permutations. The ever-increasing speed of play of modern soccer bombards a constant flurry of stimuli at players that are difficult for some to absorb and process. Coaches themselves can't seem to reach a definite conclusion as to the level of complexity of soccer. On the one hand, they claim that soccer is really a "simple game", but on the other hand, one of their favorite expressions is that "No two situations are alike in soccer".

In reality, the game can get quite complicated. It's multidimensional in spatial terms and complex in terms of all the possible solutions for each situation. It's also getting faster and more athletic, with less time to dwell on the ball. For this reason, soccer is an ideal sport for the 'whole-part-whole' teaching approach. When the 'whole' is too complex, you take it apart and work on each part separately until it is performed properly. **The 'whole-part-whole' method of coaching is to simplify the game for the players, to cut it down to smaller pieces that can each be more easily chewed, and then bring it all together again.**

Coaches provide constant feedback to players. The traditional way to provide feedback is to use **'coachable moments'** at practices and games. A 'coachable moment' in coaching parlance refers to a moment when a skill executed or a decision made by a player triggers coaching feedback or correction. When a coach tells his player that he "should have passed to X instead of Y" or that he "should have turned to his right with his first touch" or that he "needs to tuck inside more", he is giving his player a coaching tip aimed at influencing the players' performance, hopefully in a positive way. But coaches need to give careful thought on the impact and effectiveness of their corrections.

It is obviously impossible to correct every mistake made by every player. It would take too long and undoubtedly irritate the players. Given the time constraints and the need to keep players motivated and active, coaches should develop a methodical approach for providing feedback. **Judicious feedback, targeting situations that repeat themselves often in a game would be more effective in the long run.** For example, advising a player that he "should have turned one way instead of another" might have been a technically correct observation for that moment. But, given that no two situations in soccer are exactly alike, would this piece of advice ever be useful to the player in the future? How often would this exact situation occur in the rest of the game, in the rest of the season?

Once a coach decides on a system of play, he needs to plan how he would teach the players to solve soccer problems within the system. A logical sequence of teaching is required, one that would give the players the basic framework and help them deal with the most commonly occurring situations. Giving feedback to players in a random fashion, without any clear planning or method is not effective, even if the information given is tactically correct. A sporadic approach to coaching, where the coach reacts to the players' actions, as opposed to a proactive, methodical approach, could result in valuable time wasted on marginal points. Without a clear plan, the following tends to happen: Coach stops play in a scrimmage to make a correction on a minor point. A minute later, a mistake of major relevance occurs, but the coach leaves it uncorrected because he doesn't want to stop too often and irritate the players. The end result is a wasted practice that fails to address the most important areas. It's akin to fixing the window trimming before taking care of the foundation. **This can be avoided by prioritizing**. If the coach could identify a few situations that keep repeating themselves in key areas of the field, he could devote a pre-determined amount of time on each situation and prepare his team to react to it. This methodical approach would accelerate the transfer of learning to the game.

Selecting Key Situations to Serve as 'Coachable Moments'

Match analysis of games suggest that there are a few 'situations' or 'scenarios' that recur time and again in the course of the game that are ideally suited to serve as 'coachable moments'. For example, a typical situation that repeats itself is the 'wide back with the ball in the defending third' scenario. This is especially true in formations with a back line of four, where the wide backs are used as a springboard to attack, almost like a quarterback in American football. Because of the frequency of this situation and its importance to the flow and success of the attacks, it merits a special attention by the coach.

If the players learn what is expected of them when the wide back has the ball, it will help the team immensely since it happens so often. There is a definite, optimal team shape associated with the moment when the wide defender has the ball that would allow a good balance between possession and penetration options. If the team has a clear picture of this optimum shape and each player understands where he fits in the overall scheme, then every time the wide back gets the ball, everyone on the team will be on the same wavelength and immediately move to attain this shape. This would put the wide back in a great position to choose the best passing option, based on the opponents' reaction.

What are some of the other situations that coaches could focus on? The specific situations that are ideal as coachable moments by virtue of their recurrence and potential impact on the game depend to some degree on the system of play. Using the 4-4-2 formation as an example, the following tactical situations could form the basis for the attacking related coachable moments:

1. Ball with the wide back in the defending third (Diagram 303)
2. Ball with the wide midfield in the middle third (Diagram 304)
3. Ball with a central midfield, under pressure and facing own goal (Diagram 305)
4. Ball won/received by a central midfield, facing up field (Diagram 306)
5. Player with the ball in the attacking third flank (Diagram 307)
6. Goalkeeper catches a cross (Diagram 308)

A separate list of tactical scenarios could be selected as coachable moments for teaching the defensive strategy. Situations 1 and 2 above are meant to focus on the instances when the wide players receive a pass and have the time and space to control the ball and play it forward. Situation 3 replicates a moment of possession in a crowded midfield by a player with no time to look up who is prevented from turning and playing it forward. Situation 4 creates the moment a midfielder has possession, resulting from either a pass or a turn over, and is facing up. This is a classic 'transition from defense to attack' moment, a very key moment that teams should learn to exploit. Situation 5 describes the moment a player, having succeeded in penetrating into the attacking third and with the ball at his feet, is in a position to cross the ball. Situation 6 zeros in on the moment the keeper successfully gathers a cross. This is another potential 'transition' situation that can be exploited by a direct and swiftly executed counterattack.

It is worth noting that the six scenarios between them cover quite a large portion of the game. If the coach could successfully teach the tactically correct response for these six situations, the team's performance is bound to reach a high tactical level. This approach, which in essence is a 'whole-part-whole' method, can be described as a 'situational' approach to coaching tactics. By methodically concentrating on a few key situations in practice sessions, the team's tactical framework is constructed like a jigsaw puzzle, with all the biggest pieces inserted first, one at a time, leaving only small gaps to be filled in later on.

In order to help coaches understand how to use the situational approach, we will first examine each of the six situations described above, and demonstrate an example of a good team shape for each one. Later on, we will explain the process for using these situations as coachable moments to elicit and ingrain the appropriate response from the players.

Diagrams 303 through 308 recreate the six situations and show a team shape that would be desirable for that moment. In diagram 303, the left defender has the ball in the defending third. The diagram shows a good team shape that has the central defenders supporting the ball from behind, the outside midfielders providing width, and the forwards stretching the field. If, every time the ball finds its way to the wide back, the rest of the players have the presence of mind to quickly adopt a shape similar to that shown, the defender will have plenty of good passing options. The best passing choice will be dictated by the movement of the players off the shape, and by the opponents' reaction.

Once the players routinely attain the desired shape, the coach could observe and suggest which players should look to make runs. Possible runs are shown by the dotted lines and include one forward checking towards the ball, one forward attacking the space behind the defense, and the outside midfielders running through. Ultimately the players would have to read the situation in the real game to decide on the most suitable runs and the defender would have to choose the correct pass.

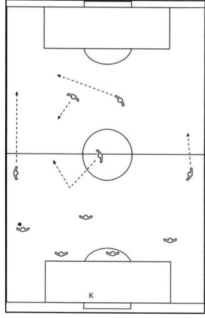

Diagram 303
Wide back with the ball

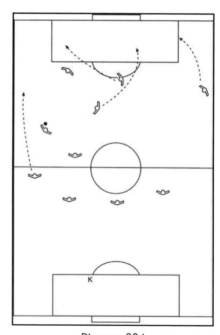

Diagram 304
Wide midfielder with the ball

Diagram 304 depicts the wide left midfielder with the ball and the associated desired shape. Notice how the defensive midfielder's supporting position close to the ball and slightly behind allows him to receive the ball and switch it to the right if needed. Notice also that, even with one defender overlapping, the defensive midfielder and the three defenders form a solid four-man block to cover against a counterattack. This gives the team a very balanced shape. Additionally, the keeper would be positioned on the edge of the penalty area in this scenario, acting as a sweeper-keeper.

Since the ball is in the middle third, the movement off the ball should aim to penetrate into the attacking third. Some of the best options are shown, including the overlapping defender, the forward's blind side diagonal run, the attacking midfielder's run into the space created by the forward, and the wide right midfielder's run. Of course, the option to dribble and take players on or use combination plays such as wall passes, should always be considered by the player on the ball.

The penetrating run by the right midfielder through the 'back door' is potentially very dangerous but alas is under-utilized and not exploited enough by many teams. Teams that have wide players who can whip accurate long diagonal or bent passes should take more advantages of the 'back door' run by the opposite-side midfielder. The element of surprise of this back door run presents a very powerful attacking tool.

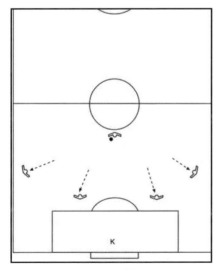

Diagram 305
Central mid facing own goal

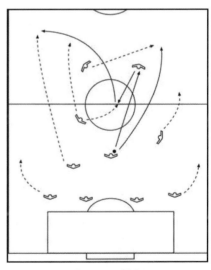

Diagram 306
Central mid facing up field

Diagram 305 deals with the scenario when a midfielder either receives a pass or wins the ball in the center and is under pressure. Every time this happens, the defenders should automatically back-pedal and communicate to the midfielder to pass the ball back rather than turn into pressure and risk losing it. This would provide the team a momentary relief from pressure and allow time for the mid-fielders and forwards to regain an attacking shape while the defenders keep the ball in the back. This is also a good tactical choice for a team who, having finally won the ball after intense and prolonged pressure, needs to 'take the sting out of the opponents' by keeping the ball for a little while and catching their breath.

Diagram 306 looks at the situation where a midfielder has won the ball, is fac-ing up field and has the space to play it forward. This 'transition' moment should be all about quick and decisive penetration. The coach must emphasize positive runs into space that get opponents 'turned'. Every time a player is 'faced up' with the ball in midfield, he should look to play it forward. Players in advanced positions should be making runs behind defenders while players behind the ball or in line with the ball should be making outward runs to create team width. Notice in diagram 306 that one of the forwards stays to provide a stationary support. If all the players ran away from the ball, the player on the ball could become isolated. There always needs to be a balance between checking to the ball and running away from the ball.

Diagram 307 shows the moment a player is wide, in a position to cross the ball. The team shape for this scenario should accomplish four aims: 1) To get players into the box to meet the cross; 2) To provide a safe support behind the ball in case there is too much pressure on the ball to cross; 3) To have enough players outside the box positioned to pounce on clearances; and 4) Maintain a covering block against a counterattack. The shape shown in diagram 307 clearly accom-plishes all these objectives. There is a tendency for inexperienced players to all sprint into the box at the same time and not leave a couple of players outside the penalty area to take care of clearances. This potentially leaves a gaping hole between the attack and the defense that often allows opponents to chase their own clearance and counterattack.

And finally, diagram 308 depicts the scenario where the keeper has just caught a cross. Here again, the transition to attack should be the paramount thought, with most of the runs aimed at penetration. As a general rule, the keepers' first glance should be cast long to see if the quick long throw or punt is the best choice. If that's not on, the next best option is usually wide to the flank, oppo-site to the origin of the cross.

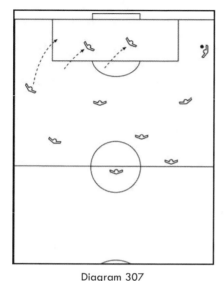

Diagram 307
Player wide, crossing the ball

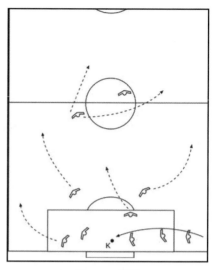

Diagram 308
Goalkeeper catching a cross

Using the Key Situations as Coachable Moments

There are a number of ways coaches can teach the ideal shape for a specific situation. One of the most effective ways and most commonly used is the 'freeze' method stoppage. Since we are talking about large group tactical situations, the freeze method would need to be applied in an 11-a-side scrimmage. Let's use the situation from diagram 303 (wide back with the ball) as an example. In this method, the coach waits for the moment when one of the wide backs gets the ball, shouts "freeze!" to get all the players to stop and stand still, and then proceeds to show each player the best position in relation to the wide back and the opponents. The coach can then step back, restart the scrimmage and observe to see whether the players heed the cues and adopt the right shape every time a wide back gets the ball. If necessary, the coach will freeze play a number of times in the scrimmage when the wide backs have the ball to reiterate the concept.

As long as the coach doesn't stop the session too often and each stoppage lasts no more than 30-60 seconds, the players will respond to the freeze method and learning will take place. In every stoppage, the desired positions of the players will vary slightly due to the fluid shifting movements of both teams. But the overall team shape should always manifest the fundamental attacking principles of depth, width, support in front of the ball, and support behind the ball.

This process of observing and stopping would be ongoing until the players instinctively move into the right positions and the optimum shape for this situation becomes ingrained. As mentioned earlier, teaching the correct shape is the first step in the feedback sequence. This would be followed by observations and corrections of the movement off the ball and the appropriate decision on the ball. Depending on the maturity level of the players, ingraining an optimum shape for a specific situation could take as little as one session, or take a whole season.

Another method for ingraining team shape for a tactical situation, where there is no need to have 22 players available, is the 'shadow play' or 'functional practice' method, which is explained in more detail later on in the book.

To summarize, soccer is a very fluid game, requiring constant surveying and reappraisal by players. The speed of play in the modern game does not allow players to dwell on the ball and forces quick decisions. Match analysis tells us that the ball changes possession a few hundred times per game and that no two situations are exactly alike. In order to simplify the game for the players, especially young players, and train them to solve soccer problems, coaches can use frequently recurring scenarios as coachable moments and teach players the correct tactical response to these scenarios.

This methodical approach, which we call a situational approach to coaching tactics, can start at the pre-season stage. Once the coach decides on the playing system, he can select the key situations that merit this approach and use scrimmages to address the optimum shape, movement off the ball, and decisions on the ball. This approach will prevent coaches from getting bogged down making corrections of limited benefit. It will accelerate the team building process and facilitate reaching a tactical cohesiveness in a shorter time than in a random approach.

FUNCTIONAL VS GENERIC TRAINING

Given that **technical training** is geared towards improving the players' control of the ball, the purpose of **tactical training** is to teach the players to make decisions. Tactical training sessions can take the form of either **generic** training or **functional** training. A generic approach to tactical training involves activities that are not position-specific. For example, playing six versus six in a grid without goals where the objective for each team is to string 10 consecutive passes to score a point, is an example of a generic activity aimed at working on possession. In this example, the players are making tactical decisions, off the ball and on the ball, which are based on the demands of the activity, with an emphasis on NOT giving the ball away. Such activities are good for teaching the basic principles of play discussed in the beginning of the book, but without any relation to formations or positions. On the other hand, functional training teaches the players to play specific positions. Functional tactical training replicates the tactical demands of the game that are specific to each player's position. It means that each player practices in the area of the field that he would normally occupy in the real game and is required to make decisions in situations similar to those imposed on him in the game.

Experts in coaching methodology point out that effective training cycles need to include both general and specific (functional) training and that, ideally, general training should precede specific training. The general training lays the foundation of performance whereas the specific functional training maximizes the transfer of learning to the game. Both general and functional training are vital for the team's success. One without the other does not develop the full performance potential, individually or collectively.

Many coaches do not spend enough time, or any time, on functional training, either because they do not understand the benefits or they are not sure how to do it properly. General training alone, without a progression into specific 'functional' practices, would not prepare players sufficiently. Without functional training, most players would experience difficulties applying the general principles to the game. The implication for tactical training is that the pre-season should start with an emphasis on generic tactical activities that sharpen up the players' decision making around the ball, followed by a gradual progression towards functional training as the season approaches.

Once the season starts, the tactical planning should be aimed at striking a balance between generic activities and functional training. The generic training would continue to dwell on general topics such as possession, penetration, support, pressure, cover, balance, using fun games and a variety of activities. The functional training would zero in on position-specific roles, specific patterns, and on organized, rehearsed collective movement designed to maximize team efficiency. It would make sense to start the weekly cycle with generic type training and switch to functional training at the end of the week just before the next game. The functional training could focus on the strategy and patterns deemed by the coach as the most likely to succeed against the next opponents, or it could serve to work on a specific weakness detected by the coach in previous games. A few examples of generic and functional tactical training are provided below, in order to illustrate the differences. Those will be followed by examples of 'shadow training', which is a form of functional training.

GENERIC TACTICAL ACTIVITIES

Generic Activity: Penetration

Diagram 309 shows a set up for an activity designed to stress penetration. Team X versus Team O, where each team must first pass the ball to one of the two target players standing on the end lines before they can score. The keepers are not allowed to pass to the target players. Penetration is emphasized by making the grid narrow and long and by using the target players as a condition for scoring.

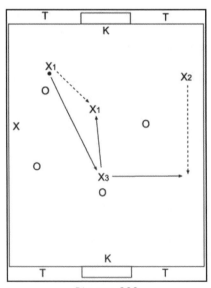
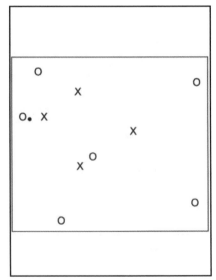

| Diagram 309 | Diagram 310 |

The coaching points are:

■ The team in possession should try to work the ball to a player who is 'faced up', meaning facing the opponents' goal and who has enough time to play it forward. Diagram 309 contains two examples of a passing sequence that accomplish this. In one sequence, X1 passes to X3 and follows the pass to receive a return ball. In another sequence, X3 gets the ball from X1 and lays it for X2.

■ Every opportunity to play the ball forward to a target player should be taken. In other words, don't play square if you can play it forward.

■ Immediate sprint to support the forward pass.

Generic Activity: Possession

Diagram 310 is an example of an activity that focuses on possession. In a 30-40 yard grid, 6 versus 4 play possession. The O players have a two touch maximum limit each, while the four X's are allowed unlimited touches. The coaching emphasis is different for each team. The O's are coached to use the whole area and to quickly move the ball around with one and two touch passing, while the X's learn to shield and dribble out of trouble and keep possession in tight areas with numbers down. Diagram 310 shows a good possession shape exhibited by team O, with good support angles and intelligent use of the whole grid. If the O players lose their shape by moving towards the ball and get bunched up, the 'freeze play' method can be used to step in and show the players the proper shape. Games like this teach the players to 'read the pressure', knowing when to put their foot on the ball and hold it, and when to get rid of it first time.

Possession games with uneven teams are extremely useful tools that are under-utilized by many coaches. Teams encounter many uneven number situations in the course of a game, such as numbers up in their defensive third or numbers down in the attacking third, but the players are not always prepared to deal with these situations. Activities such as this should be a regular staple of tactical training.

Generic Activity: Pressure on Transition

Diagrams 311 and 312 contain the organization of a game designed to develop the instinct to close the ball and apply immediate pressure upon loss of possession.

The organization in diagram 311 is as follows: Two teams of four players. Each player has a ball. Play starts with a 1v1 inside the grid, where the objective is to score on the goal on the opposite end line. All the other players are behind the end lines as shown and are not allowed to interfere or join in until the ball crosses an end line. Every time the ball goes across an end line or out of bounds, a new player from the defending end line immediately dribbles into the grid and tries to score on the opposite goal. Diagram 312 depicts the moment of transition. In the diagram, if X1 beats O1 and shoots the ball across line AB, even if he misses, O2, O3, or O4 immediately go to goal (on line CD) while X1 must now defend and O1 returns to his ball behind line AB. If, on the other hand, O1 steals the ball from X1 and shoots on goal, O1 remains in the grid to defend and either X2, X3, or X4 become the new attacker. It is important for the new attacker to immediately go for goal as soon as the ball goes out of bounds. No need to wait for a coach's signal as it will defeat the purpose of this game.

Variations:

- Add a keeper. All other rules are the same as before but if the keeper catches the ball he must roll it to a new attacker stepping into the grid.
- Play the same rules, but make it a 2v2 game. Every time the ball crosses an end line, 2 new attackers step in.

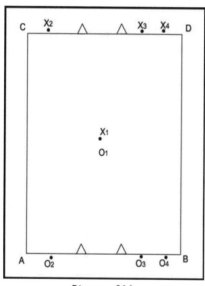

Diagram 311

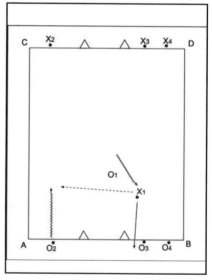

Diagram 312

Generic Activity: Pressing in Defense

Diagram 313 depicts the organization of this activity, which focuses on applying immediate pressure to stop the forward pass.

This is a 3 teams activity, in which two teams play each other while the third team rests. The diagram shows 4 X's versus 4 O's in a grid approximately 25 yards wide by 35-40 yards long, with a target area 2 yards by 5 yards

marked at each end and occupied by 2 Y players. Each team defends one target area and attacks the opposite one. In the diagram, the O team tries to get
the ball to the Y1 players and the X team tries to pass the ball to the Y2 players. If team X succeeds in passing the ball to one of the Y2's, they get a point
and the Y2 who caught the ball immediately serves it to the O team who tries
to play it to the Y1's. Obviously, if the O team steals the ball from X, they can
score by getting it to Y1. There are no throw-ins and everything starts with a
serve from a Y player. For example, if the ball goes out of bounds and an O
player last touched it, a new ball is served by Y1 to the X team. The Y players
must stay inside the target areas and catch any passes successfully played into
the area.

This is a fast paced game that teaches players to put immediate pressure upon
loss of possession or upon scoring, in order to prevent a forward pass to the Y's.
The coaching points will emphasize the speed of closing the ball down on transition from attack to defense, applying pressure frontally in order to prevent a
penetration pass to the target area, forcing back passes or square passes and
pressing all over the grid to win the ball. After 5-10 minutes, the Y team
replaces the losing team. In order to maintain a fast tempo, plenty of balls
should be placed behind each target area so that if a ball is kicked out of
bounds, a Y player can serve a new ball immediately. This game could be
played with 4 teams, with 2 teams playing and 2 teams resting inside the target area. It could be played 3v3, 4v4, or 5v5.

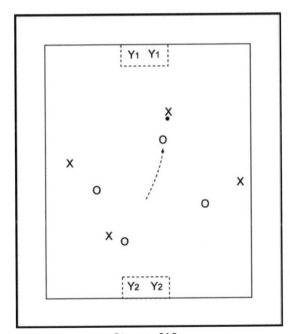

Diagram 313

Generic Activity: Cover in Defense

The previous activity dealt with immediate pressure. This activity takes it a step further and focuses on providing cover for the pressuring player. Diagram 314 shows the organization of an activity that teaches players to cover for each other when defending in small groups.

In diagram 314, the O's defend against the X's in 3v3 play that always goes in one direction. The grid size is 30-40 yards wide by 20-30 yards deep. The O team starts play by passing the ball to one of the X's and coming out to challenge the X team who tries to bring the ball across line AB under control. If the ball goes out of bounds or if the O team wins the ball, the game restarts with the next group of O players passing to the next group of X players. Note that instead of having players alternate between attacking and defending, this set up keeps the O players repeating the defending roles. This is done to provide the O players with continuous repetitions in defending, to maximize learning. However, in order to keep the O team motivated to defend with intensity, the coach can give them a goal, such as win the ball ten times and they switch roles and become attackers.

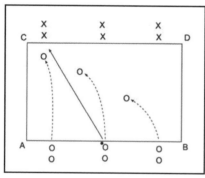 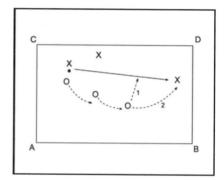

Diagram 314   Diagram 315

Since the topic of this activity is cover, the coaching points will focus on the covering players in terms of positioning, angle of cover, and communication to the pressuring defender. In diagram 314, the left sided O applies immediate pressure on the ball, the central O adopts a covering position behind the pressuring defender, and the right sided O slides inside and slightly behind the central O. The stance of the 3 defenders provides solid cover, discourages a pass behind them and invites a square pass across the grid.

Diagram 315 shows what happens when a square pass is made. The right-sided O must decide instantly whether he can intercept the pass (run 1) as this would be the best result. If he cannot intercept, he then pressures the ball (run 2) and waits for his teammates to slide behind him to provide cover. This activity is ideal for midfielders to work on pressuring and covering for each other in the midfield area.

Generic Activity: Setting a Defensive Trap

The previous two activities were typical examples of games that teach players how to apply immediate pressure and how to cover for each other. Modern defending strategies often demand from groups of players to channel the ball into a pre-determined zone of the field, flood the zone to create 'numbers up', and win the ball. The following examples are small group generic activities aimed at improving the players' ability to channel, slide and win the ball. The concepts learned in these small group activities can then be transferred to the 11-a-side game using functional tactical activities or scrimmages.

Activity #1: 2v2 with one goal

Play takes place in a grid 30 yards wide by 15-20 yards long, with one goal 3-4 yards wide at one corner (corner D in diagram 316). Two defenders play against one attacker who tries to score through the corner goal. The attacker has a partner (X1 in diagram) who cannot enter the grid and can only support the attacker from line AB. Play starts with a defender O passing to X. Attacker X enters grid and tries to score while two O's come out to defend. Attacker X can shoot or pass to X1 and use him as support. X1 can either pass back to X or score himself from line AB. Play stops when the defenders win the ball or when the ball goes out of bounds. The O's and the X return to their respective lines. The O's can rotate as follows: The first O is usually the pressuring defender and the second O is the covering defender. The covering defender becomes the pressuring defender on the next turn, while the first defender goes to the back of the line.

The key coaching points are:
- The line of approach of the defenders should be bent in order to quickly get in between the ball and the goal and prevent an early shot into the goal.
- The first defender channels the ball towards line AC. As X gets closer to line AC, the first defender shifts his stance to prevent a pass to X1 and continues to channel the ball away from goal. The covering defender must be aware of the best positioning to block a shot on goal.
- The objective of the two defenders is to corner the attacker and win the ball or at least tackle it out of bounds. Diagram 317 shows a successful attempt to corner the attacker, get him isolated, and prevent a shot on goal or a pass to X1. This is the point when the first defender can attempt a tackle.
- Covering defender needs to communicate to the first defender when to tackle. The distance and angle of the covering defender should be consistent with the objective of channeling towards corner C yet staying close enough to pounce on a loose ball and prevent a shot on goal.
- The two defenders must choose the right moment to commit to winning the ball, the 'point of no return', bearing in mind that if the defenders let X off the hook and allow him to pass back to X1, the open goal could be exposed.

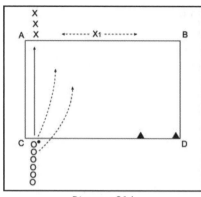

Diagram 316

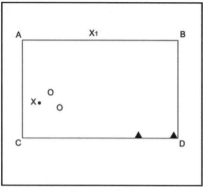

Diagram 317

Activity #2: 3v3 with one goal

A similar set up to activity 1 but this time there are three defenders versus three attackers in a grid 20 yards long by 30 yards wide and one goal in the corner. This time, the coach serves the ball to the three X's who try to score on the corner goal. As soon as the ball is served, the three O's come out to challenge. By serving the ball, the coach can vary the starting location of the ball.

Diagram 318 shows the set up and closing runs by the defenders who try to shepherd the ball towards line AC. It is recommended to keep the O's as defenders and put them through many repetitions to fully absorb and perfect the defensive principles before switching roles with the X's.

The key coaching points are:

■ Immediate pressure on the ball must be achieved as the X's inter-pass, in order to deny any goal attempts and to punish a poor first touch by winning the ball.

■ Communication among defenders is crucial. Defenders must exchange quick signals as to who is putting pressure on the ball and who is covering using short, single or double word calls. Otherwise, they are likely to duplicate runs and leave opponents open.

■ As before, the defenders' first task is to channel the ball towards line AC, away from the goal. The objective is to create a 2v1 situation in favor of the defense. This is the 'point of no return' cue for the two defenders to close the ball and cause a turnover while the third defender provides cover/balance and is blocking a possible shot on goal. Diagram 319 illustrates the 'point of no return' scenario.

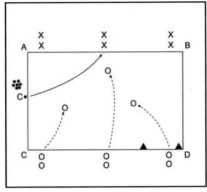

Diagram 318

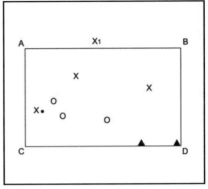

Diagram 319

Activity #3: 5v5 or 6v6 with two goals

Increase the size of the grid to accommodate 5v5 or 6v6 and play a regular game. The only special organization for this game is that the goals are offset to the corners. Each team tries to steer the ball into the 'dead end' corner, away from goal, isolate the ball carrier, and pounce on the ball to win it. Diagram 320 shows a successful isolation of the ball. Notice how X has nowhere to go and would require all his skills to get out of this trap.

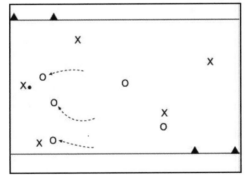

Diagram 320

Generic Activity: Switching the Point of Attack

Diagram 321 shows the organization of this activity. The game can be played 4v4 to 8v8 in a rectangular grid that is wide and short, emphasizing the concept of switching the ball from side to side. Each team attacks two goals and defends two goals, with all the goals in the corners, to emphasize switching play. The coaching points will focus on the presence of mind to switch to the other side if the nearest goal is too heavily defended. The team shape will need scrutiny and correction by the coach. If all the attacking players are too close to each other on one side, they will not be able to switch play. In diagram 321, the X players are too bunched up with a poor team shape that is not conducive to scoring on the left goal or switching to the right side. Diagram 322 shows a much better shape that enables the X's to quickly switch the ball and score. X2 is the key player here, providing safe support behind the ball and presenting an easy outlet for a switch.

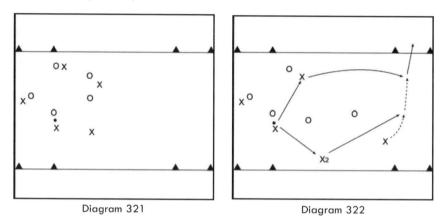

Diagram 321   Diagram 322

FUNCTIONAL TACTICAL ACTIVITIES

The sample activities from the preceding chapter were generic in nature and did not focus on any specific team formation or playing system. We now shift our attention to the functional training method, which is an approach geared to solving soccer problems specific to a position and a formation.

There are many ways to design functional activities. One obvious functional training opportunity would be an exhibition game or an inter-squad game. The best way to learn how to play a certain position is through playing it in real games. But the main disadvantage of a regular game is that the 11v11 environment generally does not afford enough repetitions for each player to experience. In order to accelerate learning, players need more repetitions than that provided by the game itself. This is part of the 'overload' principle of training. Practice sessions can be designed to focus on one or two players and create a sequence that repeatedly passes through them and provides them the scope for making decisions in game like situations. The following examples illustrate the functional training approach.

Functional Activity: Wide defender Playing Out of the Back

Diagram 323 illustrates an example of a functional tactical session that is designed to train the left defender to initiate attacks. D1 is the defender being trained in a session that always starts with a throw from the keeper, and with the objective for the team to bring the ball into the other half, under control.

Every time the team succeeds, or if the ball goes out of bounds, everyone returns to the starting position shown in diagram 323 and the keeper throws it again. If the black team wins the ball, they play it to the keeper and the sequence is repeated. In the beginning of the session, Forward 6 can be omitted so that D1 will have the time to make decisions without having to deal with immediate pressure. Later on, forward 6 can be added and positioned as shown and instructed to apply pressure on D1 once the keeper throws the ball.

Every time he has the ball, defender D1 has a few passing options that replicate the game. Diagram 324 shows all his passing options, including the wide midfielder, the forward's feet, the second forward's run, the attacking midfielder, or the defensive midfielder. He can also dribble the ball forward if time and space permit. Once 6 is added, D1's options are also to pass it back to the keeper or square to the central defender. After passing the ball, D1 can also be asked to decide when to step up into midfield or when to overlap into attack. Although the session is live until the ball is worked into the attacking half, the coach's attention and instruction will be centered on D1's decisions and executions. The key coaching points would focus on the quality of his first touch, the correct passing choice, the quality of delivery and his subsequent movement to support the attack.

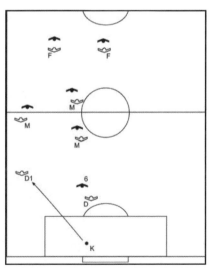

Diagram 323

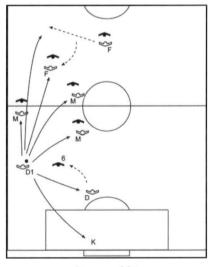

Diagram 324

A similar session can be created for each position. Careful planning of these sessions is required to make it realistic to the game and prepare the player to solve the same kind of problems that he would be required to solve in the game. This is the essence of functional tactical training.

Functional Activity: The Back 3 Playing Out of the Defense

This is an example of a session designed to train the 3 defenders in a 3-5-2 formation to build up attacks out of the back. Diagram 325 shows the starting point for the exercise. The team being trained is playing 11 versus 6. The six-player opposition includes two forwards, two midfielders and two defenders. The coach starts play by serving a long through ball behind the defense. Play ends when the ball is brought across the half way line under control, at which point everyone returns to the starting point for a new serve.

The starting position of the 11 players is shown in diagram 325, where every-one is concentrated in the middle to simulate a defensive shape. If the six opponents (black) win the ball, they can attack the goal and attempt to score. The coach's serves are most likely to be collected by the keeper or the sweeper and this will be the cue for the team to open up and adopt the shape shown in diagram 326.

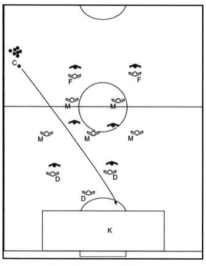

Diagram 325

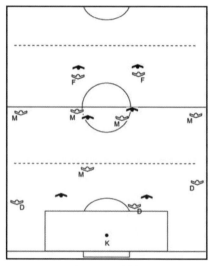

Diagram 326

In diagram 326, the two outside defenders push out wide and as high as possi-ble. The central defender/sweeper and the defensive midfielder stay central in staggered positions, one high and one low. The rest of the midfielders push up just below the half line, and the forwards stretch the field by stepping into the other half. This movement creates a 5v2 situation in the defending third, which will enable the keeper to play the ball to a defender and start the build up. The objective is to play the ball to a defender who has enough time and space to deliver a quality forward pass.

Diagrams 327 and 328 are just two examples of possible passing combinations. In both of these examples, the ball is worked into the middle third first, into a midfielder who is faced up. From there, the final pass into the other half can find the runs of the forwards or the attacking midfielders. The midfielders on the team of 11 must play two touch maximum since it is unrealistic to let players dribble at will when playing with an 11v6 advantage.

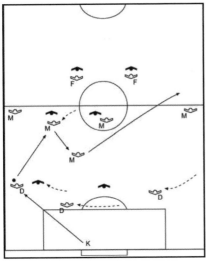 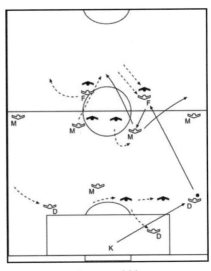

Diagram 327   Diagram 328

The coach can focus on the positioning of the defenders and show them how to get wide quickly and push as high as possible while still giving the keeper a safe passing angle. All three defenders should open their bodies to the field so that they can assess their options while the ball travels. The central defender and midfielder should adopt a sideways-on stance that allows them to see as much of the field as possible. If the keeper can send a quality serve to a defender and the defender can use his first touch to get into the middle third and lose the chasing forward, that would be the best option. If the forwards are spread wide, making it risky to pass to the wide defenders, the keeper can pass the ball to the sweeper or, even better, to the defensive midfielder.

Particular attention should be given to the quality of the first touch, with the aim of preparing for a forward pass. The quality and choice of the pass out of defense is crucial and the communication between the passer and the receiver needs to be clear and early. Composure on the ball needs to be stressed as well as speed of thought and speed of play. Awareness of options before the ball arrives is important. If a forward pass is not on, the defender on the ball should quickly use the other defenders or the keeper to switch to the other side and not get caught in possession.

Functional Activity: Switching Play Using The Back Four

In this activity, the coach works with the back lines on both the offensive and defensive aspects of switching the play. Two sets of back four are involved in this exercise, which takes place in the middle third. As the ball is passed across one back line, the line in possession learns to adopt a bowl shape for switching play while the opposite line learns to follow the ball by sliding across the field and staying compact. The ball is then played long to the opposite back line and the roles reverse.

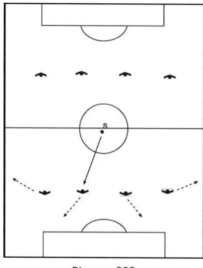

Diagram 329

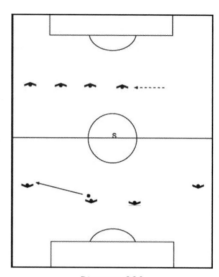

Diagram 330

Diagram 329 shows the starting position for this exercise. A server is in the center circle with a supply of balls and a back line of four defenders is positioned flat and squeezed close together, about 15 yards from the midfield line in each half. Play starts when the server passes to any one of the defenders. Diagram 329 shows what happens when the ball is played to a central defender. The line that receives the ball drops back and spreads into a bowl shape. Note that the server's pass needs to be soft to allow the defender receiving the pass to back-pedal as the ball is traveling towards him.

Diagram 330 continues the sequence, showing that, as the ball is played wide, the opposite back line slides across, staying compact and goal-side of the ball. Notice that three defenders on the line without the ball are flat, but slightly behind the wide right defender, in a covering position.

Diagram 331 shows how the roles are reversed when the ball is played to the opposite back line. The line receiving the ball is immediately spreading out into the bowl shape, and the line that just passed the ball pushes up quickly into a flat shape, and moves across towards the ball for compactness. Diagram 332 depicts the movement of the line without the ball as they follow the passes by sliding across to their right.

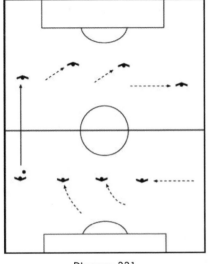

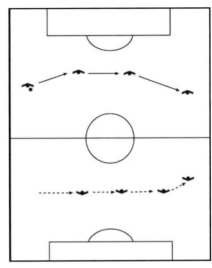

| Diagram 331 | Diagram 332 |

As the back lines play the ball across, the coach observes and instructs, as needed, the following key coaching points:

- The shape of the back lines, in terms of the angle and distance between the players. The quality of the passes should be crisp and accurate and played in front of the players' feet so they can always face up field.
- The rhythm of passing should be quick, with the first touch used to control and the second touch to pass to the next player.
- The passes can occasionally 'skip' one central defender as the ball is switched from one side to the other.
- The movement of the players as they transition back and forth, from attack to defense.

Once the eight players achieve a quick tempo of passing and movement with flawless execution, midfielders and forwards can be introduced to the activity. First, a midfielder is added to each back line as shown in diagram 333. The midfielders can be used in many ways. Diagram 333 shows a couple of sequences that involve the midfielders. One sequence has M1 linking the two central defenders. The other sequence shows an interchange, with M2 taking the place of a central defender who dribbles up into the midfield before sending the ball to the opposite line.

In Diagram 334, two forwards are added, one for each back line. The forwards move laterally, one pressures the ball and the other one checks for the ball, depending on which line has possession. The two midfielders don't try to defend and are mainly used to support the play. Diagram 334 shows how M2 is involved twice in the passing sequence, once in the back and then supporting the drop pass by the checking forward and playing it to the other back line. F1 and M1 would participate in a similar fashion when their back line has the ball.

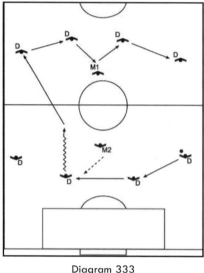

Diagram 333   Diagram 334

The key coaching points for the midfielders and forwards are:

■ The midfielders should slide to follow the ball and make themselves available without staying too close to the back line.

■ When a midfielder receives the ball from a defender, he should play it to another defender on the same line but keep the ball moving in the same direction. This keeps the switching rhythm going.

■ When the midfielder gets the ball from a forward, he should play it to some one in the opposite line to reverse roles.

■ The defenders on the line without the ball should be actively marking the forward as he checks for a pass (If the defenders are arranged in zonal defending, this activity gives them the added opportunity to work on communicating and handing the marking over to the adjacent defender as the forward moves across).

■ The forward can pass it back to the supporting midfielder or to any defender moving up to support.

■ The quality of the passes into midfield such that the pace and accuracy allows first time passing by the forwards and midfielders.

Functional Training:
Zonal Defending With 4-4-2 Formation

The following practice progression is an example of how to systematically develop a team's ability to defend zonally within the 4-4-2 formation, using the functional training approach. The first step is to get the back four working together as a unit. From there, the coach can start adding the other units, progressing until the whole team is integrated into the training. The activities that follow are not necessarily meant to represent a progression for a single practice session. The amount of time spent with each progression depends on the ability and maturity of the players. With some teams, certain concepts could require a mere 20 minutes to get across while other teams might need a couple of weeks, or even a whole season, to accomplish the same thing. It is up to the coach to decide how much time is needed to devote to each activity and how often to use it. In fact, a coach who works with a mature team can choose to skip the first activity and start with activity #2.

Activity #1: Teaching Central Defenders to Mark the Target Player

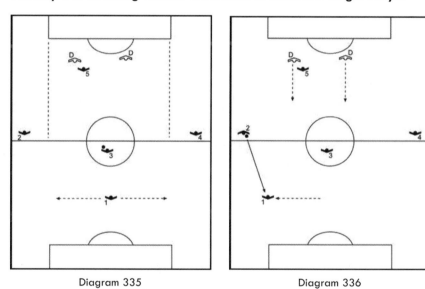

Diagram 335   Diagram 336

The objective of this activity is to fine tune the partnership of the two central defenders as they share the marking responsibility of a target player and learn where to hold the line, when to push up to squeeze space, and how to cover for each other. Organization of the activity is shown in diagram 335. The two central defenders are marking the target player 5. Four other players are positioned as follows: 2 and 4 are wide on the half way line, 3 is inside the center circle, and 1 is about 20 yards behind the half way line. 5 is instructed to push up as high as the defenders would allow him and to constantly move laterally, staying within the width of the penalty area as shown by the dotted lines. 3 can only move within the center circle. The wide attackers (2 and 4) must remain stationary and 1 can move from side to side, keeping a distance of about 20 yards behind the midfield line. A few balls are placed just below the center circle.

Diagram 335 shows the starting, or 'reloading' arrangement of the players: The ball always starts with 3, the defenders start by holding the line about 5 yards in front of their penalty area and the target player pushed high against them. 3 begins the sequence by passing the ball to any teammate, including the target player. The attackers pass the ball to each other and look to feed the target player. The target player plays with his back to goal and shows for the ball asking for a pass to feet. Initially, the target player cannot turn and go to goal but is restricted to just playing it back to any teammate. The two central defenders can only intercept the ball when it is played to the target player. The objective for the central defenders is to win the ball and play it to 1, or at least clear it away from their own half. If the ball gets cleared out of bounds, the two defenders resume the 'reloading' position as shown in diagram 335 and 3 starts another passing sequence.

To replicate game conditions, the attackers should pass the ball crisply and at game speed, using one or two touches. Also, the target player needs to push up against the defenders as he would in the game and the defenders need to stay goal-side of him until the pass is made to him. The coach might have to occasionally ask the players to 'reload' to the starting position if the players get all bunched up and flat. The attackers should play a variety of balls to the target player, including ground passes, lofted balls to the head, and hard driven low balls. Suggestion to coaches: Another forward could be used as 1 and he and 5 can switch when 5 gets tired. Also, 2 and 4 could be the team's alternate central defenders, so that they too can benefit from switching with the defenders.

Coaching points:
- Whenever an attacking player passes the ball back to 1, the central defenders should **push up immediately as a unit** and hold their line about 10 yards off the half way, as shown in diagram 336. The defenders need to move up while the ball is in transit but stop and hold a line or even drop a little when the ball arrives at 1's feet.
- Whenever the defenders win the ball and play it to 1, they should also push up immediately the same way. By always **taking up positions of no more than 40 yards from the ball**, the defenders maintain team compactness. One defender should be the leader who decides and commands when to push up and how far.

- The defenders need to **communicate** as they pass the target player on to each other. It is important not to leave him unmarked.
- The defenders should adopt a **marking angle and distance** that maximizes the chance of interception. This is demonstrated in diagram 337. Notice that defender 1 marks on the forward's right shoulder, within hand-touching distance, from where he can pounce on the ball. If he were positioned right behind the target player, he would not be able to attack the ball without fouling the player.
- Between them, the two defenders are **'sandwiching' the forward,** while still maintaining their flatness. In diagram 337, defender 1 is ready to intercept any ball played into the area in front of the target player while defender 2 is ready to pounce on any ball played into the space behind the forward. This approach allows defender 1 to mark tight and challenge aggressively in the knowledge that defender 2 will take care of the dangerous space behind.
- The moment the ball is played to the target player, the **free defender should drop back behind the marking defender,** into a covering position (diagram 338). If the target player plays the ball back, the free defender immediately steps up and resumes his position in line with his partner. Defenders must learn to read body language and cues, such as an opponent dropping his eyes to focus on the ball just before passing. This will help defenders anticipate opponent's next move, react early, and time their challenge. Although at this stage of the session the target player is not going to goal, dropping into a covering position is an important habit to ingrain.
- When the target player checks to the ball, his marker must **follow him tightly** and try to win the ball. The free defender stays and covers.

Diagram 337

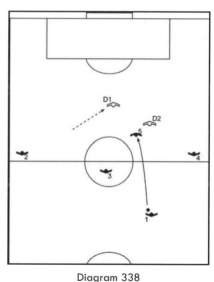

Diagram 338

Progression

Once the central defenders are comfortable marking, moving as a unit, and stepping up, the activity can progress where the target player can now turn and attack the goal. A keeper is added to the activity and 3 is now allowed to move up and support the target player from behind, without running ahead of him. Balls played into 5 can now be to feet or to space behind defenders. If the keeper catches the ball, he throws it to 3 and everyone 'reloads' and restarts. Similarly, if the ball goes out of bounds, 3 restarts. The activity needs an assistant coach to make the offside calls. Everything else is the same as before. All **coaching points** are still applicable, with a stronger emphasis on the free defender dropping to provide cover for the challenging defender and pick up balls played into space behind the marker.

Progression

Add a second forward. Now the two central defenders are marking two forwards. As before, play starts with 3. The forwards can combine to attack the goal or they can play the ball back to any teammate. 3 can move up to support play but cannot run past the forwards. The defenders try to win the ball and play it to 1 and the rest of the organization is the same. The **coaching points** are still the same, but now the emphasis is on learning to switch back and forth from marking to covering on the fly and making quicker decisions on when to drop and cover and when to let the forward run into offside. Diagram 339 and 340 illustrate the shifting roles of the two defenders. In diagram 339, the ball is played to the forward and the other defender drops to provide temporary cover. Diagram 340 continues the sequence, with the forward playing it back to the supporting midfielder and the covering defender quickly pushing up to mark his own opponent tight.

In this activity, the central defenders should maintain flatness for as long as possible and let the forwards run into offside. Obviously, tracking the forward or letting him run into offside will depend on whether the ball was released and will require split second decisions. Staying flat is also crucial here otherwise the second defender will keep the forward onside. If it does break down and a forward is chasing a through ball, the keeper will have to be alert and charge out to intercept the pass. A flat defense requires a quick, mobile keeper who can come off his line and play an effective sweeper-keeper role. The defenders' positioning and marking distance will also depend on their speed. If the forwards are faster, the defenders will have to drop and hold their line a couple of yards behind the forwards to avoid losing a foot race.

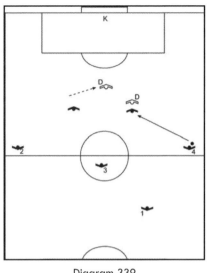

Diagram 339   Diagram 340

The activity explained above is just one of many ways to introduce zonal marking to the central defenders. The key consideration is to replicate the game situations in terms of the technical and tactical demands of the game, and practice within the area of the field where it would normally take place in the real
game.

Activity #2: Teaching the Back Four to work as a Unit

This activity focuses on developing cohesion in the back. The four defenders
learn to move up, down and sideways as a unit, and pass on the forwards to
each other. The starting and 'reloading' position is shown in diagram 341. 3
starts in the center circle, with a supply of balls. 3 could either be the coach or
one of the team's central midfielders. The advantage in the coach taking on the
role of 3 is that he can dictate the passing sequences and create the desired
specific situations that he wishes to go over. The four defenders start on a line
about 5 yards in front of the penalty area, with the two forwards pushed up
against them. There is a keeper in the goal. There are two wide midfielders
and 1 stays about 20 yards behind the midfield line. 3 can move around to
support the ball from behind but not run ahead of it.

This activity is simply attack versus defense. 3 starts the sequence by passing to
any teammate. If the defenders or the keeper win the ball, they pass it to
either 3 or 1 and push up immediately as a unit. If the ball goes out of bounds,
the players reload as in diagram 341. **The first stage is to teach the defenders to adjust to the location of the ball.** To this end, the coach should initially
restrict the attackers to stay in their areas, receive balls and return passes back
to 3 without going to goal. This would allow the coach to freeze play and show
the defenders how to adjust to every situation as the ball is circulating.

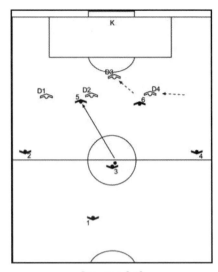

Diagram 341   Diagram 342

Diagram 341 shows the location of the defenders when the ball is in the middle of the field, for example with O3. Notice how close together the four defenders are. If the defenders were too spread across the width of the field, the gaps between them would be too big, and even bigger when a central defender leaves the line to follow a checking forward. Such huge gaps would be ideal for opposing attackers and must be avoided by staying close as shown. Notice also the marking position of the central defenders, on the inside shoulders of the forwards.

Diagram 342 shows how the defenders should adjust to a pass to one of the forwards. Notice how the back four's flatness is broken for a few moments, with D3 dropping to cover, and how D4 slides a little inside. The covering position adopted by D3 will depend on the type of ball played into the forward. A ground ball to feet would require a covering distance of 3-4 yards behind D2, while a high ball for an aerial duel would require a deeper covering position to deal with a possible flick on. Once the ball is cleared, D3 would quickly resume his old position in line with the other defenders.

Diagram 343 shows how the defenders would adjust to the ball played wide. In this system, the wide defenders are responsible for closing down the opponents' wide midfielders. Hence, D1 would dash towards 2 to close him down while the ball is in flight. Notice D2's marking position off the outside shoulder of the forward and within hand-touching distance. This allows him to intercept the ball if it is played to 5's feet.

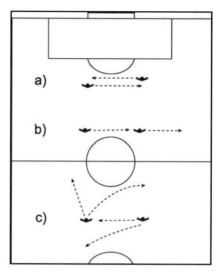

Diagram 343   Diagram 344

It is important to explain to the defenders the 'sandwich' approach. That is, when one defender marks tight, the next defender in line is responsible for the space behind the tight defender. In diagram 343, D2 must focus on intercepting a possible ball to the forward's feet, hence he cannot be expected to also worry about the space behind him (area 1). It is D3 who must be ready to attack balls played into area 1. Between them, D2 and D3 are essentially 'sandwiching' 5, with D2 ready to attack the space **in front** of 5 and D3 ready to charge into the space **behind** 5. The same relationship exists between D3 and D4, where D3 is responsible for balls played into 6 and D4 is responsible for balls played behind (area 2). D2 must mark 5 very closely, whereas D3 can mark 6 more loosely, since 5 is closer to the ball.

D3 is also responsible for tracking a possible run by 6 into area 1. If 6 makes a diagonal run through area 1, D3 would have to make an instant decision on whether to follow him or let him run offside. If the ball has not been released yet, D3 can let 6 run into offside, but if the ball has already been played, D3 will have to stay with the forward. The key is for D4 to hold the line by positioning himself flat with D3. Otherwise, the offside line would be destroyed and D3 will not be aware of it. D4's responsibilities also include picking up 4 if he runs into area 2.

Once the coach is satisfied that the four defenders understand how to adjust to the location of the ball, he can switch his focus to **teaching the defenders how to adjust to the attackers' movement off the ball**. Diagram 344 illustrates the typical off-the-ball movements of twin strikers. The forwards' movement will generally fall into one of the following patterns: (a) lateral runs in opposite directions across each other to switch positions, (b) both forwards run across the field in the same direction, and (c) one forward running into midfield, to check to the ball or to create space, while the second forward runs into the space created.

At this stage, the coach would encourage the two front-runners to increase lateral movement across zones and randomly recreate the movement patterns shown in diagram 344. This will force the defenders to deal with tracking the forwards and passing them on from one to another while maintaining awareness of the ball. Also, the coach can instruct 2 and 4 to move up and down the flanks just like wide midfielders. 2 and 4 should start very wide when 3 has the ball and only cut inside to meet a cross or take a shot. All these movements will provide the coach plenty of scope for stopping and teaching.

Dealing with the forwards' straight lateral runs (a) and (b) would require constant communication between the defenders, as they avoid being dragged out of position and maintain their alignment by passing on the attackers to each other. As long as the forwards stay in front of the defenders, the task of handing them over to each other is relatively easy. Movement patterns (c) are more difficult to handle and would require a momentary break in alignment to make sure that the checking forward cannot receive the ball and turn. Top level forwards will often drop into midfield to escape tight marking, hoping that defenders will be reluctant to break their alignment and follow them. It's imperative that defenders stick to their mark, follow him, and not allow him to turn with the ball.

There will be times when one of the forwards will drift wide and be picked up by the wide defender while the ball is in a central area. Diagram 345 illustrates this situation, where D4 is marking one of the forwards. If the ball is passed to 4, D4 must leave the forward and close the ball down while D3 must immediately pick up the forward.

The four defenders must be careful to avoid potentially dangerous 1v1 situations near goal. For example, the situation depicted in diagram 346 presents a defensive liability since 4 could send an early cross into the weak side (dotted) area where 5 could beat D1 to the ball. D2 must recognize the danger early and call D3 back to mark his forward so he could be free to slide into a more central covering role, as shown in diagram 347.

Once the four defenders learn to cope with the movement patterns, the four attackers should be allowed to go to goal and try to score, with 3 supporting the attack from behind the ball. Every time the defenders win the ball, they try to play it out to 1 and push up as a unit. Every now and then, 3 should surprise the defense and dribble the ball forward in order to teach the defense to deal with the situation of a midfielder breaking through. When this happens, one of the free defenders must step up and close down on the ball to prevent a shot on goal.

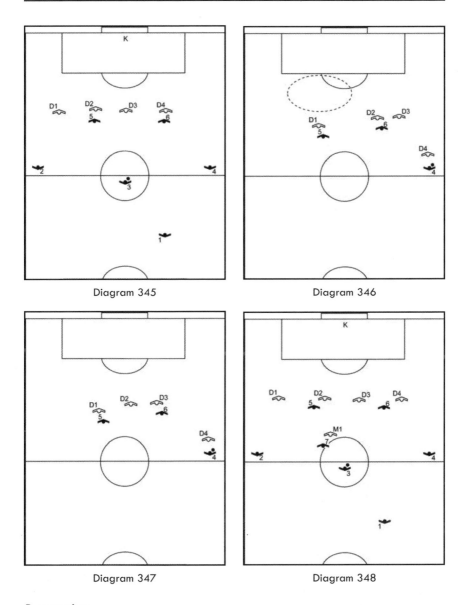

Diagram 345

Diagram 346

Diagram 347

Diagram 348

Progression

The next progression would be to incrementally add midfielders for both teams. The first step would be to add an attacking midfielder, 7, and a defending midfielder, M1, to mark him, as shown in diagram 348. 7 is free to move anywhere, including making runs in behind the defenders. M1 would need to track him down and make decisions on whether to let him run offside or hand him over to a free defender or stick to him.

More players can be added gradually, depending on the number available in the squad. Diagram 349 illustrates how to use 16 players and a coach to replicate the full-game environment. The defending team has a keeper, four defenders, one defensive midfielder (M1), and two wide midfielders (M2 and M3), playing against two forwards, four midfielders and three defenders (1, 8, 9). Here play can start with 1 (the coach), who has a double role. He starts the black team's attacks and supports it from the back but is not allowed to run forward and join the attack. His second role is that of a counterattacking outlet for the defending team, meaning that whenever the defending team wins possession, they try to play the ball to him. Everyone else is free to move as they would in the game, with 8 and 9 acting as attacking fullbacks, moving up on the overlap. All the **coaching points** previously discussed would apply, with the following additional points:

■ As explained before, the **wide defenders would mark the wide midfielders**. For example, D4 would close down 4. But should 9 make an overlapping run, M3 would slide over and pick him up to prevent a 2 v 1 situation on the flank.

■ The three midfielders, M1, M2, and M3, start out **compact in the center** when the ball is with 1, as shown in diagram 349. The midfield's compactness can be used to create numbers-up around the ball. Since M2 and M3 don't have a specific opponent to mark, they give the team defensive flexibility. They can be used to double team on the ball. For example, if the ball is played to 2, both D1 and M2 could close him down quickly and try to steal the ball. They can be used to hunt down the ball in twos and threes anywhere in the midfield area. For example, they can double up on 7 or 3, or they can turn and sandwich a forward just when he receives a ball. If a ball is played to 6, either M1 or M3 or even both of them can jump in and surround the forward who is already under pressure from D3.

■ There must **always be immediate pressure on the ball** anywhere in the defensive half. This is the most important point and it overrides any predetermined marking assignments. For example, normally D4 would be expected to apply pressure on 4, but should M3 or any other player be much closer to 4 when he gets a pass, it would be foolish for M3 to hold back and wait for D4 to arrive. Pressure must be immediate, regardless of marking assignments. To this end, midfielders should always be ready to shift over and release a teammate to apply pressure. Diagram 350 shows such a situation. M3 runs wide to double team against 4, but cannot prevent 4 from passing to 3 who proceeds to dribble into the defending half. M2 immediately shifts over to pick up 7, thus releasing M1 to apply immediate pressure on 3. This is the kind of quick reaction thinking that must be ingrained into the midfielders' defensive mentality. Activities such as the ones described here create ample repetitions of game-like situations and allow for problem solving by the players with immediate feedback by the coach.

Diagram 349   Diagram 350

- Good defending is all about positioning and anticipation. For example, M2 and M3 can position themselves to cut out dangerous passes to the forwards by blocking the passing lanes. Good anticipation, based on reading the passer's body language, allows defenders to 'cheat' and move early towards the next recipient of the ball. In fact, the best defenders can use deception to intercept the ball. They invite a pass to a specific opponent by positioning, wait for the passer to look down and fix his eyes on the ball, and quickly close down on the intended receiver to steal the ball.

- The central defenders need to learn when to drop off their mark and when to step up and mark tight. Generally speaking, when there is no pressure on the ball, the central defenders should drop off their mark. Dropping off increases the likelihood of a challenge for the ball while facing up field, thus preventing them from 'getting turned' towards their own goal to chase a through ball. If they do have to chase a through ball, dropping off will allow them to be first to the ball. Diagram 351 shows defenders D2 and D3 dropping off because there is no pressure on the ball and 1 has the time to measure a dangerous through pass. Diagram 352 shows the defenders holding the line flat and marking tight because there is pressure on the ball by a midfielder.

- It is much easier for the defense to step up and let forwards run offside if the wide defenders stay in line with the forwards. To illustrate this point, refer to diagrams 353 and 354. In diagram 353, the defenders are lined diagonally, with the wide right defender in the deepest position. This alignment makes it easy for the attackers to make dangerous forward runs since D1 will keep them onside. It's also hard for all three defenders to coordinate stepping up together should they want to play the offside trap. Diagram 354 shows a better alignment, with only the central defender dropping back to cover. Now, if the central defender wants to step up, he can easily do it, with the knowledge that the wide defender will not be stuck behind him, putting everyone onside.

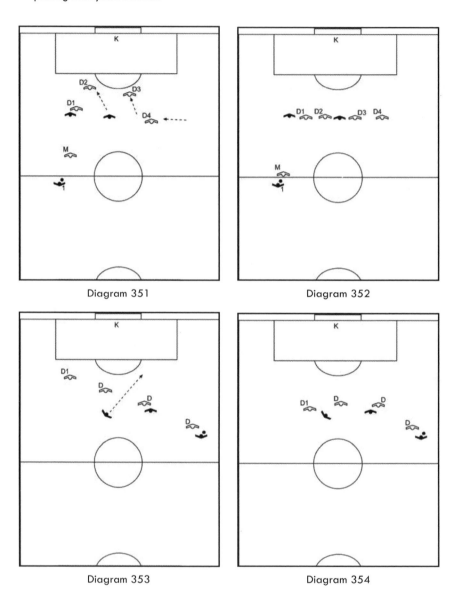

Diagram 351

Diagram 352

Diagram 353

Diagram 354

Activity #3: Teaching The Forwards To Apply First Pressure

Activities #1 and #2 illustrated a method for coaching the back and midfield units to defend zonally. Since, in the modern game, the forwards are referred to as the first line of defense, they need to be integrated into the team's defending strategy. The following activity is just one example of how to go about teaching the forwards their defensive duties. In this activity, the two strikers are coached on how and where to apply pressure on opposing defenders as they are building up from the back, assuming both teams play 4-4-2. The specific objective in this exercise is to teach the forwards to squeeze play to one side and force the ball down the flank. When forwards are able to keep the ball on one side and limit the passing options, it makes play predictable and helps the team gain possession.

Working within the constraints of having no more than 16 players available, the activity takes place in the attacking third, where the players are arranged as shown in diagram 355. The 16 players are positioned in a way that best replicates the 4-4-2 system. The team being coached contains two forwards (F1, F2), two midfielders (M1, M2), and three defenders (D1, D2, D3). The opponents have a keeper, four defenders, a defensive midfielder (5), two wide midfielders (6, 7), and a forward (8).

Not having 22 players available, certain positions can be omitted without conceding the realism of the 11-a-side game. For example, the absence of a second forward as well as an attacking midfielder does not hinder the session since 8 can roughly represent the combined effect of the two forwards and the attacking midfielder. Since the session will focus on the forwards defending against a build up by the other team's defenders, it is more relevant to include the full complement of players in that part of the field.

Diagram 355 shows the starting positions, and is also the 'reloading' arrangement. Notice the central location of the F strikers when the keeper has possession. By taking up a central position, the forwards invite the ball to be played out to one of the wide defenders. The keeper always starts the action by serving the ball to one of his defenders. The attacking team works the ball from the back and attempts to penetrate into the other half. If they succeed, all the players reload and start again from the keeper. The defending team tries to win the ball and, if they succeed, they play it back to the black team's keeper and retake the starting positions. If the ball goes out of bounds, everyone reloads as shown in diagram 355. Diagram 356 shows how the forwards close down the ball as it's played to 1. Forward F1 applies pressure on 1, trying to win the ball or at least keep it on the right flank. F1's angle of approach makes it difficult for 1 to play it across the field. F2 moves quickly towards 2 to prevent a switch through the back line. The forwards' movement forces the ball down the line where D1 and D2 are waiting to pounce on any passes. The coach should make it clear to his forwards at what point they should make their first challenge. Typically, it would be 10-20 yards above the half line.

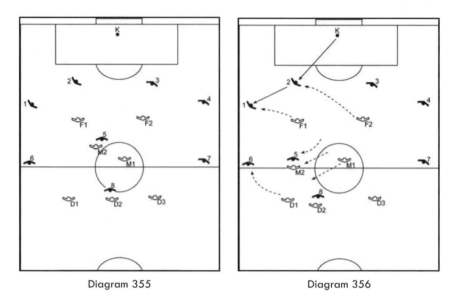

Diagram 355   Diagram 356

The **key coaching points** are for the forwards to close the ball quickly, win the ball if they can or force the defenders into rushing their passes and prevent the ball from finding its way to the other side, where 4 and 7 lurk unmarked. It is important for the forwards to stay on their feet and not slide tackle, unless they are absolutely sure of making contact with the ball. A miss-timed tackle will let the attackers off the hook and allow them to switch the ball to 7. F2 should be aware of both 2 and 3's positions. If either one of them steps into the midfield space vacated by 5, F2 should adjust his position to block that outlet, otherwise the ball will end up with 7. If the ball is passed back to the keeper, both forwards should quickly slide back to their original central positions from where they can wait to re-apply pressure.

The element of transition can be added to the exercise by allowing the defending team to go to goal if they win the ball. This will take more time away from the main objective and stray somewhat from the topic, but it will certainly increase the motivation and enjoyment for the players and that is always desirable.

Functional Activity: Attacking From Middle Third in 3-5-2

The 3-5-2 formation demands from the midfielders to make penetrating runs into the attacking third. This activity can be used to teach the midfielders to do just that. The organization and starting positions of the players are shown in Diagram 357.

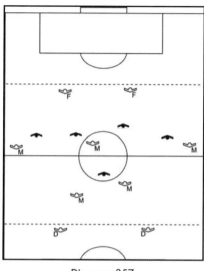
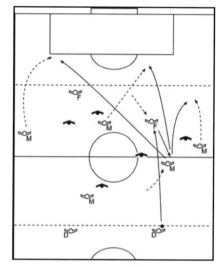

Diagram 357   Diagram 358

The team being coached has two defenders (D), five midfielders (M) and two forwards (F) as shown. There are five opposing midfielders matched up against the five M's. The M's are arranged in the formation they would normally adopt in a game. For instance, in diagram 357, the midfield arrangement has two defensive midfielders, two wide midfielders, and one attacking midfielder. The objective is to bring the ball into the attacking third either by passing or by dribbling but only the midfielders can enter the attacking third. The attacking team gets a point if they succeed in sending a midfielder, with the ball under control into the attacking third. Players from the defending team can chase the midfielders into the attacking third but once the midfielder has the ball under control, the players stop and restart a new attack from the D's. The defending team gets a point if they win the ball and play it back to the D's.

Every attack starts with a serve from one of the D defenders. The D's support the midfielders, can receive back passes and switch the point of attack, but they cannot enter the middle third. The two F's roam unmarked around the upper edge of the middle third and can be used in the build up, but they cannot turn with the ball, cannot make runs into the attacking third and are restricted to two touches. The forwards are so restricted because the purpose of the exercise is to teach the midfielders to make the attacking runs. Note how this exercise creates the 11v11 environment with only fourteen players.

For realism, the offside rule is applied. The offside line can be represented by the location of the highest F or, alternately, cones can be placed across the field to designate a static offside line, approximately where the dotted line is shown in diagram 357.

The coach can guide the attacking team through some passing patterns that finish with a final pass into the attacking third. The passing permutations are many. It could be as simple as a long diagonal pass from D straight to a midfielder running into the attacking third, or it could involve a succession of passes and runs. The key is for the coach to observe and assist the team in maintaining a good shape in midfield, since a balanced shape, with sufficient width and depth, will allow the forwards to play the way they are facing and automatically produce better passing options.

A five-midfield system works best in attack if the two wide midfielders use the whole width by 'hugging' the sidelines. There is no need for the wide midfielders to drift inside, as this will simply clog the already crowded central area. If they stay on the sidelines when the attack is building up, the team can instantly switch sides with one long pass and really stretch the opponents. One sure way to unbalance opponents is to start with a pass to a wide midfielder standing against the sideline. This will draw the opponents towards that side. The ball is then played back to either a defensive midfielder or a defender, who promptly sends a long diagonal pass to the opposite sideline where the other wide midfielder is waiting to penetrate.

Another major coaching point revolves around the supporting role of the defensive midfielders. The two defensive midfielders are instrumental in maintaining the correct shape in midfield. They should be constantly adjusting their positions to make themselves available for back passes from the other midfielders and from the forwards. Diagram 358 shows one such example, where play starts with D passing to a checking F who lays the ball back to a defensive midfielder who now has a number of options for the final pass. This is just one example. The reader can find additional examples of patterns conducive to the 3-5-2 formation in a later chapter titled "Passing patterns in the Middle third".

Functional Activity: The scrimmage

The tried and trusted scrimmage can also be used as a functional activity. Instead of just throwing scrimmage vests at the players and splitting them randomly into teams, scrimmages can have a functional element if all the players are arranged in a shape that resembles their normal positions. Even a five-a-side scrimmage can be organized to derive functional benefits. For example, playing five-a-side using a 2-2-1 formation with players placed in their game-like positions.

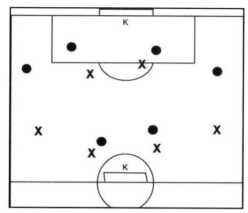

Diagram 359

It all depends on the training objective. A coach of a fourteen player squad that normally plays 4-4-2 who wishes to work on the wide defenders overlapping in attack, can use a 7v7 scrimmage as shown in diagram 359. Each team plays a 4-2 formation that recreates the back four and allows the coach to focus on the movement of the wide players. The coach can put the starting back line together on one team and the alternates on the other team and rotate as needed. If the coach has sixteen players available, he could play a 4-1-2 formation to work on the same topic. A 4-1-2 formation is probably better than a 4-2-1 formation since the coaching will focus on the defenders and it is more realistic to match up the four defenders against two forwards rather than against just one forward.

GENERIC VS FUNCTIONAL TRAINING

So far, this chapter has presented examples of generic activities as well as functional tactical activities. It was suggested earlier that for a team to reach its full performance potential, it should undergo both generic and functional training. If players are exposed to both types of training, they benefit from a well-rounded preparation and learning experience. But how does a coach divide his training volume between the two types and how does a coach decide when to emphasize one over the other?

Both types of training have their place in the annual, seasonal and weekly planning cycles. How big a dose of each depends on many factors. As a general rule, a training program should start with generic activities in order to sharpen up the players' touches and decision-making and to give the coach an opportunity to assess the players' technical, physical and tactical levels. The coach's observations during the generic activities will also help him in the planning of the functional sessions that follow.

Coaches of club teams, either youth or professional, are more likely to have the luxury of many training sessions. Whenever the training volume is high and is stretched over a period of many months, generic activities should greatly out-number functional activities, for a few reasons. Generic activities, especially when performed in small groups, yield a high volume of repetition and repre-sent an economical method of training, where all the technical, physical and tac-tical components of the game are trained. Generic activities add variety to the training, which is an important consideration over a long season. Another important distinction is that players enjoy generic activities, where they are in charge of decisions on the ball and are able to express themselves more freely than in functional sessions.

Players enjoy a greater control when engaged in generic activities, while the coach is more clearly in charge when conducting a functional tactical activity. This also makes generic activities more effective in developing the players' problem solving skills. As much as coaches would like to control the game and its outcome, soccer is unpredictable and full of surprises. Not every moment fits neatly into the collective game plan. It is ultimately a players' game and, as such, it behooves coaches to develop players who can think on their feet. Over-reliance on functional training, where the coach dictates the passing and move-ment patterns, produces robots.

Another potential problem with functional training is the necessity for a higher degree of interference and coaching stoppages by the coach, which could annoy the players. Also, functional training in the hands of an inexperienced coach could lose its effectiveness or even prove counterproductive. Incorrectly applied, a functional activity could become too static, unrealistic, and downright boring.

However, there are times when functional training takes precedence. Some situ-ations do not allow a coach many opportunities to work with his team. For instance, an all-star team that comprises players from different teams, a region-al or national team that only has a couple of training sessions before their first game, or a school team with a very short pre-season. These examples repre-sent quite a challenge for a coach whose primary task would be to build a cohesive unit in a short time. This is where functional training comes in handy. If the players are already sharp from playing regularly, the coach can immedi-ately jump into functional activities and shadow play type of drills that would meet the urgent objective of team building much better than any generic activi-ties. Even if the players are not match fit, as in a school pre-season, the coach can incorporate soccer specific fitness into the functional training and kill two birds with one stone. An example of a functional activity that combines the technical and physical demands specific to each position is illustrated in dia-gram 359A.

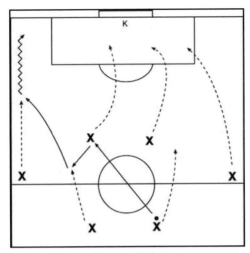

Diagram 359A

In diagram 359A, six players execute a passing pattern as shown, culminating with a cross, and immediately followed by a sprint back to the starting position to replicate a transition to defense. In this activity, the players simultaneously work on a passing move, on finishing crosses, and on soccer fitness that replicates the stamina demands of their positions. The work to rest ratio can be manipulated to design an interval training effect. For example, if it takes a total of about 10 seconds to execute the pattern at game speed and sprint back to the starting point in the middle third, a targeted work to rest ratio of 1:2 would require a 20 second rest period between each repetition.

To summarize, training programs need to include a mix of generic and functional training. Generic activities are more enjoyable for the players and are effective at developing creativity and problem solving skills. Functional training accelerates transfer of learning to the game and develops the team's tactical cohesion. Both types of training methods are necessary for teams to reach their performance potential. The challenge for coaches is to determine the optimum mix of generic and functional sessions. When many training sessions are possible, generic type activities should outnumber functional activities and should precede functional activities. When only a few sessions are possible, functional training should become a priority.

PATTERNS OF PLAY

With eleven players on the field, the passing patterns and permutations are obviously endless. But a careful study of games at the top level reveals that certain passing patterns are strung more often than others and that teams adept at possession tend to rely repeatedly on similar movement and passing sequences to maintain a rhythm of ball circulation. For example, one very common pattern can be described as the 'in-back-out' sequence. Diagram 360 shows an example of 'in-back-out', with a pass IN to feet, followed by a BACK pass to a supporting player, followed by a pass OUT of the area. This sequence is routine at the top level because it involves everyone passing the way they are facing and eliminates the need to receive and turn and risk losing the ball. It produces a high tempo of play, especially if every pass is made with the first touch. The ball is always in motion, not allowed to remain in the same area for long, making it difficult for opponents to press.

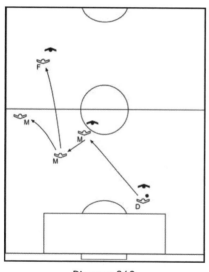

Diagram 360

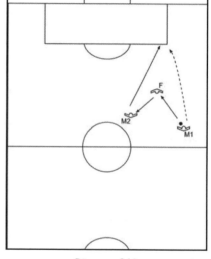

Diagram 361

Another common passing habit by top-level teams is for players not to pass the ball back where it came from, unless they have no choice. The habit of passing the ball to someone new allows a better ball circulation and makes it hard for opponents to chase the ball with numbers. The passing sequence shown in diagram 361, coined by coaches as the 'third man passing' pattern, is a great example of every pass going to a new player. It also demonstrates how a correct body position allows every player to see both the player passing to him and the player to whom he will pass.

One other point about passing patterns that bears mentioning is the advantages of diagonal passes as opposed to straight up and down passes. When passes are diagonal, as shown by the pass from D to M in diagram 360, the receiver can wait for the ball in a half-turned posture that permits his peripheral vision to check whether he can turn or not. If his marker is far enough from him that he can receive and face up, it makes him more dangerous since he can now play the ball forward. It is a lot more difficult to 'read the marking' and turn with the first touch if the pass is straight and vertical.

The passing patterns depend to a large extent on the area of the field and the amount of pressing by the other team. Coaches should study top-level soccer and try to spot the preferred patterns, making note of how they are utilized in the different areas of the field. They can then design practice sessions where these patterns are rehearsed, first in what coaches call 'shadow training' without opponents and then incrementally adding more opponents to replicate realistic game scenarios.

Coaches divide the field into thirds, namely the defending third, the middle third, and the attacking third. Teams can rehearse the passing sequences that are typical to each third in order to become more comfortable in possession and learn to advance the ball from one third to another. Examples of such practice sessions can be found later in the book in the chapter on 'shadow plays'.

The team formation also has a strong bearing on the passing patterns used. Each formation has its own unique player movements and passing selections that maximize the efficiency of that formation. There are certain passing combinations that are more effective and thus more common within the 4-4-2 system, just as there are passing sequences that are more typical in a 3-4-3 formation. The following chapters provide some of the most common patterns in each third of the field as they apply to various formations.

PATTERNS IN THE DEFENDING THIRD

When the ball is in the defending third, the main objective is of course to get it forward into the middle or attacking third. If that's not possible, then the next best thing is to switch it to the other side. Therefore, passing patterns in the defending third are mainly geared towards playing it forward quickly or a risk-free switching of the ball from side to side. Diagram 362 shows a passing sequence that would be typical within a 4-4-2 or a 4-3-3, with the back four stretched across the width in a bowl shape. If the left defender has the ball and he cannot play it forward, he could switch it to the right via the central defenders.

The three defenders in the 3-5-2 formation could do the same, or they could form a chain with the wide midfielders to switch the ball from one side to the other, as shown in diagram 363.

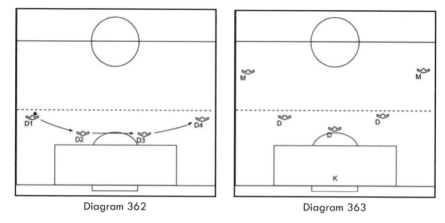

Diagram 362   Diagram 363

When the ball is played across the back, it should be switched quickly, using one or two touch passing, in order to gain time and space on the other side to play it forward. Of course, the ball doesn't have to go through each player in the chain. Good defenders can pass accurately over long distance and therefore can skip a player along the chain. For example, D2 can pass directly to D4 in diagram 362. Top-level wide backs can even bypass both central defenders and launch a direct pass from sideline to sideline.

The decisions to pass short or long would obviously depend on the pressure by opponents and the passing range of the players. The keeper could also be used in the switch sequence, which means that when teams work on these patterns, the keeper should also be part of the session to work on his passing technique and improve his decision-making.

When opponents are playing high pressure, their forwards often try to prevent the ball from being switched across the back line. A typical passing sequence that gets the ball switched against high pressure is shown in diagram 364. Here, opposing forward 1 is closing down on D2 with an angle of approach that blocks a pass to D3. The ball still gets to D3 by using midfielder M. Even though M is marked tightly, he should have enough skill and awareness to receive a ball and pass it on to D3 with one touch. Midfielder M is essentially a rebound wall, redirecting the ball within the switching sequence without needing to control and turn into trouble.

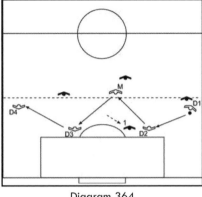

Diagram 364

Since in the modern game forwards are expected to be the first line of defense, teams should rehearse patterns that bring the ball out from the defensive third to the middle and attacking thirds against the pressure of opposing forwards. The objective of the patterns is to penetrate into the middle third, in behind the pressing forwards. The most common passing sequences from the defensive to the middle third are shown in diagrams 365 through 368, where the black players are the opponents putting pressure on the ball. Diagram 365 shows a sequence of a defender to a forward checking to the ball and laying it back to a midfielder. In Diagram 366, a defender passes to the attacking midfielder who lays it back to the defensive midfielder. In diagram 367, the defender passes to a midfielder who squares it to an overlapping fullback. Diagram 368 shows how the midfielders make space for a defender to step up into the middle and receive the ball.

In all these sequences, when the ball is played into the feet of a marked player, he does not attempt to turn into pressure but rather plays it back to a support-ing teammate. The idea here is to get the ball to someone in the middle third who is 'faced up' and who can then maintain the momentum of the attack and deliver a forward pass.

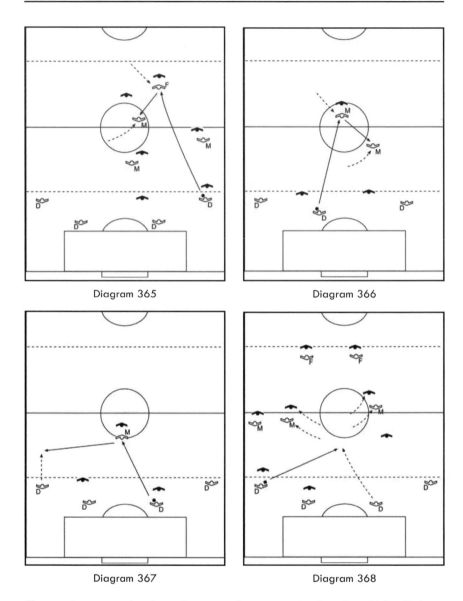

Diagram 365

Diagram 366

Diagram 367

Diagram 368

The previous examples showed patterns for penetration into the middle third. An example of a pass that brings the ball from the defending third directly to the attacking third is depicted in diagram 369. Notice how one forward is checking to the ball and dragging his marker with him in order to make space for the second forward who ends up receiving the pass. This type of pass is used frequently within the 4-4-2 formation, where the twin strikers complement their runs to create space for each other. The instant the ball leaves the defender's foot the wide midfielder would sprint forward to support the striker. British teams describe these passes as 'balls down the channels', where the space between the wide defender (1) and the central defender (2) is referred to as the 'channel'.

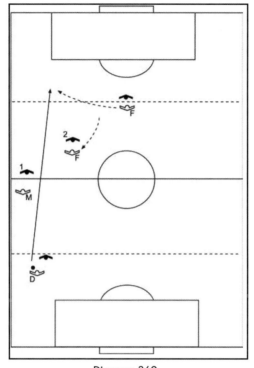

Diagram 369

It is important to note here that the patterns in diagrams 365 and 369 involve a relatively long pass from a defender to a forward. For such passes to succeed, defenders must have the technique and range to deliver quality balls on the ground, driven or floated, and the forwards must be strong enough to hold off tight markers and comfortable at receiving balls on the run or with their back to goal.

Passes from defenders to forwards are routine at the top level but they are also easy to anticipate and intercept and result in frequent loss of possession. These passes used to be a regular staple of the British game and are still more prevalent in Britain than anywhere else. Some teams in Britain still use these passes frequently, and although they often lead to turnovers, it all evens out if both teams return the favor and give the ball right back to each other. The British game is however changing and moving towards the more patient possession game, due in no small part to the influx of foreign players and coaches into the Premier League.

Continental European teams and South American teams prefer to play the ball through midfield before connecting with the forwards. This means that continental forwards tend to receive shorter passes, reducing the chance of interception. At the youth level, passes from the back directly to the front should only be used if the players have the passing range and ability to receive long balls. Otherwise it becomes a game of helter-skelter air duels and loose balls with no rhythm or flow.

It goes without saying that, during the game, if the defender in possession has time and space in front of him, he can dribble into the middle third. But in the modern game, forwards are conditioned to chase and press and midfielders close down the ball quickly and aggressively. This means that teams are well advised to spend some time working on a few patterns for passing the ball out of the defensive third. The defensive third is an area where safety in possession is of primary concern. It is too risky there to rely on individuals to figure a way out, or to play off-the-cuff. It is much safer to rehearse a few sequences, get everyone on the same page, and be prepared with collective solutions to pressure situations. Creativity and individual expression can be allowed to flourish in the other, more advanced areas of the field.

PATTERNS IN THE MIDDLE THIRD

Coaches repeatedly claim that the middle third is where games are won and lost. They have a point. The team that controls the middle of the field is more likely to dictate the game and get the result. Although passing patterns are more variable and unpredictable here, there are still certain tendencies that typify play in the middle third that coaches need to understand and utilize to their advantage. When a team has possession in the middle third, the chances are that the opponents' back line would hold their position in front of their own penalty area, somewhere in the shaded area shown in diagram 370.

The ultimate aim is to work the ball into the areas behind the defense and score a goal. That can be done either by getting 'around the defense' into the flanks (areas 4 and 5 in diagram 370) and crossing, or by using combination plays to slice through the middle into area 6 and shoot. Hence, if passing patterns in the middle third are successful, they should lead to penetration behind the defense. This can be done from anywhere in the middle third but, as mentioned before, if a team can repeatedly work the ball into the 'hole' in front of the opposing defense, denoted as area 3 in diagram 370, it can be more successful in creating dangerous scoring opportunities. From area 3, the attacker can thread a quick through pass in behind the defense, or combine with the forwards to get into area 6, or dribble and shoot.

Modern teams are well organized defensively and tend to pressure the ball quickly to prevent penetration behind the defense. Immediate pressure is applied on the ball almost anywhere in the middle third, and especially if it's played into area 3. The battle for midfield control therefore flows and ebbs with the following tendencies:

■ The attacking team tries to work the ball into area 3, from where they can spring someone through with a 'killer pass'.

■ The defending team defends ferociously with numbers, pressing the ball, trying to steal it, and fights tooth and nail to make sure no one has time to control and turn in area 3.

■ If the defending team wins the ball, they launch an immediate counterattack, trying to catch the other team off-guard.

■ If the defending team doesn't win possession but does an effective job of pressing the ball, the attacking team is forced to relieve pressure by playing it back into its own defensive third or into the wide areas denoted as 1 and 2 in diagram 370.

Since there is typically more time and space to hold the ball in areas 1 and 2, the ball does tend to find its way into these wide areas frequently, where a team can hold it long enough to regroup and launch another attack. This means that possession in the middle third often involves areas 1 and 2, with many attacks originating from these flank areas. Therefore, the implication for coaches is that it is worthwhile to rehearse attacking patterns that originate from areas 1 and 2.

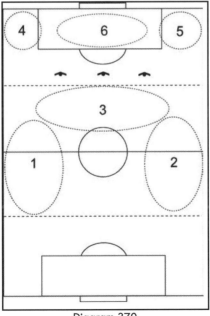

Diagram 370

Let us look at some patterns that start from areas 1 and 2. The following patterns, in which the strikers combine with the midfield to work the ball into the
attacking third, work best within the 4-4-2 and 3-5-2 systems. Diagrams 371
through 373 illustrate penetration down the flanks. In diagram 371, the in-
back-out sequence is used to spring the wide midfielder through. Diagram 372
shows a switch from one wide midfielder to the opposite side via the checking
forward and the central midfielder, followed by a wall pass with the second forward to achieve penetration. Diagram 373 shows how the overlapping fullbacks in a 4-4-2 formation can be included in the pattern. Here, following the
switch, the wide midfielder dribbles diagonally inside towards the defender to
make room for the attacking fullback and releases the ball into the overlapping
run.

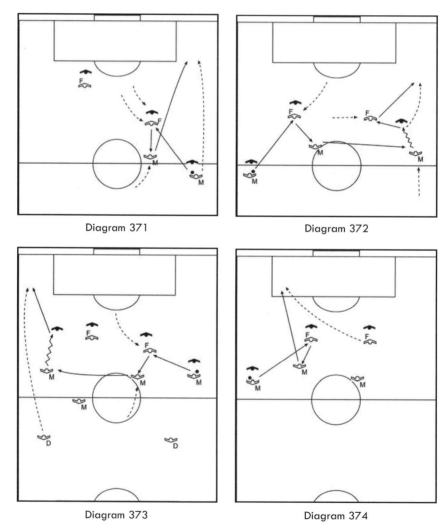

Diagram 371

Diagram 372

Diagram 373

Diagram 374

- 182 -

Diagrams 374 through 376 demonstrate combinations that spring one of the two forwards through within the 4-4-2 or 3-5-2 system. Diagram 374 shows the second forward starting with a flat run to avoid off-side and timing his cutting run for a through ball. In diagram 375, the near forward checks towards the ball, but the ball is played to the far forward. The first forward spins and attacks the space behind the defense to get a through ball either from the second forward (1) or from the attacking midfielder (2).

When two quality forwards play together long enough to develop an understanding, their awareness of each other's habits and positioning can become devastating. Andy Cole and Dwight Yorke were a formidable double act for Manchester United, as were Jurgen Klinsman and Rudy Voller for Germany in the nineties. A favorite ploy used by both of these pairs is shown in diagram 376. Both forwards would get into the same diagonal passing lane. The first forward would pretend to go for the ball but would let it run behind him and sprint for a through ball from the second forward.

Diagram 375
Diagonal ball to second forward

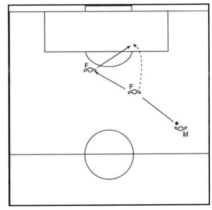
Diagram 376
Creativity by twin strikers

The attacking midfielders in the 4-4-2 or 3-5-2 systems can also rehearse runs into scoring areas within a variety of passing combinations. Diagrams 377 and 378 are just two examples among many. Diagram 377 shows how the attacking midfielder can exploit the space created by a forward, while diagram 378 shows a sequence that has one forward checking to the ball to combine with a supporting midfielder, a second forward creating space with a lateral run, and the central midfielder benefiting as the 'third man running'. It goes without saying that, although the diagrams don't show it, once the ball is played into the attacking third, the players finish the move with a cross or a shot on goal.

Diagram 377

Diagram 378

4-4-2/3-5-2, twin strikers create space and combine with central midfielders

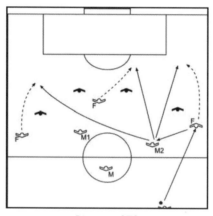

Diagram 379

4-3-3/3-4-3 combinations

Next we can look at some sequences that work best within the three forward system. The traditional way of aligning three forwards is to play with a center forward and two wingers. This alignment stretches the opponents and creates many penetration options. If your team has two wingers, it makes sense to spend time and practice on penetration down the flanks, otherwise there is no point playing with wingers. The best way to exploit the wingers' pace is to work the ball into area 3 in diagram 370. From there, the ball can be played into space towards the corner flag for the winger to chase, or it can be played to his feet to allow him to take on the defender one on one. Diagram 379 shows a passing pattern that starts with a defender feeding the winger who lays it inside to the midfielder and sprints down the flank for a through ball (1). Diagram 379 shows that the midfielder has other options, such as a pass through the gap for the center forward (2), or a switch into space on the far side for the opposite winger (3). In fact, if a three forward system works as it should, the final pass into the attacking third should often look very much like one of those shown in diagram 379.

Some variations for the 4-3-3/3-4-3 formations could include overlapping runs by the midfielders or defenders around the outside of the wingers to create 2v1 situations on the flanks. Other variations could involve an interchange between the attacking midfielder M1 and the center forward, where the forward checks into the midfield and M1 runs into the space created for a through pass.

To summarize, rehearsing passing patterns serves an important purpose in getting all the players on the same page and adding cohesion to the team. Players get a clearer understanding of their role and team shape is easier to maintain. Obviously, there are endless permutations of passing sequences that could be practiced. There is no need to have a large variety of patterns. It is quality of execution that needs emphasis, not quantity, and quality only comes from repetition in training. Coaches should select a few patterns that work best within the team's formation and profit the most from their players' strengths and get the team to do them right.

It bears reminding that players should also be given the freedom to try things instinctively and be creative. This is especially vital in the attacking third, where the unpredictability of individual initiative can result in goals as well. A forward who has the ability and confidence to turn with the ball and take on defenders, or a midfielder who is not afraid to try the difficult pass could prove priceless for the team. Defenders dread facing an unconventional attacker who possesses tricks and close control. Coaches shouldn't stifle such players. One never knows when a game, locked in a defensive stalemate, would require a brilliant individual play to tip the balance.

SHADOW PLAYS

It has been suggested earlier in the book that tactical training should include a certain amount of functional (position-specific) work, where players go through a high volume of repetitions, rehearsing passing and movement patterns in the areas of the field that are relevant to their position. 'Shadow play' in coaching parlance means playing without opponents, or against passive defenders. Shadow play is a form of functional training, but without opponents. This enables the repetitions to be successfully executed in order to paint clear pictures of the patterns, fine tune the distances and angles and integrate the movement with timing. Once the players can execute the play harmoniously and at game speed, opponents can be gradually introduced.

Every top-level team uses shadow play at some point in the training regiment. There is no one set way to conduct a shadow play session. There is no formula to apply. The key considerations are realism and potential for success against live opponents. Shadow training should replicate the game and ensure that the movement patterns rehearsed are the most appropriate ones for the area of the field in question. As well, the movement and passing patterns chosen should be the ones most likely to be successful against live opponents in general, or against the next opponents in particular.

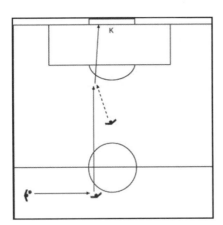
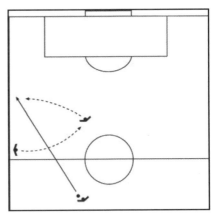

Diagram 380   Diagram 381

Examples of poorly selected shadow training sequences

Diagrams 380 and 381 are examples of poorly selected shadow training sequences. In Diagram 380, the bad sequence starts with a square ball inside, followed by a through ball to a forward who chases and shoots. This sequence is inadequate because it lacks good angles. For one thing, it is not advisable to encourage square passes in the midfield and secondly, it is not realistic to expect that a simple straight pass through the middle will often work against good opponents. In diagram 381, the sequence involves an angled pass to the flank for the striker to chase, while the outside midfielder runs inside. This sequence is inappropriate for a number of reasons: the pass's orientation directs the ball out of bounds, making it hard to reach and control; the strikers' square run has no penetration; and the midfielder's run inside isolates the striker on the flank with his back to the field and no support.

Shadow play can involve all eleven players or it can be limited to certain units of the team. It is usually executed without opponents but sometimes it can involve some opponents. If opponents are used, it is essential for the opponents to position themselves, to move and to react in a realistic way that duplicates the real game. The example below illustrates one such method for running a shadow play session.

SHADOW PLAY IN ATTACKING THIRD

Diagram 382 shows the initial arrangement of the players involved in the shadow play. Four midfielders are spread across the field, just outside the attacking third, in a 'half moon' shape. One forward and three opposing defenders positioned in front of the penalty area.

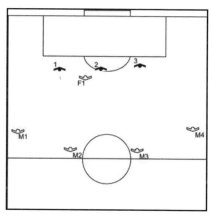

Diagram 382

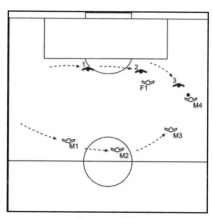

Diagram 383

Play starts with the four midfielders passing the ball from side to side in the following sequence: M1 to M2 to M3 to M4 who takes two or three dribbling touches down the wing, spins back, and passes back to M3 to M2 to M1 who in turn takes a couple of dribbling touches down his wing, turns back and passes back to M2, etc. While this passing pattern is performed, forward F1 moves laterally from side to side, following the ball to provide constant support up high. The three defenders also adjust their positions to the movement of the ball as they would in a real game, but they remain passive. For example, when M4 gets the ball out wide, 3 closes him down and jockeys him but without attempting to tackle. At this stage, the coach should emphasize the following coaching points:

- Quality crisp passing, with the ball played across the front of the players, i.e. M3 plays the ball towards M4's right foot, M1 plays it towards M2's right foot, etc.
- Inside midfielders use two touches to sustain a rhythm of passing and high tempo speed of play.
- Everything done at match speed! Even defenders, although passive, must move at match speed to maintain realism.
- The four midfielders slide across midfield to support the ball and stay compact in case of a loss of possession. This is a very important concept for the midfielders. Intelligently timed movement by the midfield can achieve two diametrically opposite aims - to move the ball across the whole width of the field, from sideline to sideline, while maintaining compactness by avoiding a stretched-out midfield. This is accomplished by having the outside midfielder slide inside when the ball is in the opposite flank. Diagram 383 illustrates this concept, showing the inside position of M1 when M4 has the ball. Notice also M3's support angle behind the ball and F1 sliding across to provide support.

Diagram 384

Diagram 385

Once the players become comfortable with the pattern, progress by bringing the forward into the scheme. F1 joins the passing sequence by showing for the ball, receiving a pass from one midfielder, and returning it to another. Diagram 384 shows how F1 checks away from the midfield while the ball travels from M3 to M2, checks back towards the ball to receive it from M2, and lays it first time to M1.

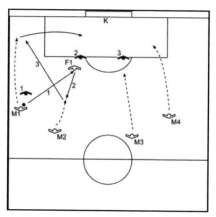

Diagram 386

Diagram 387

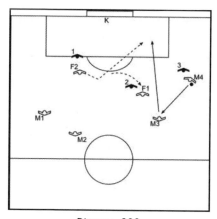

Diagram 388

Next, the coach can introduce specific combination plays with which the five attackers can penetrate and finish on goal. At this stage, a keeper is added. Diagram 385 shows a wall pass combination, Diagram 386 has a third man running combination, and Diagram 387 shows an overlapping run. All of these combinations finish with a cross, with players making near post and far post runs. In these diagrams, the opposite wide midfielder makes the far post run, the forward makes the near post run, one of the central midfielders attacks the center of the penalty area, and one midfielder stays outside the penalty area to attack clearances. Other variations can be used as well, as long as players get to the end of the cross and someone stays behind to take care of clearances.

And finally, a second forward can be inserted and another penetration option is added in the form of a through ball to the second forward as shown in diagram 388. In all these stages, the defenders are passive except when defending the cross. Eventually, the defenders can be allowed to tackle. A fourth defender and a defensive midfielder can also be added, with the defensive midfielder positioned in front of the defenders to put pressure on the midfielders as they pass it around.

Some key coaching points need to be emphasized here:
- Players need to communicate to each other both verbally and with their 'cue runs' off the ball in order to read each other and be on the same page as to which combination play is on. A sudden burst of speed and/or a shout is a great way to 'ask for the ball'. For example, in the overlapping diagram, M3 can shout to M4 "hold it" while sprinting around him.
- The timing of runs, the pace of the passes, and the distances between players all need careful attention from the coach to prevent offside runs or players running into the same space.
- The players should develop a rhythm of possession-penetration cycles by first knocking the ball around and suddenly, using verbal and sprinting cues, penetrate and finish. The players should decide when and how to penetrate and the coach observes and stops occasionally when he feels it is necessary to explain a point.

The shadow play example above uses a midfield formation of four across the field. It goes without saying that shadow play patterns should match the specific formation of the team. For example, teams that employ an attacking midfielder in the hole underneath the forwards would obviously use patterns to achieve penetration different from above. The reader can refer to Diagrams 375, 377 and 378 in the chapter on Patterns of Play for illustrations of combination plays that incorporate an attacking midfielder. These are by no means the only combinations, merely a few examples. The scope of variations is only limited by the coach's imagination. Coaches who are keen students of the game will ultimately be in the best position to combine creativity with sound principles and come up with successful shadow play patterns.

FULL FIELD SHADOW PLAY

Coaches often use the full complement of 11 players over the entire field in shadow play practices, working on building the attack from the back and finish-

ing with a goal attempt. This promotes cohesion between the units and provides
opportunities to fine-tune various passing sequences for advancing the ball
through the thirds. The coach needs to plan the session in a way that maximizes
the number of repetition, with careful consideration of the starting positions, ball
management, and the 'reloading' method.

For example, the sequence could start in the middle third, or the defending
third, or with a throw from the keeper, and finish with a shot on goal at the
other end. The players could reload by simply jogging back to the starting
position. Alternately, to accommodate all the players in the squad, new players
could take up some of the starting positions while the first group returns.

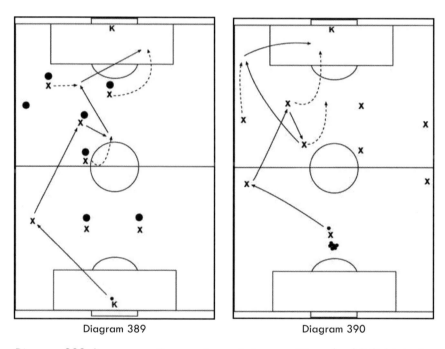

Diagram 389   Diagram 390

Diagram 389 shows a creative way to maximize repetition of a full-field shadow pattern with only 16 players. A team playing out of a 4-4-2 formation
rehearses a pattern that starts with a throw from the keeper and finishes with a
shot on goal as shown. By eliminating the redundant positions (those not
involved with the sequence), the team can go end to end without wasting time
and energy to reload. When team X executes the sequence, the defenders just
shadow mark passively. After team X shoots on goal, the keeper starts the
sequence in the other direction and team X becomes the passive shadow.
Diagram 390 demonstrates another way to keep the tempo with little time
wasted. Here, the central defender starts the sequence, and each flank attacks
separately, in groups of four. While the players on the left flank return to their
starting positions, the central defender feeds the right flank. While diagram

390 shows one passing combination, this set up could be used to rehearse a number of flank penetration patterns.

Often, the coach will want to rehearse a pattern that is designed to exploit a weakness in the next opponent. Diagram 391 shows a shadow pattern within the 3-5-2 formation that is designed to unbalance the next opponent, a team that is known to give up space on the flanks. Here, the sequence starts in the middle third with a pass from the left defender to the left midfielder and back to the defender who quickly sends a long diagonal pass to the opposite flank, where the outside midfielder delivers an early cross into the space behind the defense. The players reload and the pattern is then repeated from the right side with a diagonal switch to the left flank.

Diagram 391

In conclusion, shadow plays such as the ones described here are meant to get all the players on the same page and become more adept at recognizing collectively certain moments in the game that call for certain patterns. Shadow play helps synchronize the players to some extent and ingrain good habits until they become instinctive.

A word of advice here for coaches on effective usage of shadow plays. In the first couple of shadow play practices, many stoppages will be required by the coach to demonstrate the correct timing of runs and get his ideas across. Once the players are doing it right, less coaching will be needed. At that point, coaches might be tempted to stop rehearsing and shifting focus to other training priorities. But it must be remembered that in order for players to transfer learning to the game, they need to rehearse these patterns on a regular basis over a period of time. There is a big difference between getting it right and getting it ingrained!! There are no quick fixes here. Only a substantial volume of repetition regularly scheduled throughout the season will ingrain the patterns and translate into game performance.

SECTION FOUR

FINISHING TOUCHES

DEVELOPING FORWARDS

Forwards have three main roles: scoring goals, supporting the build up, and acting as the first line of defense. For a forward to consider himself the complete package, he must be able to contribute towards all three duties. But, needless to say, goal scoring is the key yardstick by which forwards are measured. Are goal scorers born or made? It's a question that will always trigger a healthy debate. Goal scoring instincts are, for the most part, a natural talent. Some players have an inborn composure in the penalty area or a knack for being at the right place to score. How much of this gift for scoring is inborn and how much is learned from training and observing is hard to measure.

Regardless, all top coaches agree that training plays an important part in ingraining good habits and improving the forward's effectiveness. In fact, coaches should regard the forward as a specialist, in the same way that the goalkeeper is considered a specialist. For this reason, forwards should work on finishing in EVERY practice. Just as for the keeper, work inside the penalty area should be the bread and butter of a forward's session. Many coaches neglect this aspect of training, concentrating on general team sessions, to the exclusion of specialized work in and around the penalty area. Of course, young players in their formative years need to acquire the technical and tactical foundation to play in any position, but once players are old enough to specialize, aspiring forwards need to spend considerable practice time working on all aspects of scoring goals.

The forward's position is the toughest one to fill in the modern game. That is why professional clubs are willing to pay exorbitant transfer fees for players who can stick the ball in the back of the net. Strikers at the top level not only have to contend with tough, organized defenders, they often must lead the attack isolated against superior numbers and up against double marking. The majority of balls that forwards receive need to be controlled under close pressure, in tight areas, with their back to goal or on the run.

To survive at the top, forwards should learn to make space for themselves. When their team is in possession in the build up phase, forwards must make themselves available for the ball and create a few yards of space to avoid interception. When the ball is in the attacking half, the forwards should be looking to get in behind defenders into scoring positions. The ability to create space is crucial for attackers and is certainly the hardest thing for strikers to do against modern defenses. Diagrams 127 to 129 in the section on attacking principles illustrate the kind of dummy runs attackers can use to shake off defenders.

It is worth noting that the best way to learn how to move off the ball and create space is by watching the top players. Learn from the masters. Young players can study how the best forwards make life difficult for defenders and create chances for themselves. Coaches should also make a special effort to study the art of forward play. A coach who understands the dynamics of the attacker-versus-defender duel can be invaluable to his forwards. He can point out the likes and dislikes of defenders and how to make defenders uncomfortable. He can teach his forwards how to exploit their own strengths and instill in them some good basic habits, which in turn will increase their confidence.

One of the most important habits any decent forward should acquire is to always sprint behind his marker immediately after laying a pass. Most forwards participate in the build up by routinely checking towards the ball, receiving it while tightly marked, and passing it back to a supporting player. But all too often, forwards stop momentarily after making the pass. They switch off, thinking that they have done their job. All they are doing is making it easy for the defender to keep them in check. This is the point when a forward can make life tricky for his marker. Immediately after laying off the ball, the forward should spin and attack the space behind his marker, as shown in diagram 401. This should become a habit. If it is done quickly and combined with quality passing, the forward can get a return pass and leave his defender for dead. Even if he doesn't receive a through pass, he manages to create fear in his opponent's mind since defenders don't like to 'get turned' or lose their mark.

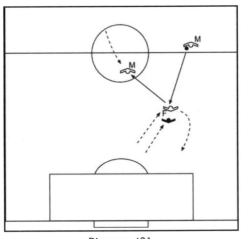

Diagram 401

When confronted with a forward who is constantly moving back and forth, trying to get goal-side of them, defenders become weary of marking tightly and back off. Now the forward has more space to receive the ball, is less likely to lose it to an interception, and could even turn and go at the defender.

Defenders are happiest if they can see both the ball and their mark at the same time and keep them both in front of them. Diagram 402 illustrates this point by showing a stationary forward doing his marker a big favor by standing right in front of him. Forwards who are constantly moving, checking into midfield and spinning back out are good at shaking off tight defenders. When a forward has the stamina to buzz around in this fashion, he can use his assets very effectively against a less mobile defender by wearing him down with non-stop movement. If the forward is blessed with speed as well, he can really become a handful. Defenders are frightened of speed. When confronted with forwards who are faster, defenders drop back and concede space, for fear of getting 'turned' and thrown into a foot race they have no chance of winning. Good coaches know the value of speed. Pace creates space and stretches the game in favor of the attacking team.

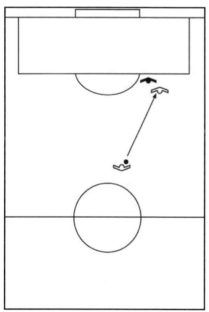

Diagram 402

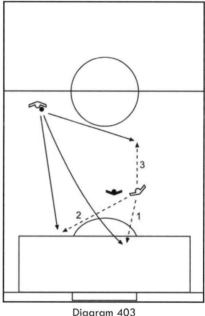

Diagram 403
Batistuta stands on blind side

When forwards do not have the stamina to run so much, they prefer to pace themselves and conserve their energy for when they need to be the sharpest - in the penalty area. Forwards who are less mobile by choice or by athletic limitation must still find ways to become elusive and shake off defenders. One of the best examples of a forward who runs 'smart' rather than 'hard' is the Argentine Gabriel Batistuta. Batistuta tends to stay high and central and wait for the opportunity to poach at goal. His style is more predatory than busy. But this doesn't mean that he is easier to mark. Batistuta stays as high as possible, beside the last defender, and positions himself on the back shoulder of his marker, as shown in diagram 403, making it tough for the defender to watch both him and the ball at the same time. From there, Batistuta can sprint to goal (1), or diagonally (2), or come off his marker for a pass to feet (3).

It helps that Batistuta is blessed with quickness over the first few yards, which makes him very dangerous around the penalty area. Most defenders marking him would instinctively drop back to regain sight of Batistuta, but that only plays into his hands since he would adjust and line up with the defender again, creating more space in midfield and inching closer to goal. If the ball were switched to the left side in diagram 403, Batistuta would shift his position and stand beside the defender's left shoulder, so that he is always on the side opposite to the ball. Playing against a forward like Batistuta may not be physically tiring for a defender, but it's a mental challenge that requires great concentration. The defender is left to guess and Batistuta is winning the mind games without expending too much energy. He is the ultimate, opportunistic goal poacher.

As mentioned before, forwards must learn to hold the ball under the close attention of defenders who are physically strong. Some forwards are blessed with size and strength and therefore, do not always need to escape tight marking. They revel in physical battles and are not afraid to receive the ball with a defender breathing down their neck. Instead of running off their marker, they step back and lean into him. They have the strength to hold off the defender's challenge, control and shield the ball with their immense frame and make their next move. But the modern game sees fewer forwards like this at the top level since they tend to be less mobile, too one-dimensional, and thus, too predictable.

So far, we have illustrated three techniques used by forwards to receive balls:
-       Constant movement into and out of midfield,
-       staying as high as possible on the blind shoulder of the last defender,
-       using physical size to push up against the marking defender.

Intelligent use of angled, or diagonal passing. Romario of Brazil is a master at positioning and moving off defenders to invite angled passes. Romario is small in stature but in his prime he was blessed with quicksilver acceleration. When he played for Brazil in the 1994 World Cup, he used a ploy that was devastating against most defenders. Romario did not exert too much energy running about. Instead, he stayed mostly central, always looking to create the best angle for himself.

Diagram 404 shows how Romario played up front. As his team knocked the ball around in midfield, and Brazilian teams tend to do that a lot, Romario looked to position himself diagonal to the ball. Diagram 404 shows how Romario moves from right to left as the ball is moving from left to right. Diagram 405 shows how he then came off his marker in a sideways-on posture that allowed him to see the defender while the ball was traveling towards him. Defenders feared Romario's speed. This meant that, when he came off defenders, they didn't follow him closely for fear he might sprint behind them. This allowed him to receive the ball with his front foot, facing the goal. Now Romario could use his close dribbling and change of pace to go at the defender. The result was a penetrating dribble or a combination play with the other forward to get into the penalty area. Many times, the desperate defender challenging Romario's dribble would foul him and concede a free kick close to goal, which is tantamount to a dangerous goal chance for Brazil.

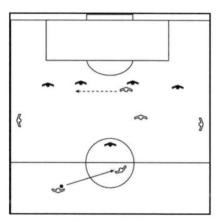

Diagram 404

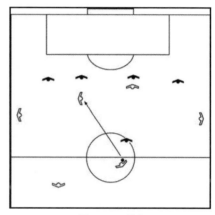

Diagram 405

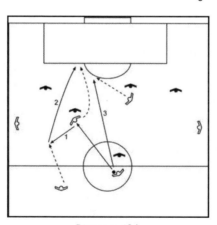

Diagram 406

The defender marking Romario had a real quandary since Romario's combination of speed and excellent ball control made it difficult to contain him. If, as shown in diagram 406, he stayed close to Romario to prevent him from receiving and turning, Romario would lay the ball back (pass 1) and sprint into the space behind the defender to receive a through ball (pass 2). The second

Brazilian forward could also exploit the space created by Romario's movement and attack a through ball himself (pass 3).

As mentioned before, forwards are always trying to find space. Often, the best time to find space is when the other team has possession. While the other team is spreading out to build up their own attacking moves, the forward on the defending team can sneak away from opponents so that, when his team wins the ball, he is free to receive it. Space is most likely to open up either in the 'hole' between the defense and the midfield, or on the flanks vacated by attacking fullbacks. Intelligent strikers are always thinking ahead and looking to drift into these spaces while their own team is defending.

 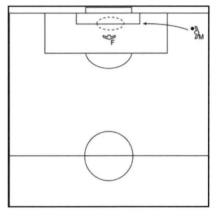

Diagram 407   Diagram 408

Another important aspect of attacking play is the quality of runs to meet cross-es. Coaches should spend significant time in practice teaching their forwards to attack crosses. There are basically three types of runs that attackers make to score on crosses: The near post run, the far post run, and the central run into the six yard box. Diagram 407 shows the near post and far post runs. F1 is mak-ing the near post run, making sure to time his run so that he arrives into the six yard box at the same time as the ball. The near post run is usually the more aggressive, direct, and quickest run. The intent is to get into the near post space first and either redirect the ball into the goal or flick it to the far post. F2 is making the far post run. Usually, the far post run is a delayed run which is meant to attack the ball that is played high over the defense or the ball that everyone else misses as it zooms across the penalty area. F2 would need to hold his run on the edge of the penalty area long enough to judge the flight of the ball and the likely landing area. If F2 runs in too soon, the ball might land behind him.

Diagram 407 shows the likely landing areas of the near and far post crosses. Also, note that both runs start with a bent run that initially takes the forwards away from the ball. Moving away from the ball first is another good habit for strikers to adopt. It confuses the defenders, gets the forwards momentarily out of sight of their marker, and allows the forwards to attack the ball on the run, adding momentum to their jump and power to their heading. The near post runner might not always have the time to make a bent run, but the far post runner should have enough time to start his run by drifting away from the ball first.

The central run into the six yard box, shown in diagram 408, is also a dangerous choice. Here, the idea is to get into the penalty area, somewhere around the penalty spot depending on the origin of the cross, wait there to judge the cross, and attack the balls that skim though the six yard line between the near post and the far post. Again, the timing of the run is meant to gain maximum advantage from the momentum of the run. An attacker arriving into the six yard box will be have more power to his jump than a defender who is standing still.

So far, this section has dealt briefly with the nuances of striker play, providing coaches with tips on maximizing the effectiveness of the forwards in attack. Forwards must learn to create space for themselves. They must develop an understanding of when to go towards the ball and when to move away from the ball. But, most of all, they must practice finishing on a regular basis. This is an area of coaching that is often neglected at the junior level. Since the game is all about scoring more goals than the opponents, it is an area that needs most attention. To illustrate how coaches can design sessions that hone their forwards' finishing skills, a few sample practice activities are described below.

Activity #1: Combination Plays on the Edge of the Penalty Area

The objective of this activity is to learn to create goal scoring chances and work on finishing in 2v2 games that start outside the penalty area.

Diagram 409 shows the organization of the activity. The O's are the defenders and the X's are the attackers and a keeper is in goal. The attackers chosen for this session would be all the team's forwards and attacking midfielders. The grid size has the width of the 6 yards box and extends about 10 yards outside the penalty area. The line of O1 defenders has all the balls. Play starts with O1 passing the ball to X1 and closing in to challenge him. As soon as the ball is passed to X1, O2 and X2 step inside the grid to make it a 2v2 situation. The X's combine to create a goal chance and score. The defenders try to win the ball or at least kick it out of the grid.

To make the activity competitive, the coach can use a point system that would motivate the defenders to work hard. For example, if the defenders win the ball and pass it to the coach denoted as C in the diagram, they get a point. If the ball goes out of bounds or the keeper catches it, the defenders do not get any points. If the forwards shoot on target, they get a point. If the forwards score, they get five points. If the forwards lose the ball, they can try to get it back before the defenders pass it to the coach. To add realism, the offside rule should be applied. Initially, the penalty area line can be used as a static offside line and eventually the deeper of the two defenders could become the offside line, just like in the game.

Diagram 409

Diagram 410

This activity is an ideal environment to teach attackers to combine, using wall passes, crossovers and overlapping runs to get behind defenders. The key coaching points are:

- X1 should go straight to goal with his first touch, forcing O1 to commit.
- X2 should look for ways to gain a couple of yards on his marker O2. He can do this by taking a couple of quick steps in one direction and then changing to another direction as shown in diagrams 410 and 411.
- The angle and distance between the two attackers is crucial. Too close or too narrow and there is no room to combine or slot a through ball. Too far and the passes could be intercepted. Constant repetition and trial and error will teach the attackers the ideal distance and support angle for each moment.
- The attackers need to read the cues, such as the defenders' positions and marking distance, to decide the best combination. For example, Diagram 412 shows an ideal situation for a through ball. The key is for the attackers to recognize instantly the best option and act quickly before the defenders see the danger themselves and adjust.
- Attackers should always look to beat opponents with a dribble. The player on the ball could use his partner's run as a decoy and take it in himself.
- Overlapping runs and crossover runs are very effective when playing in tight areas against an offside line. Diagram 413 shows an overlapping run. X2 can either slot a through ball or dribble inside, depending on how the defenders react.

■ The coach must emphasize that this activity is a penetration game, not a pos
session game. The attackers need to take chances and get behind the
defenders quickly, not resort to a succession of square and back passes.
Remember that this activity replicates action on the edge of the penalty
area.

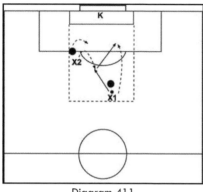

Diagram 411

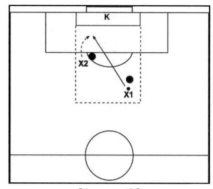

Diagram 412

The activity can be expanded to 2v3 and eventually 3v3 as shown in Diagram
414. The 2v3 situation has two attackers playing against two defenders and a
sweeper (O3). The width of the area would have to be increased by about 10
yards. The 2v3 scenario would be quite a challenge for the attackers but modern forwards have to deal with being outnumbered in the penalty area. The
next progression could be 3v3, where X3 is added to the set up as shown in
diagram 414. This would replicate an attacking midfielder combining with the
two frontrunners against three defenders. The coach should encourage the
attackers to shoot on sight and use the defenders to block the keeper's vision.
And, lastly, the habit of following shots and pouncing on rebounds should be
instilled, since many goals are scored from rebounds and loose balls.

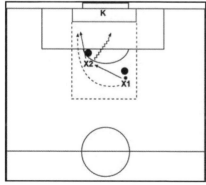

Diagram 413

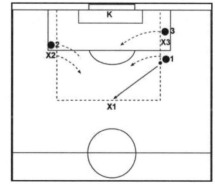

Diagram 414

Activity #2: Forwards Receiving and Turning

This is a functional session that teaches the frontrunners to create space to receive the ball, turn and shoot. Diagram 415 contains the set up for this activity.

Diagram 415   Diagram 416

The sequence starts with F1 passing to either one of the midfielders M, who control the ball with the first touch and pass to F2 with the second touch. F2 turns with his first touch and shoots with his second touch. The number of players involved in this session is designed to create a balance between work and rest for the forwards. Quality must be emphasized, but for quality to be sustained, the work-to-rest ratio has to be carefully monitored or else fatigue will get in the way of technique. Therefore, the activity utilizes three forwards, with F2 and F3 working and F1 resting as he is used to feed the midfielders.

Each turn involves two goal attempts. For example, F2 receives a pass from the left midfielder, turns and shoots, then he gets a ball from the right, turns and shoots and then changes with F3 who proceeds to have his two attempts. After 5 minutes or so, F1 switches position with one of the forwards.

The following key coaching points should be explained and observed by the coach:

■ Although this stage of the session has no opponents, the forwards should get into the habit of creating space for themselves by taking a few steps in a direction away from the space and suddenly checking into the space to meet the ball. This will help them gain a couple of yards on a tight marking defender. Diagram 416 shows the spaces in which the forwards would receive the ball and the movement patterns aimed at gaining the time and space to turn.

■ The timing of the runs is crucial. The initial run away from space should be made just as the midfielder is controlling the pass with his first touch. The minute the midfielder looks up to make eye contact the forward should switch into his final run. The sudden change of pace and direction should be the main cue for the midfielder. To facilitate the development of timing and understanding between the midfielders and the forwards, the coach can instruct his forwards to first make runs to receive the ball in the space outside the penalty area. Once the timing is successful, the forwards can switch to runs into the space in the penalty area. Eventually, the forwards progress to deciding on their own between the two options and relying on the movement cues to have the ball played into the correct area.

■ When receiving balls in the spaces outside the penalty area, the forwards will meet the ball with their back to goal. The technical demands imposed on the forwards are to turn with the ball in one touch and one motion and shoot with the second touch. The mechanics of the first touch should send the ball away from the 'hypothetical' defender. For example, the forward receiving the ball in space 1 in diagram 416 could either use the outside of his right foot to cut towards the 'D' and shoot, or use the inside of his right foot to turn into the penalty area.

■ When receiving the ball in the space inside the penalty area, the forwards should shoot first time on the run and should aim low and to the far post unless the keeper leaves a big gap at the near post.

■ Either way, the key is to receive the ball within shooting range. The forwards should develop an awareness of space, distance to goal and angles in and around the penalty area. Using quick glances over their shoulder, the forwards should be aware of the keeper before shooting in order to pick their spot and either power the ball or bend it around the keeper.

■ It is important to get the shot off quickly. This calls for sharp, economical movement and a clean, sure touch on the ball. This session is aimed at sharpening the skills required for successful execution in the game.

The next stage of the practice introduces a defender who marks the forward tightly. The organization of the practice is the same except that now the midfielder who passes the ball to the forward can step up to support from behind the ball. This means that the forward has the option of turning on the defender or laying it back to the midfield and sprinting into the space behind his marker for a second ball.

Since this practice is geared towards teaching the forwards to create shooting angles, the coach can restrict the supporting midfielder from shooting and allow only the forward to finish. With the introduction of a live defender, the coach can teach the forward to position himself on the blind shoulder of the defender in relation to the ball. From there, the forward can keep it unpredictable by sometimes attacking the space behind the defender and other times checking into the space in front of the defender. Tip for the coach: use the penalty area line as a static offside line. In other words, the forward can only be offside inside the penalty area.

In all these exercises, the coach must always insist on quality execution and work to instill in his forwards a desire to perfect technique. Repetition is the key, as long as it is done at match speed and with attention to technical details. It should be easy to motivate players in activities that involve finishing since players love to put the ball in the net. This type of training is sure to pay dividends in the long run.

DEVELOPING A POSSESSION RHYTHM

Superior possession of the ball has always been a coveted aim of coaches and the subject of many a practice session. The challenge for today's coach is the same as it was for his predecessors, namely, how to strike the right balance between possession and penetration. On the one hand, swift and direct attacks can slash through opponents like a knife, but they lack punch if only two or three players are involved. Slow deliberate attacks can mobilize the whole team, but the element of surprise is missing. Hence, the universal conundrum of possession: when to go forward and when to go sideways?

Over the years, the weighting of the possession-penetration scale has modulated back and forth. There was a period in the 1970's and 1980's when possession was so much in vogue that it came at the expense of penetration and attacking play suffered. Square passes and back passes were seen as tactically justifiable in the name of possession, with some coaches taking the concept to such an extreme that keeping the ball almost became the 'end' rather than the 'means'. 'Negative Soccer' was the term used to describe the preference for 'safe' passes, born out of the obsession to not give the ball away.

But, thankfully, the game has evolved in a positive way, towards a more adventurous, attacking soccer. The pendulum has swung back towards penetration, and the credit for this welcome change is equally shared by FIFA, the sport sciences, and modern coaching innovations. It was FIFA who kick-started the shift towards attack by changing the point system and awarding three points for a win. Meanwhile, advances in the sports sciences played their part, virtually rendering the soccer field smaller by making players bigger, stronger and faster. And innovative coaching methods produced more intelligent players and better team organization.

All these changes made possession for the sake of possession unprofitable. FIFA's new rule meant that the single point gained by playing for a draw was not as attractive when a win yielded three. Better team organization meant that every square pass or back pass gave opponents more time to regroup and organize, making it that much harder to penetrate. And as the field 'shrank', it meant that keeping the ball in one's half increased the risk of losing it in one's half.

As a result, modern soccer is a more direct game, where teams look to attack the minute they win the ball. Possession is still important, but the ball is played forward more quickly, passes are longer, and the game oscillates faster from one end to the other. Now, if a back pass is given, it is a prelude to a forward pass. The mindset has changed. We don't go back in order not to lose the ball, we go back in order to enable us to go forward.

Coaches can't agree on many things, but on one topic they all agree: Teams can never work too much on possession. The longer the team can keep the ball, the less opportunities for opponents to score. The team without the ball has to do all the chasing and, in a fast paced encounter, the extra running can take its toll towards the end of the game. The modern game is quicker, requiring instant decisions on the ball and continuous adjustments of support angles to get out of pressure and keep the ball. Possession requires weaving passing patterns that keep the ball constantly moving, always looking to get it into less congested areas. No matter what formation is used, for teams to keep the ball, they need to learn how to develop a **possession rhythm**.

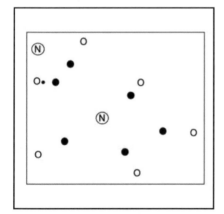

Diagram 417
Neutrals inside grid

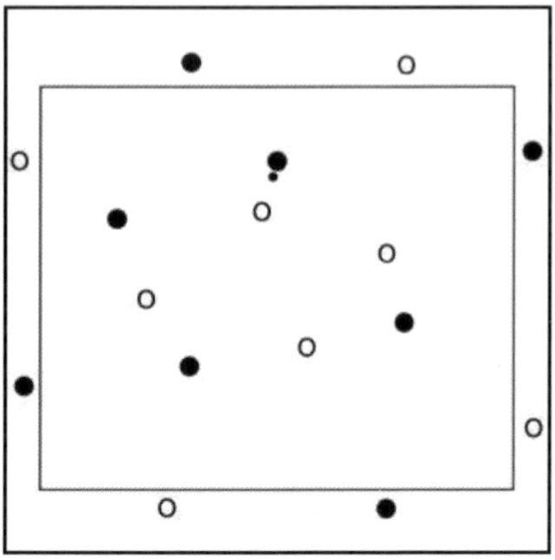

Diagram 418
Neutrals outside grid

A possession rhythm can be established and ingrained in practice and fine-tuned in games. Coaches need to utilize a variety of conditioned games in training. Players, for their part, enjoy playing possession games in grids, where each team tries to string a certain number of consecutive passes to score a point. The better the players, the more they relish the challenge of playing games in tight areas, games that demand concentration, where their first touch must be clean and their passing options assessed before they even get the ball.

There are as many possession game variations as there are coaches. Using the universally accepted concept of progression, a coach could start a possession game with a 'numbers-up' advantage, where the team in possession outnumbers the defenders. The numerical advantage provides a soft introduction to the topic and can be gradually lifted as players become successful in achieving a rhythm. Many coaches commence by using neutral players, or 'floaters', that always play with the team that has the ball. For example, diagram 417 shows a 6v6 plus 2 arrangement, meaning that there are two teams of six playing each other, with two additional players designated as floaters, essentially making it an 8v6 game.

Coaches usually use their midfield generals as floaters, since they are the team's playmakers in charge of dictating a rhythm. The practice games can be conditioned in a variety of ways, depending on the training objective. For example, a one-touch limitation imposed on the floaters teaches them to think ahead and play first time passes. Alternatively, a one-touch limitation on all the players except the floaters teaches the floaters to provide immediate support and gives them a bigger influence on the flow and rhythm of play. Other conditions that are commonly used by coaches are: cannot pass back to the player that passed to you; every third pass must be long; can only pass the ball the way you are facing.

Another way to create a numerical superiority is by placing neutral players around the perimeter of the grid in which two teams compete. The training squad can be split into three teams, with two teams inside the grid and the third team spread outside the perimeter to serve as neutrals. For instance, an 18-player squad playing 6v6 inside a 30yds by 30yds grid plus six neutrals, making it a 12v6 game. This method achieves a numbers-up situation while giving each team an active rest period when used as neutrals. Another variation is to split the squad into two teams, and place half the players from each team inside the grid and half outside. The players can only pass the ball to their teammates, inside or outside. Diagram 418 shows such a set up, with a 4v4 game inside the grid and 4 players from each team outside the grid, essentially making it an 8v4 game. The size of the grid can be adjusted to fit the level of the players. Once the playing rhythm is attained, the numbers advantage is removed and the teams continue to work on a possession rhythm, playing with equal numbers.

Games that use neutrals around the perimeter can be conditioned to challenge the players in the technical and tactical nuances of possession play. For example, using conditions such as: cannot play to the same outside player twice in succession; outside players have one touch only; outside players cannot pass back to the same inside player; when an inside player passes to an outside player, he takes his place and they switch roles, etc. The variations are unlimited and can serve to focus on specific aspects of possession while keeping the players from getting bored.

As explained above, the purpose of possession games is to improve the team's ability to keep the ball under pressure and develop a passing rhythm that is transferable to the real game. This is done by using the practice activities to instill possession-oriented good habits and later reinforcing those habits in games. The habits that are conducive to possession are always the same, regardless of formation. Hence, they can be instilled using generic activities as well as functional activities. A rhythm of possession is attained when players consistently do the following:

- **Stretch the field** - the team in possession spreads out and uses the whole grid area, providing width and depth.
- **Support the ball** - teammates should provide passing options on either side of the ball, behind the ball, in front, close and far.
- **Play the way they are facing** - with good support, players won't have to look hard for teammates and should be able to play the ball in the direction they are facing and not have to turn into pressure and risk losing the ball.
- **Play one and two touch** - players don't hold on to the ball or take too many touches before passing it.
- **Play short-short-long** - the ball doesn't stay in the same area for long, just enough time to draw opponents and then quickly switched with a long pass to a less congested area.
- **Communicate** - players talk to each other and give each other specific information early, using short words such as "time!" or "man on!" or "hold it!".

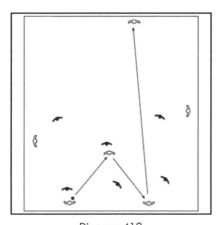

Diagram 419
Possession rhythm

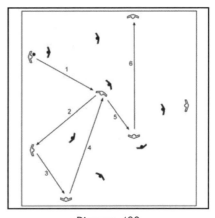

Diagram 420
Possession rhythm

Diagrams 419 and 420 illustrate examples of the passing rhythm that would typically be produced if players follow the six golden habits mentioned above. In diagram 419, the players play the way they are facing, using a short-short-long sequence to get the ball from one end to the other through one-touch passing. In diagram 420, a six pass sequence has similar attributes, namely, one-touch passing, pass the way they are facing, good support angles, and the ball doesn't stay in one area of the field for long.

Another point worth noting is the different roles played by the players inside the grid and those on the periphery. The players on the outside have a better vision of the field and are usually not closely marked. Hence they play the role of 'pressure relief' and ball switching. They also act as the 'eyes' of the inside players by communicating to them when to control the ball and turn and when to 'first-time' it. The inside players are more tightly marked, see less of the field and have less time on the ball. They play the role of a 'rebound wall'. They do this by checking to the ball and re-directing it into a new player with one touch passing. Hence, a successful passing rhythm has the ball moving all around the grid with one and two touch passing and frequently finding its way to outside players away from congested areas. Whenever the ball is played inside, it is quickly re-directed outside to avoid dispossession. Whenever opponents close in with numbers, the ball is quickly switched to the other end for pressure relief. In both diagrams 419 and 420, the last pass in the sequence finds an outside player with time and space to hold the ball and wait for support. The end result: A possession rhythm that will stand the team in good stead.

The last and most crucial step in the process is for the team to carry the possession rhythm into the actual game. In the eleven-a-side environment of the real game, the 'outside-player' role rests on the shoulders of the back line and the wide midfielders. The 'inside player' roles are in the hands of the central midfielders and the forwards. The same good possession habits learned in the practice grids can now be transferred to the game to achieve a possession rhythm, where the ball is knocked around the field with one and two touch passing, going through the midfield but never staying in the congested center for too long, players playing the way they are facing, passes inside are delivered with the appropriate communication, and the ball going often to the wide or back players for pressure relief.

Once a team can consistently reach a possession rhythm in games, penetration will become that much easier. As the ball is knocked around and switched from one side to the other with speed and precision, opponents will get stretched, spaces will appear and goal chances will be carved. And scoring goals should always be the ultimate objective.

THROW INS

Earlier in the book it was suggested that there are certain situations in the game that keep repeating themselves and, therefore, merit special attention in training. The throw-in situation is one very important moment that deserves more attention than it normally gets. Throw-ins occur too frequently in the game to ignore and leave their execution to chance. Too often, teams give the ball away at throw-ins and even concede goals from the ensuing counterattack. This happens when not enough thought and practice is devoted to this very basic situation. Its hard enough to maintain possession in soccer during the run of play. Hence, considering that the thrower is under no pressure, losing the ball straight out of a throw-in is downright criminal. Coaches should make it a priority to work on this aspect of 'dead ball restarts'. With a little bit of organization and minimal practice, the throw-in should no longer be a vulnerable moment.

Whenever the ball goes out of bounds for a throw-in, the player who picks up the ball should immediately assess whether a quick throw-in is the best option. If opponents are slow to react and are leaving players unmarked, then a quick throw is probably the best bet. However, most teams are well organized and are usually not so generous. Most of the time, opponents will quickly close down and mark all the players within throwing distance. Coaches need to prepare their teams for such moments and rehearse throw-ins in practice in order to successfully deal with tight marking.

Let us first look at throw-ins in the defensive and middle thirds. If a quick throw-in is not the best option, the following strategies are recommended. Assuming that the opponents have congested the area around the throw-in with the clear intent to win the ball, the main objective would be to get the ball into play safely and pass it immediately out of the area. If successfully executed, the ball can be played to the other side of the field as quickly as possible, where the open spaces can be exploited. This can be accomplished by spreading out quickly and stretching the field, as shown in diagram 421.

As a general rule, teams that play with four at the back should assign the wide defenders to take the throw-ins in the defensive and middle thirds. This will still leave three defenders in the back and render all the midfielders available for the throw. Teams that play with three at the back should let the wide midfielders take the throw-in to ensure that the three defenders remain behind the ball should the team lose possession.

Throw-ins in the middle third are the easiest to handle, since it is possible to stretch the field in every direction. Diagram 421 shows the team shape that could be adopted every time there is a throw-in in the middle third. Notice how deep the three defenders dropped. If the opposing forwards don't follow them, they would have plenty of time to receive and settle the ball. If the opposing forwards follow the defenders as they drop, it opens up acres of space in the midfield. Next, note how forwards F pushed up high. Since there is no offside on a throw-in, the forwards can also stretch the field, even if they take themselves out of throwing range. This again serves to create space in the middle. With so much space in the middle, it becomes quite easy for the midfielders to check to the ball, receive a throw and play it back to the thrower.

The central midfielders must resist the impulse to run towards the thrower too soon. They should first clear the space near the thrower and start off at least 20-30 yards from the ball as shown. One of them should then dart towards the ball. Based on how the opponents react and position, the thrower could either throw the ball to the checking midfielder or wait for the second midfielder to make a run, or simply play it back to the closest defender. With the team spread out as shown, it will be extremely difficult for opponents to cover all the outlets.

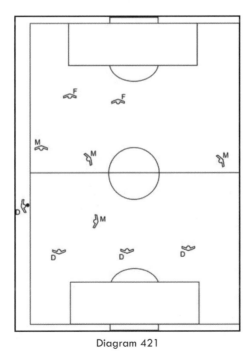

Diagram 421

The following additional points are worth noting in diagram 421. The closest defender is positioned as much inside the field as possible, as opposed to near the sideline. This enables him to switch the ball with one long pass to the opposite side and possibly unbalance the other team. Note that the forward is also positioned inside the field, leaving space on the flank for a possible run. And finally, note the wide position of the right midfielder. This forces the other team to spread out as well or risk getting caught unbalanced on a switch.

The key to success hinges on the defenders dropping early every time there is a throw-in. It should become second nature for them. If they get into the habit of dropping deep, they will either pull the opposing forwards with them or become available for a safe throw. The drop distance needs to be exaggerated for this strategy to be effective. The thrower will not risk throwing the ball back if the defenders do not keep a safe distance from their opponents.

Diagram 422

Diagram 423

The same concept can be applied with throw-ins in the defensive third, although there it is more confined and difficult to stretch the field. Diagram 422 illustrates the positions that could be adopted for a throw-in in the defensive third. Here again, three defenders should drop to create as much space as possible for the midfielders. One defender should always stand behind the thrower as done by D1, even if it means standing right on the end line.

Assuming that everyone is marked, the midfielders should create as much space as possible, denoted by the dotted area, and use this space intelligently. For instance, D2 or M1 could run into the space to receive a throw and play it forward or back to the thrower. Another option could have M2 checking towards the ball and M1 running into the space vacated by M2 to receive the ball. A third option is shown in diagram 422 and involves a throw to M3 who lays the ball back to M1. To disguise the intent, M1 could start with a dummy run towards the thrower and change direction as soon as the ball is thrown to M3. Diagram 423 shows yet another ploy, where the team has two players on the flank and, as the ball is thrown to the further player, the closer one spins and gets a back pass. If none of these options are possible, the thrower can always throw to D1 who simply kicks the ball high and long towards the forwards. As they say, when in doubt, clear it out!

Now let us look at throw-ins in the attacking third. The same principle of deep support behind the ball can be used here as well. But throw-ins in the attacking third present a great opportunity to get the ball into the penalty area and basically create a corner kick situation. Almost every team has at least one player who can throw the ball far. With this weapon at one's disposal, it is foolhardy not to use it. Long throw-ins into the penalty area can cause havoc because they are difficult to clear away. Even if a defender wins the heading duel, the ball will not travel far because a thrown ball does not have the same speed and power as a crossed ball.

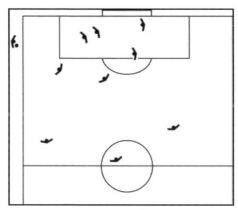

Diagram 424

Diagram 424 shows a possible placement of players to get the most out of a throw. Two players are positioned next to each other inside the penalty area near the six-yard box. These two players will undoubtedly attract two or three opponents, making it a very crowded spot. If the ball is thrown into this human pile and they all jump up to get their heads to it, it doesn't really matter who touches the ball. The chances are the contact will not have any power to it and the ball will likely drop somewhere close, within shooting distance. The rest of the players could be positioned around the heading duel in anticipation of the most likely landing areas. For instance, diagram 424 has one player standing inside the six yard box near the goal, always a good idea in case the ball gets flicked towards goal, and three other players around the duel spot ready to pounce on a loose ball. The rest of the players can position themselves to defend against a counter.

In conclusion, throw-ins occur too often to leave to chance. There is no excuse for losing the ball from a throw-in. In the defending and middle thirds, throw-ins need to be rehearsed with the key points being to spread the field, drop defenders deep, and switch the ball quickly to the other side, where there is more space. In the attacking third, the throw-in should be exploited to the fullest by treating it like a corner kick with a long throw into the penalty area.

THE OFFSIDE TRAP

The offside trap can be defined as the deliberate action by the defense to sprint up as a block in order to leave opposing attackers behind in an offside position. The offside trap should not be confused with the modern strategy of pushing up to squeeze space. Modern defending is based on compactness by stepping up and keeping the gap between the units to a minimum. Team compactness is one thing. Playing the offside trap is altogether a different strategy.

The offside trap is a tactical ploy used by coaches for a number of reasons. Some coaches use the trap as a means of winning back the ball. Other coaches employ it in conjunction with a pressing game. Although the offside trap has been a mainstay defensive tool since the beginning of tactics, one of the most celebrated and admired examples of the trap was seen in the 1974 World Cup Finals by the Dutch National Team. The Dutch Team displayed an almost perfect execution of the offside trap. The '74 team, famously dubbed 'Clockwork Orange', played a high pressing game combined with an offside trap that often left three to five bemused opponents stranded offside.

The Dutch back line was very well synchronized in its actions. They knew when to rush forward to trap opponents. They waited for specific moments ideal for the simultaneous application of pressing and trapping, such as an opponent's back pass or a long square pass. While the ball was traveling between two opponents, the nearest Dutch players would rush towards the receiver to apply immediate pressure with numbers, while the back line would sprint up to trap the forwards. The opponent receiving the ball had to get rid of the ball quickly and invariably played it forward to teammates stuck in an offside position. The Dutch defenders did not just sprint up in a straight line when trapping. They angled their run to converge towards the ball carrier. This tactic ensured that the ball carrier did not beat the offside trap by dribbling through. Those old enough to have watched the Dutch team play in 1974 against teams such as Argentina and Uruguay will probably remember the incredible sight of a Uruguayan in midfield with the ball, being charged by four Dutch players while three Uruguayan attackers are caught out in offside territory.

The trap is also used to nullify superior speed. Defenders who are marking faster attackers have basically two choices. When asked to defend an imminent forward pass, they can either drop back a few yards to get a head start in a foot race towards goal, or they can step up and play the offside trap.

The offside trap has seen better days. The new rule changes, coupled with the savvy of modern players, render heavy reliance on the trap somewhat risky. With many teams employing a lone striker supported by withdrawn attackers or attacking midfielders, the offside trap is proving less effective. Players running through from midfield are likely to beat the trap and latch on to penetrating passes. Although the trap has its place and could be utilized at certain times, such as when pressing the ball, over-reliance on the trap will ultimately be punished by teams who are trained to deal with it. The offside trap's unnerving dependence on the Assistant Referee's judgment and split second decision is another detractor for adopting it as a main defensive weapon. The soccer graveyard is littered with famous defeats caused by 'offside' goals that were allowed to stand by referees who missed the correct call.

Still, there are certain situations in the game in which teams are trained to push up quickly in order to catch opponents offside. Diagram 425 shows a typical moment that often triggers an attempt to trap. In this diagram, team X attacks and penetrates deep into the opponent's half, with the ball on the flank. Attacker X1 is unable to cross and decides to pass the ball back. Many teams are conditioned to sprint out and clear the penalty area in order to catch the attackers offside when X2 crosses the ball. But if midfielders X3 and X4 are ready and alert, they could run into the penalty area as everyone else is running out, and gain a free shot on goal. In fact, astute coaches who are familiar with the tendencies of their opponents could deliberately invite this situation by instructing their team to play the ball back from deep flank positions and teach their midfielders to take advantage of the anticipated response. Corner kicks and free kicks from the flank present additional opportunities to lure defenders to clear the penalty area in a similar ploy by passing the ball back instead of crossing it right away.

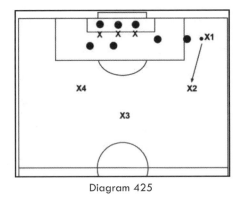

Diagram 425

Let us look at some situations that render an offside trap effective. One of the most appropriate times for the trap is when opponents are using a very direct and fast attack with long passes. Since this style of attack presents little danger of midfielders running ahead of the forwards, the offside trap is less risky. The trap is also likely to be more successful when playing against three forwards since, with so many opponents committed to attack from advanced positions, it is easier to catch some of them offside. Also, a team facing a physically fitter opponent might choose to use the less tiring option of a trap rather than chasing players to exhaustion. And, as mentioned before, for teams that play a high-pressure game that requires players to push up high into the attacking half, playing the trap also makes sound strategic sense.

In conclusion, coaches should be careful about using the offside trap and weigh the pros and cons. The trap is viable against certain attacking styles and formations but over-reliance could backfire. Alert coaches should prepare their team to take advantage of opponents who routinely use the offside trap by springing players through from midfield. Coaches could even go as far as invite opponents to play the trap and exploit it with players running through from behind.

SUBSTITUTIONS

Many youth, school and college leagues around the world allow unlimited substitutions during games. The main driving force behind the liberal substitution rules is to promote equal playing time for all participants and to provide ample development opportunities to all the players. Although these substitution rules are well intentioned, the end result is not always conducive to player development. When substitution is taken to excessive levels and players are rotated in and out like a revolving door, the rhythm of play breaks down, games become too helter-skelter, and player development suffers.

The fundamental process of tactical development hinges on the cycle of playing-receiving-feedback-playing. This cycle is already naturally inherent in the current format of the game. Players play the first half, receive immediate feedback from the coach at half time, and return in the second half to apply the coach's instructions. When unlimited substitutions are literally applied, the tactical learning cycle is interrupted. For instance, the half-time talk loses its effectiveness if many players are replaced for the second half. The new players cannot relate to the coach's feedback since they didn't experience the problems of the first half and the non-returning players lose an important opportunity to put into use the coach's feedback.

One feature of unlimited substitution often seen in North American youth games is the constant re-entry of players to play in 10-15 minute shifts. This seemingly pre-determined player shifts do little to teach players the tactical intricacies and nuances of the game. It takes at least ten minutes to get into the rhythm of the game. Just as a player settles into a position, he gets pulled out. This strategy does not allow players to develop a feel for the pace of the game. Knowing that one has only 15 minutes before coming out, players tend to run 'hard' rather than run 'smart'. To make matters worse, coaches often send players back to play a different position from the one they occupied in the previous shift.

Tactical development is all about learning the right angles and support distance relative to teammates and to the ball. In other words, it is about learning to maintain a good team shape. Every position has it own specific angles to discover. Players, especially inexperienced ones, need time to learn how to contribute to the overall team shape with their own positioning, and how to adjust to the game's ebb and flow. Good coaches observe their players' positioning and provide brief but relevant feedback while the game is going on and at half time. The purpose of the feedback is to help the players understand team shape. This is the essence of tactical development. Constant substitutions, with players thrown into different positions within the same game, hinder players' tactical growth.

A much better approach is to allow players to play entire games, or at least most of the game, and let each player remain in the same position for the whole game. In fact, in an earlier chapter, it was suggested that allowing players to play the same position for the whole season will produce better long-term results in terms of individual and team tactical progress. A player rotation system can be used to make sure every member of the squad gets to play full games. The volume of playing time over the course of the season will still be the same, regardless of substitution method, but leaving players on for entire games will accelerate their tactical development.

Another consideration relating to second half substitution warrants a mention. In games with no re-entry, should coaches send new players in at half time or should they wait until the second half is under way? Sometimes, waiting until about ten minutes into the second half allows the coach to better assess which players are losing their effectiveness. It also allows the coach to check what changes his counterpart has introduced and respond with an appropriate substitution of his own.

Lastly, coaches should prepare the bench players physically and mentally for action before sending them into the field. The players on the bench should go through a warm up routine and stretch periodically, especially in frigid weather. Sending players cold into a game straight from a sitting position is likely to cause injuries. When working with young players, the coach can point out to the bench players certain tactical aspects in order to help them read the game and prepare them for entry. If the substitution is a tactical one, it always helps to have a quick word with the player just before sending him into the game to make sure he understands his role.

CONCLUSION

Coaching is one of the most challenging, yet fulfilling, human-interaction endeavors. Whether coaching seasoned professionals or working with pre-puberty beginners, the feeling of satisfaction following a successful game or a rehearsed move can be intoxicating. Soccer is a players' game, but coaches are responsible for pointing the players in the right direction and giving them the encouraging nudge to 'go for it'.

This book was written for the benefit of coaches who are seriously committed to improving themselves. It is hopefully not the first book, nor should it be the last book that a coach reads. Humility is a desirable attribute, since good coaches never stop learning. After every training session or game, the coach should ask himself/herself the following two questions: What did I learn about myself as a coach today? And what did I learn about my players today?

In the beginning of the book it was noted that coaching is about improving players' performance, but that performance perfection is never achieved. The same can be said about coaches' performance. The perfect practice session has never been conducted, nor will it ever be. After every practice, coaches should reflect on the session and ask themselves in hindsight what could have been done to improve it, and what changes could have been imposed to extract more from each activity. This ongoing process of planning, conducting and evaluating oneself is the essence of coaching excellence. It is not the number of trophies won that makes a coach, but rather the unrelenting quest for that elusive perfection.

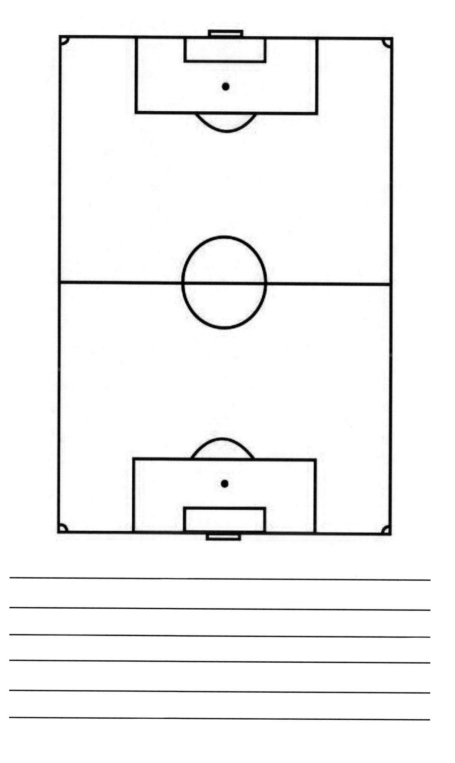

_____
_____
_____
_____
_____
_____
_____

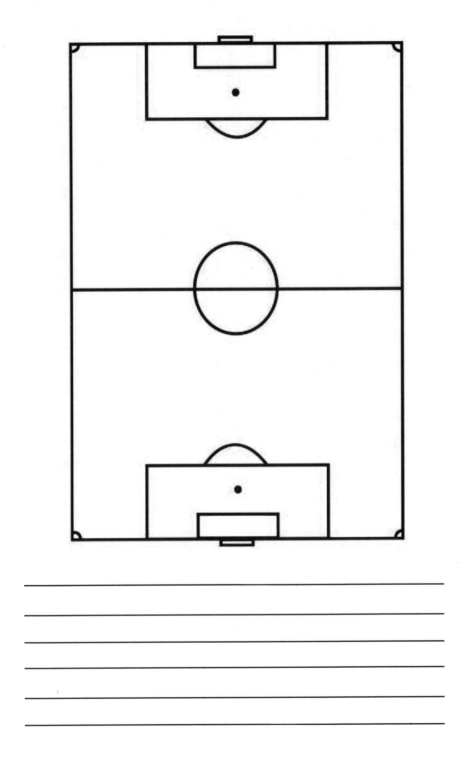

_____

_____

_____

_____

_____

_____

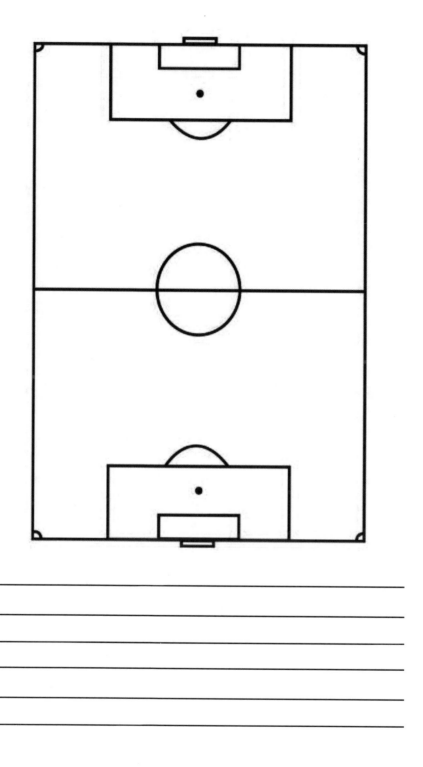

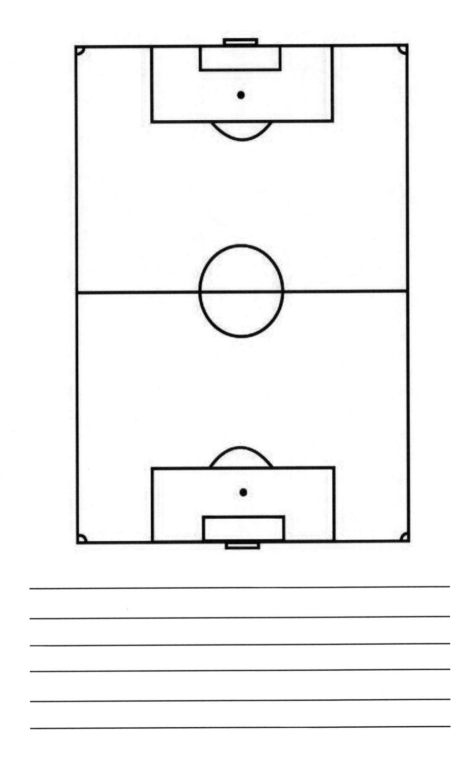

_____

_____

_____

_____

_____

_____

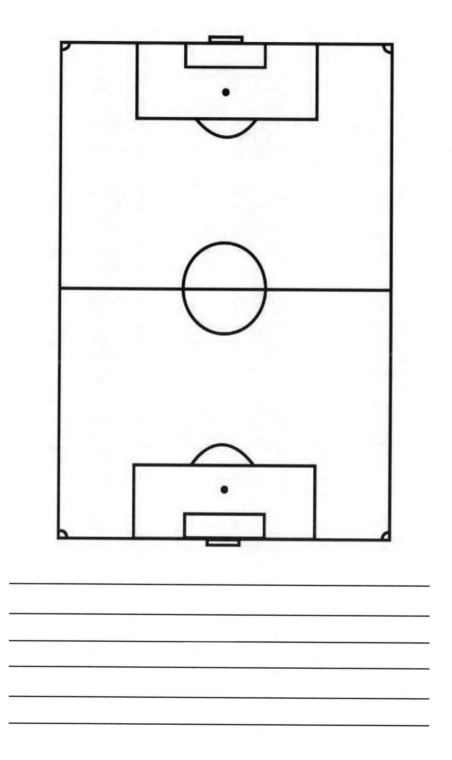

_____

_____

_____

_____

_____

_____

Also available from Reedswain Publishing:

 SOCCER'S
4-4-2 SYSTEM

 FITNESS
TRAINING IN
SOCCER
A Scientific
Approach

 COACHING
THE 3-4-3

 PRESSING

 COACHING
SOCCER:
MATCH
STRATEGY
AND TACTICS

 SOCCER
TACTICS
An Analysis of
Attack and
Defense

 FITNESS
TRAINING FOR
SOCCER

 TRANSITION
AND
COUNTER
ATTACKING

 CONDITIONING
FOR SOCCER

 COACHING
THE 3-4-1-2
AND 4-2-3-1

 TOTAL
SOCCER
COACHING
Combining
Physical,
Technical and
Tactical Training

 COORDINATION
AND SPEED
TRAINING FOR
SOCCER

 DUTCH
SOCCER
DRILLS
VOLUME 4

 EFFECTIVE
USE OF THE
AGILITY
LADDER FOR
SOCCER

 SOCCER:
ATTACKING
SCHEMES
AND TRAINING
EXERCISES

 COACHING
TEAM SHAPE

 THE CREATIVE
DRIBBLER

 248 DRILLS
FOR
ATTACKING
SOCCER

www.reedswain.com or 800.331.5191